3 Longman Academic Reading Series

READING SKILLS FOR COLLEGE

N
loss

V
lose

ADJ
losing

Adv
X

Make a sentence. Choose just one.

Judy L. Miller
Robert F. Cohen

Dedication

To my daughter, Ariana Miller, with love.
Judy L. Miller

In loving memory of my mother, Lillian Kumock Cohen, and my uncle, Julian Kumock.
Robert F. Cohen

Longman Academic Reading Series 3: Reading Skills for College

Copyright © 2017 by Pearson Education, Inc.
All rights reserved.

No part of this publication may be reproduced, stored in a retrieval system, or transmitted in any form or by any means, electronic, mechanical, photocopying, recording, or otherwise, without the prior permission of the publisher.

Pearson Education, 221 River Street, Hoboken, NJ 07030

Staff Credits: The people who made up the *Longman Academic Reading Series 3* team, representing editorial, production, design, and manufacturing, are Pietro Alongi, Margaret Antonini, Stephanie Bullard, Tracey Cataldo, Rosa Chapinal, Aerin Csigay, Ann France, Pam Kirshen-Fishman, Françoise Leffler, Amy McCormick, Liza Pleva, Massimo Rubini, Robert Ruvo and Joseph Vella.

Cover image: The Loupe Project/Shutterstock
Text Composition: TSI Graphics

Library of Congress Cataloging-in-Publication Data
  Böttcher, Elizabeth.
   Longman Academic Reading Series / Elizabeth Bottcher.
      volumes cm
   Includes index.
   ISBN 978-0-13-278664-5 (Level 1)—ISBN 978-0-13-278582-2 (Level 2)—
   ISBN 978-0-13-276059-1 (Level 3)—ISBN 978-0-13-276061-4 (Level 4)—
   ISBN 978-0-13-276067-6 (Level 5)
   1. English language—Textbooks for foreign speakers. 2. Reading comprehension—Problems, exercises, etc. 3. College readers. I. Title.
   PE1128.B637 2013
   428.6'4—dc23

                                           2013007701

ISBN 10: 0-13-466337-3
ISBN 13: 978-0-13-466337-1

Printed in the United States of America
14 2022

CONTENTS

Welcome to the *Longman Academic Reading Series,* a five-level series that prepares English-language learners for academic work. The aim of the series is to make students more effective and confident readers by providing **high-interest readings on academic subjects** and teaching them **skills and strategies** for

- effective reading
- vocabulary building
- note-taking
- critical thinking

Last but not least, the series encourages students to **discuss and write** about the ideas they have discovered in the readings, making them better speakers and writers of English as well.

High-Interest Readings On Academic Subjects

Research shows that if students are not motivated to read, if reading is not in some sense enjoyable, the reading process becomes mechanical drudgery, and the potential for improvement is minimal. That is why high-interest readings are the main feature in the *Longman Academic Reading Series.*

Varied High-Interest Texts

Each chapter of each book in the series focuses on an engaging theme from a wide range of academic subjects, such as art history, nutrition studies, American literature, and forensics. The reading selections in each chapter (two readings in Level 1 and three in Levels 2–5) are chosen to provide different and intriguing perspectives on the theme. These readings come from a variety of sources or genres — books, textbooks, academic journals, newspapers, magazines, online articles — and are written by a variety of authors from widely different fields. The Level 3 book, for instance, offers a short story by writer Ernest Hemingway, an interview with nutritionist Michael Pollan, a book excerpt from scientist James Watson, and letters from painter Vincent Van Gogh — all challenging reading selections that spark students' interest and motivate them to read and discuss what they read.

Academic Work

The work done in response to these selections provides students with a reading and discussion experience that mirrors the in-depth treatment of texts in academic course work. Although the readings may be adapted for the lower levels and excerpted for the upper levels, the authentic reading experience has been preserved. The series sustains students' interest and gives a sample of the types of content and reasoning that are the hallmark of academic work.

Skills and Strategies

To help students read and understand its challenging readings, the *Longman Academic Reading Series* provides a battery of skills and strategies for effective reading, vocabulary building, note-taking, and critical thinking.

Effective Reading

The series provides students with strategies that will help them learn to skim, scan, predict, preview, map, and formulate questions before they begin to read. After they read, students are routinely asked to identify main ideas as well as supporting details, progressing through the chapter from the "literal" to the "inferential." Students using this series learn to uncover what is beneath the surface of a reading passage and are led to interpret the many layers of meaning in a text. Each text is an invitation to dig deeper.

Vocabulary Building

In all chapters students are given the opportunity to see and use vocabulary in many ways: guessing words in context (an essential skill, without which fluent reading is impossible), identifying synonyms, recognizing idioms, practicing word forms, as well as using new words in their own spoken and written sentences. At the same time, students learn the best strategies for using the dictionary effectively and have ample practice in identifying roots and parts of words, recognizing collocations, understanding connotations, and communicating in the discourse specific to certain disciplines. The intentional "recycling" of vocabulary in both speaking and writing activities provides students with an opportunity to use the vocabulary they have acquired.

Note-Taking

As students learn ways to increase their reading comprehension and retention, they are encouraged to practice and master a variety of note-taking skills, such as highlighting, annotating, paraphrasing, summarizing, and outlining. The skills that form the focus of each chapter have been systematically aligned with the skills practiced in other chapters, so that scaffolding improves overall reading competence within each level.

Critical Thinking

At all levels of proficiency, students become more skilled in the process of analysis as they learn to read between the lines, make inferences, draw conclusions, make connections, evaluate, and synthesize information from various sources. The aim of this reflective journey is the development of students' critical thinking ability, which is achieved in different ways in each chapter.

Speaking and Writing

The speaking activities that frame and contribute to the development of each chapter tap students' strengths, allow them to synthesize information from several sources, and give them a sense of community in the reading experience. In addition, because good readers make good writers, students are given the opportunity to express themselves in a writing activity in each chapter.

The aim of the *Longman Academic Reading Series* is to provide "teachable" books that allow instructors to recognize the flow of ideas in each lesson and to choose from many types of exercises to get students interested and to maintain their active participation throughout. By showing students how to appreciate the ideas that make the readings memorable, the series encourages them to become more effective, confident, and independent readers.

The Online Teacher's Manual

The Teacher's Manual is available at www.pearsonelt.com/tmkeys. It includes general teaching notes, chapter teaching notes, answer keys, and reproducible chapter quizzes.

CHAPTER OVERVIEW

All chapters in the *Longman Academic Reading Series, Level 3* have the same basic structure.

Objectives

BEFORE YOU READ

A. Consider These Questions/Facts/etc.

B. Your Opinion *[varies; sometimes only Consider activity]*

READING ONE: [+ *reading title*]

A. Warm-Up

B. Reading Strategy

[Reading One]

COMPREHENSION

A. Main Ideas

B. Close Reading

VOCABULARY *[not necessarily in this order; other activities possible]*

A. Guessing from Context

B. Synonyms

C. Using the Dictionary

NOTE-TAKING *[in two reading sections per chapter]*

CRITICAL THINKING

READING TWO: [+ *reading title*]

A. Warm-Up

B. Reading Strategy

[Reading Two]

COMPREHENSION

A. Main Ideas

B. Close Reading

VOCABULARY *[not necessarily in this order; other activities possible]*

A. Guessing from Context

B. Synonyms

C. Using the Dictionary

CRITICAL THINKING

LINKING READINGS ONE AND TWO

READING THREE: [+ *reading title*]

A. Warm-Up

B. Reading Strategy

[Reading Three]

COMPREHENSION

A. Main Ideas

B. Close Reading

VOCABULARY *[not necessarily in this order; other activities possible]*

A. Guessing from Context

B. Synonyms

C. Using the Dictionary

D. Word Forms

NOTE-TAKING *[in two reading sections per chapter]*

CRITICAL THINKING

AFTER YOU READ

BRINGING IT ALL TOGETHER

WRITING ACTIVITY

DISCUSSION AND WRITING TOPICS

Vocabulary

Self-Assessment

Each chapter starts with a definition of the chapter's academic subject matter, objectives, and a Before You Read section.

A short **definition of the academic subject** mentioned in the chapter title describes the general area of knowledge explored in the chapter.

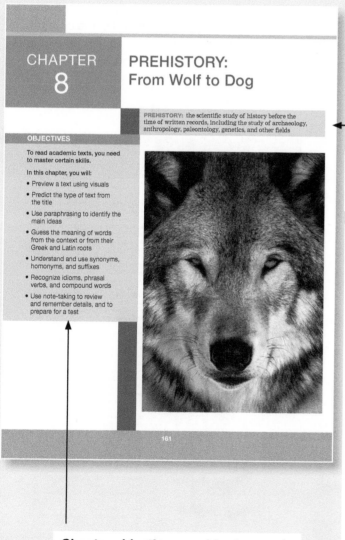

CHAPTER
8

PREHISTORY:
From Wolf to Dog

PREHISTORY: the scientific study of history before the time of written records, including the study of archaeology, anthropology, paleontology, genetics, and other fields

OBJECTIVES

To read academic texts, you need to master certain skills.

In this chapter, you will:

- Preview a text using visuals
- Predict the type of text from the title
- Use paraphrasing to identify the main ideas
- Guess the meaning of words from the context or from their Greek and Latin roots
- Understand and use synonyms, homonyms, and suffixes
- Recognize idioms, phrasal verbs, and compound words
- Use note-taking to review and remember details, and to prepare for a test

161

The **Before You Read** activities introduce the subject matter of the chapter, using a mix of information and questions to stimulate students' interest.

BEFORE YOU READ

Consider These Facts

There were no dogs on earth 20,000 years ago, only wolves. Somewhere and sometime after this point, a new animal evolved from the wolf — the dog. In a sense, dogs are domesticated wolves. Were the wolves tamed by humans, or did some wolves tame themselves to survive better?

Look at the timeline showing two eras of the past: the *Paleolithic* and the *Neolithic*. Read some of the characteristics of each era.

2.5 million years ago — 12,000 years ago — Present

Paleolithic Era
(Old Stone Age)

hunter-gatherers
- take food they find
- go from place to place following animals (nomadic)
- use stone tools
- hunt animals
- started use of fire

Neolithic Era
(New Stone Age)

farmers
- grow their own food
- live in one place (settling down in permanent homes)
- use digging tools and plows
- herd animals
- started domestication of animals

Now read each statement. Decide if the activity mentioned was more common in the *Paleolithic* or the *Neolithic* era. Check (✓) the appropriate box. Discuss your answers with a partner.

	PALEOLITHIC	NEOLITHIC
1. Humans hunted for food and primarily ate meat.	☐	☐
2. Humans began to eat wheat and other grains.	☐	☐
3. Humans lived in permanent settlements.	☐	☐
4. Humans began to cook their food.	☐	☐

Chapter objectives provide clear goals for students by listing the skills they will practice in the chapter.

Each of the three reading sections in a chapter starts with a Warm-Up activity and a Reading Strategy presentation and practice, followed by the reading itself.

The **Warm-Up** activity presents discussion questions that activate students' prior knowledge and help them develop a personal connection with the topic of the reading.

Reading One sets the theme and presents the basic ideas that will be explored in the chapter. Like all the readings in the series, it is an example of a genre of writing (here, a journal article).

READING ONE: More Than Man's Best Friend

Ⓐ Warm-Up

Discuss the questions with a partner.

1. Thousands of years ago, human beings dreamed about animals as protectors and allies, even as the ancestors of their clans. Why do you think animals had this important place in the human imagination? Do you know any myths about wolves?

2. Do you think there is a special bond between dogs and man? Can you describe it? Why do we say that dogs are "man's best friend"?

3. Do you have a pet? Would you like to have a pet? What pets, if any, are popular with people you know?

Ⓑ Reading Strategy

Previewing Using Visuals

Looking at the pictures (drawings or photographs) that illustrate a text first, before you read the text, can help you **predict what the text is about.**

1 Look at the pictures of a wolf and a dog that illustrate the reading. List the ways that dogs differ from wolves. Share your answers with a partner.

WOLVES	**DOGS**
1. _Wolves have a long, narrow "nose."_	_Dogs have a shorter, wider "nose."_
2. _____	_____
3. _____	_____
4. _____	_____
5. _____	_____

2 Look again at the pictures in the reading. What do you think you will learn from this reading? Discuss your answer with a partner. Write it on the line.

_____

Now read the text to find out if the pictures that illustrate it give you a good idea of its contents.

Prehistory: *From Wolf to Dog* **163**

The **Reading Strategy** box gives a general description of a reading strategy, such as previewing using visuals, and the reasons for using it. The **activities** below the box show students how to apply that strategy to the reading.

More Than Man's Best Friend

By Jarrett A. Lobell and Eric A. Powell, *Archaeology*

1   Today there are some 77 million dogs in the United States alone. But 20,000 years ago, it's possible there wasn't a single animal on the planet that looked like today's *canis lupus familiaris*. All scientists today accept the fact that dogs descend from the gray wolf, *canis lupus*. But biologists and archaeologists still debate when, where, and how gray wolves first evolved into dogs. Were the dogs first domesticated in China, the Middle East, or possibly Africa? The answers are important since dogs were the first animals to be tamed by man. They probably played an important role in what is called the "Neolithic Revolution," the time when human beings began to settle down in permanent homes and grow their own food instead of wandering around from place to place as they did in the Paleolithic era.

A wolf

A dog

2   What is it that tells us this animal is a "dog" and that one is a "wolf"? Modern wolves and dogs can be easily identified by their appearance. The most important difference is in the snout or nose area. In almost all dogs, the snout is shorter and wider than wolf snouts. Another crucial difference is the animal's manner and attitude toward humans. Dogs are genetically predisposed to want human attention and approval and to accept human leadership. Wolves are not.

3   Because early dogs looked more like wolves than dogs do today, it can be difficult to distinguish between wolf and dog skeletons from the far past. But recently, a team led by paleontologist Mietje Germonpré of the Royal Belgian Institute of Natural Sciences reported a stunning new finding in the February 2009 issue of *Journal of Archaeological Science*. Her team found a nearly complete fossil dog skull dating back 31,700 years ago. The skull, found in the Goyet Cave in Belgium, could represent the change from wolf to dog. However, there is a large gap in time between the age of the Goyet Cave "dog" and the next oldest dog-like skeletons from western Russia dating from 14,000 years ago. Was the appearance of the Goyet skull just an isolated event? What happened in between? We don't know.

4   Another way to estimate when and where domestic dogs originated is to study the genetic differences between dogs and wolves from different locations. In 2009, Peter Savolainen of the Royal Institute of Technology in Sweden published a genetic analysis of DNA indicating that dogs were first

164 CHAPTER 8

Domesticating Wolves

By Meg Daley Olmert, from *Made for Each Other*

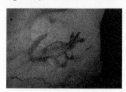

1 Paleolithic humans, as cave paintings show, were brilliant students of animal behavior. The first human hunters probably observed the wolves' cooperative strategies for hunting. Wolves are watchful, too. Rather than compete with these new hungry hunters, wolves may have chosen to give them their trust and work with them. They would join these humans in their chase, combining their better sense of smell and speed with the deadly aim of human weapons. They may have hoped that these two-leggers would prove trustworthy and share with them.

2 Humans didn't just hunt like wolves; they lived like them as well. Humans lived in "packs" or groups and cooperatively cared for their young. Besides being socially compatible, these two-legged carnivores[1] cooked their kill, offering a smell that some wolves probably couldn't resist. Those wolves that dared to come near discovered that these cooking animals threw away some of the best parts. (Early human hunters seem to have been more interested in bone marrow[2] than meat). Scavenging the garbage from early human camps may be what lured wolves into cave dwellings as long as 400,000 years ago. That's when wolf bones started appearing in the caves humans lived in.

3 If some wolves entered human dens voluntarily, they must have been the boldest, most genetically predisposed to be adventurous. It would have been the least nervous wolf, or the hungriest, who made the most successful cave raids. If their presence kept more dangerous animals away, humans may have repaid this service by throwing these adventurous animals a bone. Soon the animals would decide to stay. Eating leftovers doesn't make a wolf into a dog, but it's a start. A bone or two would have sent a powerful trust symbol to the wolf. What we do know is that perhaps as early as 40,000 years ago, something environmental, social, or both started some Eurasian wolves on their genetic journey toward dogdom.

4 The gentlest wolves followed us into our new homes.[3] The final transformation wouldn't have taken long once we began to selectively mate our favorite — most cooperative — wolves and help raise their young.... Sometime between 40,000 and 15,000 years ago, genetic tuning knobs started turning and wolves became affectionate to people and youthful in their personality and bodies. They came to lick the hand that fed them.[4] They also kept their best wolf manners, offering their services to their new human family.

[1] *carnivores:* meat-eaters (humans are omnivores and will eat everything; most animals are either herbivores like cows and eat only plants, or carnivores like wolves and eat meat)

[2] *bone marrow:* the soft tissue inside bones

[3] Human societies eventually moved away from caves.

[4] *lick the hand that fed them:* The expression is "Don't bite the hand that feeds you," which means "Don't be ungrateful." Daley Olmert is making a play on words meaning "love the hand that feeds you."

172 CHAPTER 8

Reading Two addresses the same theme as Reading One, but from a completely different perspective. In most cases, it is also an example of a different genre of writing (here, a book excerpt).

Reading Three addresses the same theme as Readings One and Two, but again from a different perspective from the first two. And in most cases, it is also an example of a different genre of writing (here, an online article).

Most readings have **glosses** and **footnotes** to help students understand difficult words and names.

All readings have **numbered paragraphs** (with the exception of literary readings that have numbered lines) for easy reference. The **target vocabulary** that students need to know in order to read academic texts is set in boldface blue for easy recognition. Target vocabulary is recycled through the chapter and the level.

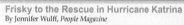

Frisky to the Rescue in Hurricane Katrina
By Jennifer Wulff, *People Magazine*

1 His neighbors tried to get him to leave, but lifelong Biloxi, Mississippi resident George Mitchell, a widower, insisted on riding out the storm. Yes, that terrible storm Katrina. "I said, 'Nope, Hurricane Camille[1] was as bad as it gets,' says Mitchell, 'and I survived it.'" He turned 80 the day Katrina[2] hit. Stubbornly, he took his schnauzer-poodle mix Frisky (who was a senior citizen himself for a dog at age 18) to an empty neighbor's home and waited. Soon Mitchell was chest-deep in water. He put Frisky on an inflatable mattress and hung on to keep himself afloat. "It was like being in a washing machine," says the retired Navy man turned real estate agent.

2 After treading water[3] for hours, he began to fade. "I was ready to let go," says Mitchell, who was on the verge of passing out. Not if Frisky had anything to do with it. The dog, which Mitchell found on his porch in 1987 as a stray puppy, went to the corner of the mattress and began frantically licking his master's face. "He would not stop licking until I snapped out of it," says Mitchell. Realizing his best friend's own life would be in danger if he died, Mitchell fought to stay alive. Finally, at daybreak, the water began to recede, and Mitchell could once again stand.

3 He spent the next 12 days at a nearby hospital being treated for dehydration[4] and cuts. Frisky was right by his side. "He slept on me the whole time," says Mitchell, who now lives in a Biloxi retirement community[5] with his pup. "He's quite a boy. I wouldn't give him up for a million dollars."

[1] *Hurricane Camille* was a category 5 hurricane that hit the Gulf states in 1969, killing more than 200 people and causing more than $8 billion of damage.

[2] *Hurricane Katrina,* one of the worst hurricane disasters in U.S. history, hit the Gulf states in 2005, killing 1,800 people and causing $81 billion of damage due to flooding. The river levees (walls) broke, and water flooded 80% of New Orleans and many cities along the Mississippi River.

[3] *tread water:* to stay floating upright in deep water by moving your legs as if you were riding a bicycle

[4] *dehydration:* if you don't drink enough water, you will suffer from dehydration.

[5] *retirement community:* a place where senior citizens choose to live together

Prehistory: *From Wolf to Dog* **181**

Each reading in the chapter is followed by Comprehension and Vocabulary activities.

COMPREHENSION

Ⓐ Main Ideas

Work with a partner. Complete the sentences that reflect the steps Malcolm X went through in teaching himself to read.

1. When Malcolm X went to jail, he _____

2. The first thing he did was _____

3. In his own handwriting, he _____

4. Then, after a night's sleep, he would _____

5. He learned not only words but _____

6. Reading became _____

Ⓑ Close Reading

Read the quotes from the reading. Circle the statement that best explains each quote. Share your answers with a partner.

1. "So I had come to the Norfolk Prison Colony still going through only book-reading motions." (*paragraph 1*)

   a. Malcolm had limited reading skills.

   b. He could read the words and understood what he was reading.

2. "In my slow and terrible handwriting, I copied into my notebook everything printed on that page, down to the punctuation marks." (*paragraph 3*)

   a. He copied everything but the punctuation marks into his notebook.

   b. He also copied the punctuation marks into his notebook.

3. "With every succeeding page, I also learned of people and places and events from history. Actually, the dictionary is like a small encyclopedia." (*paragraph 6*)

   a. By reading the dictionary, he learned a lot more than just words.

   b. Reading the dictionary helped him read the encyclopedia.

4. "There was nothing you could have done to take me away from my books. Between my correspondence, my visitors, and my reading of books, months passed without my even thinking about being imprisoned. In fact, up to then, I never had been so truly free in my life." (*paragraph 7*)

   a. According to the author, reading is part of the pathway to freedom.

   b. According to the author, freedom is having time to read.

Education Studies: *Overcoming Inequalities* **197**

The **Comprehension** activities help students identify and understand the main ideas of the reading and their supporting details.

The **Vocabulary** activities focus on the target vocabulary in the reading, presenting and practicing skills such as guessing meaning from context or from synonyms, using a dictionary, and understanding word usage.

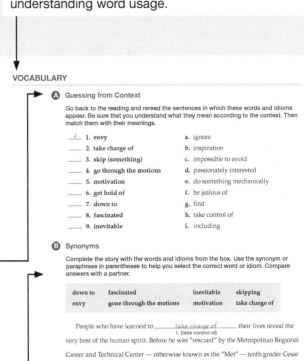

VOCABULARY

Ⓐ Guessing from Context

Go back to the reading and reread the sentences in which these words and idioms appear. Be sure that you understand what they mean according to the context. Then match them with their meanings.

_f_ 1. envy		a. ignore
___ 2. take charge of		b. inspiration
___ 3. skip (something)		c. impossible to avoid
___ 4. go through the motions		d. passionately interested
___ 5. motivation		e. do something mechanically
___ 6. get hold of		f. be jealous of
___ 7. down to		g. find
___ 8. fascinated		h. take control of
___ 9. inevitable		i. including

Ⓑ Synonyms

Complete the story with the words and idioms from the box. Use the synonym or paraphrase in parentheses to help you select the correct word or idiom. Compare answers with a partner.

down to	fascinated		inevitable	skipping
envy	gone through the motions		motivation	take charge of

People who have learned to ___*take charge of*___ their lives reveal the
                                   1. (take control of)
very best of the human spirit. Before he was "rescued" by the Metropolitan Regional

Career and Technical Center — otherwise known as the "Met" — tenth grader Cesar

had only _____ of going to school. Between hanging out
         2. (attended school in a mechanical way)
on street corners with fellow gang members, getting into trouble with the police,

and visiting his father and brother in jail, he never did his homework and had very

limited reading and writing skills as a result. Dropping out of school was surely

going to be the _____ consequence of this lifestyle.
                3. (impossible to avoid)
However, at the Met, Cesar found the _____ to turn
                                       4. (inspiration)
his life around and become an exceptional student. The Met was a unique public

high school in Providence, Rhode Island, where students received a lot of personal

198 CHAPTER 9

Guessing from Context helps students guess the meaning of the target vocabulary by encouraging them to go back to the reading to find clues in the context and base their guesses on these clues.

Synonyms also helps students understand the meaning of the target vocabulary in the reading, but here for each target word students are given synonyms to match or choose from.

that such a feeling is _____, but the conditioning remains.
9. (unreasonable)
In other cases, children may observe parents or other close adults who are deeply and permanently afraid of the water, and copy their reactions. Such phobias may diminish with patience and time. Yelling at children or punishing them will do no good.

B Word Usage: *be characterized by*

> In a **definition**, we often include a **description of the main characteristics** or qualities of the thing being defined, and we use the idiom *be characterized by*.
>
> **EXAMPLE:**
> - A phobia **is characterized by** intense and irrational fear.
>   *This means that the main characteristic of a phobia is a feeling of great fear.*

Work with a partner. Take turns describing the main characteristics of the phobias mentioned in the reading.

1. Social phobia: *A social phobia is characterized by . . .*

2. Specific phobia: _____

3. Claustrophobia: _____

4. Zoophobia: _____

5. Agoraphobia: _____

6. Aerophobia: _____

C Using the Dictionary

Read the dictionary entry for *disorder*.

> disorder *n.* **1** [C] a mental or physical problem that can affect your health for a long time: *a serious heart disorder* | *After two years of therapy, Duane was able to conquer his eating disorder.* **2** [U] a situation in which many people disobey the law, especially in a violent way and are difficult to control: *Most urban areas were generally free of civil disorder.* **3** [U] a situation in which things are not organized at all: *The smallest problem can throw all their services into disorder.*

Now answer the questions. Share your answers with a partner.

1. Which definition of the word is used in this chapter?
2. How are the three definitions related? What do all "dis-orders" have in common? [*dis-* is a prefix meaning "not"]
3. Why do we refer to phobias as "disorders," and not "diseases"?

Psychology: Fears and Phobias **33**

Word Usage shows students some of the ways English speakers use a word or idiom featured in the reading, and then checks students' understanding.

Using the Dictionary shows students how to understand a dictionary entry for one of the target words. Students choose the appropriate meaning of the word as it is used in the reading and in other contexts.

Word Forms helps students expand their vocabulary by encouraging them to guess or find out the different forms some of the target words can have. Then students are challenged to use the forms correctly.

C Word Forms

1 Fill in the chart with the correct word forms. Some categories can have more than one form. Use a dictionary if necessary. An *X* indicates there is no form in that category.

	NOUN	VERB	ADJECTIVE	ADVERB
1.	anxiety	X	*anxious*	
2.		fear		
3.			intense	
4.	phobia	X		X
5.		dread	dreadful /	
6.		X	psychological	
7.		X	severe	
8.	depression			X

2 Complete the summary of the main points of the reading with the correct form of the words. Choose from the forms in parentheses.

Many people are _____*anxious*_____ about something, but this
1. (anxiety / anxious / anxiously)
_____ does not prevent them from functioning normally
2. (anxiety / anxious / anxiously)
in everyday life. An anxiety of overwhelming _____ is
3. (intensity / intense / intensely)
called _____. People who are suffering from phobias
4. (a phobia / phobic / phobias)
_____ being in certain situations, such as riding in elevators
5. (a fear / fear / fearful)
or making speeches. This makes it difficult for them to function in school or at work.

These anxiety disorders, which affect people _____
6. (psychology / psychological / psychologically)
undoubtedly have a _____ impact on the quality of their
7. (severity / severe / severely)
lives. People with phobias live lives filled with _____ and are
8. (dread / dreadful / dreaded)
often very _____.
9. (depress / depression / depressed)

Two of the three reading sections in a chapter have a Note-Taking activity. All three reading sections end with a Critical Thinking activity. The Linking Readings One and Two activity comes at the end of the Reading Two section.

NOTE-TAKING: Circling Names and Writing Margin Notes

1 Go back to the reading. Circle the names of the important people in the Pixar story. Then write notes in the margin about the role of each person.

EXAMPLE:

> The Pixar team began in 1979, when (George Lucas) needed special effects for *Star Wars*. He **enticed** [Edwin Catmull], a PhD in computer science, to Lucasfilm. Over the next few years, Catmull and his ensemble created innovative computer graphics programs and equipment. This included an imaging computer, the "Pixar," which could create high-resolution color images of anything from buildings and cars to tornadoes and aliens.

filmmaker, needed special effects for "Star Wars" — hired Catmull
Computer scientist, created innovative imaging computer: the "Pixar"

2 Match the people in the Pixar story with their roles.

_____ 1. George Lucas   a. owner of Pixar as of 2006
_____ 2. Edwin Catmull   b. head of Pixar's computer animation department
_____ 3. John Lasseter
_____ 4. Roy Disney   c. sole owner of Pixar in 1991
_____ 5. Steve Jobs   d. filmmaker, needed special effects for *Star Wars*
   e. computer scientist, created the "Pixar," an innovative imaging computer

CRITICAL THINKING

Discuss the questions in a small group. Be prepared to share your answers with the class.

1. Apple was the first of the digital giants (before Amazon or Google) to make a wide-ranging deal with music companies, which led to iTunes. What in Steve Jobs's previous experience with Pixar helped him understand how to build bridges between creative people and "techies"?

2. Because Pixar wasn't making any profit, most management advisers would have told the owner to get rid of it. Why was Jobs the kind of person who would stick with Pixar?

3. Look up some information on the life of Steve Jobs. Try to answer the questions you might have had when you did the readings. Many people have said that Steve Jobs was a more complex and contradictory person than we think. Do you agree or disagree? Why or why not?

14   CHAPTER 1

The **Note-Taking** activity teaches students to use skills such as circling, underlining, writing margin notes, categorizing, outlining, and summarizing information to increase their reading comprehension.

The **Linking Readings One and Two** activity leads students to compare and contrast the ideas expressed in the first two readings. It helps students make connections and find correlations between the two texts.

The **Critical Thinking** activity encourages students to analyze and evaluate the information in the reading. This activity develops students' critical thinking skills and their ability to express their opinions coherently.

LINKING READINGS ONE AND TWO

Work in groups of four. Role-play an interview with Jonathan Kozol and Malcolm X about educational issues. Two journalists ask the questions suggested below.

Fill in the chart to prepare for the role-play. The group should add one or two "journalist's questions" and answer all questions based on information in Readings One and Two .

	JOURNALIST'S QUESTION	JONATHAN KOZOL'S ANSWER	MALCOLM X'S ANSWER
1.	Do you believe that education leads to freedom?	*"Yes I do. Education provides our young people with opportunities for better jobs and more freedom of choice in life."*	*"Yes I do. When I taught myself to read in prison, I never felt freer in my life. Reading gave me intellectual and spiritual freedom even though I was in prison."*
2.	Do you believe that children who don't go to good schools might end up in prison?		
3.	If the schools aren't good, should people teach themselves?		
4.			
5.			

Now role-play the interview.

Each chapter ends with an After You Read section, a Vocabulary chart, and a Self-Assessment checklist.

The **After You Read** activities go back to the theme of the chapter, encouraging students to discuss and write about related topics using the target vocabulary of the chapter.

AFTER YOU READ

BRINGING IT ALL TOGETHER

Work in groups of three or four. Discuss each quotation to explain what it means. Then decide how Kozol, Malcolm X, and Scibona would respond to it. Be prepared to share your point(s) of view with the class. Use some of the vocabulary from the chapter (for a complete list, go to page 210).

1. "It is not the biggest, the brightest or the best that will survive, but those who adapt the quickest."
   — *Charles Darwin, English naturalist, 1809–1882*

2. "A mind is not a vessel to be filled but a fire to be ignited."
   — *Plutarch, Greek historian and biographer, 46–120 A.D.*

3. "It was in making education not only common to all, but in some sense compulsory on all, that the destiny of . . . America . . . was practically settled."
   — *James Russell Lowell, American poet and diplomat, 1819–1891*

4. "It is only the ignorant who despise education."
   — *Publilius Syrus, Latin writer, 1st century B.C.*

5. "The direction in which education starts a man will determine his future life."
   — *Plato, Greek philosopher, 429–347 B.C.*

WRITING ACTIVITY

Write a report about a book you read or were forced to read. Answer these questions:
- Did you like the book or not?
- What did reading the book bring to you?
- Did you experience Scibona's "intense and enigmatic joy"? Why or why not?

Use at least five of the words and idioms you studied in the chapter.

DISCUSSION AND WRITING TOPICS

Discuss these topics in a small group. Choose one of them and write a paragraph or two about it. Use the vocabulary from the chapter.

1. How could more funding make schools better? Give some concrete examples. Use your experience as a guide.
2. If Malcolm X was able to teach himself to read, why do we need schools to educate people? Is there a danger in having a society of only self-taught people?
3. Why is it important for a free society to have good public schools?
4. Would you recommend that future teachers be asked to read Kozol, Malcolm X, and Scibona? What could they learn from these writers about their job as teachers?

Education Studies: *Overcoming Inequalities* **209**

The **Vocabulary chart**, which lists all the target vocabulary words of the chapter under the appropriate parts of speech, provides students with a convenient reference.

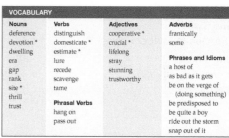

VOCABULARY			
Nouns	**Verbs**	**Adjectives**	**Adverbs**
deference	distinguish	cooperative *	frantically
devotion *	domesticate *	crucial *	some
dwelling	estimate *	lifelong	
era	lure	stray	**Phrases and Idioms**
gap	recede	stunning	a host of
rank	scavenge	trustworthy	as bad as it gets
site *	tame		be on the verge of
thrill			(doing something)
trust	**Phrasal Verbs**		be predisposed to
	hang on		be quite a boy
	pass out		ride out the storm
			snap out of it

* = AWL (Academic Word List) item

SELF-ASSESSMENT

In this chapter you learned to:
- ○ Preview a text using visuals
- ○ Predict the type of text from the title
- ○ Use paraphrasing to identify the main ideas
- ○ Guess the meaning of words from the context or from their Greek and Latin roots
- ○ Understand and use synonyms, homonyms, and suffixes
- ○ Recognize idioms, phrasal verbs, and compound words
- ○ Use note-taking to review and remember details, and to prepare for a test

What can you do well?

What do you need to practice more?

The **Self-Assessment** checklist encourages students to evaluate their own progress. Have they mastered the skills listed in the chapter objectives?

186 CHAPTER 8

SCOPE AND SEQUENCE

CHAPTER	READING	VOCABULARY
1 BUSINESS: **Steve Jobs,** **Innovator and CEO** **Theme:** How to be successful in business **Reading One:** *The Extraordinary Life of Steve Jobs* (a magazine article) **Reading Two:** *The Pixar Story* (an online article) **Reading Three:** *The Map of Innovation: Creating Something Out of Nothing* (a book excerpt)	• Understand and practice different reading strategies • Predict the author's point of view from the title of a text • Predict the content of a text from the first paragraph • Skim a text by reading the topic sentence in each paragraph • Identify the main ideas of a text • Understand the details that support the main ideas	• Guess the meaning of words from the context • Use dictionary entries to learn the meanings of words • Understand and use synonyms and different word forms • Use the Vocabulary list at the end of the chapter to review the words, phrases, and idioms learned in the chapter • Use this vocabulary in the After You Read speaking and writing activities
2 PSYCHOLOGY: **Fears and Phobias** **Theme:** What a phobia is and how phobias can be treated **Reading One:** *When Does a Fear Become a Phobia?* (a textbook excerpt) **Reading Two:** *Case Studies* (a textbook excerpt) **Reading Three:** *Treatments for Phobias* (a textbook excerpt)	• Understand and practice different reading strategies • Scan a text to find specific information • Preview a text using visuals like charts and graphs • Understand scholarly references (in-text citations, bibliography) • Identify or complete the main ideas of a text • Understand the details that support the main ideas	• Understand and use synonyms, collocations, and different word forms • Guess the meaning of words from their Greek or Latin roots • Use dictionary entries to learn the meanings of words • Study the usage of certain phrases and idioms • Use the Vocabulary list at the end of the chapter to review the words, phrases, and idioms learned in the chapter • Use this vocabulary in the After You Read speaking and writing activities
3 NUTRITION STUDIES: **Food Rules** **Theme:** What we should eat to be healthier and how we should treat the animals we eat **Reading One:** *An Interview with Michael Pollan* (an online article) **Reading Two:** *Bad Food? Tax It, and Subsidize Vegetables* (a newspaper article) **Reading Three:** *Humane Treatment for the Animals We Eat* (a magazine article)	• Understand and practice different reading strategies • Skim an interview by looking at the questions asked by the interviewer • Scan a text for specific answers to a question in the title • Understand the tone of a text and identify the author's point of view • Identify the main ideas of a text • Understand the details that support the main ideas	• Guess the meaning of words from the context • Use dictionary entries to learn the meanings of words • Understand and use synonyms, prefixes, and antonyms • Use the Vocabulary list at the end of the chapter to review the words, phrases, and idioms learned in the chapter • Use this vocabulary in the After You Read speaking and writing activities

NOTE-TAKING	CRITICAL THINKING	SPEAKING/WRITING
• Use underlining and margin notes to identify and remember important facts in a story • Use circling and margin notes to identify and remember important people in a story	• Express your opinions and support them with examples from a text or from your own experience and culture • Analyze and evaluate information • Infer information not explicit in a text • Draw conclusions • Hypothesize about someone else's point of view • Find correlations between two texts • Make connections between ideas • Synthesize information and ideas	• Role-play an interview with Steve Jobs and Kevin O'Connor about business • Write two paragraphs about business management • Discuss in a small group a number of topics about business • Choose one of the topics and write a paragraph or two about it
• Fill out an organizer with study notes from the readings to prepare for a test • Organize and categorize the material in the reading to understand it better	• Answer questions based on information in a text or on your own experience and culture • Analyze and evaluate information • Infer information not explicit in a text • Draw conclusions • Find correlations between two texts • Use a chart to contrast negative and positive thoughts • Make connections between ideas • Synthesize information and ideas	• Discuss a list of questions about phobias in a small group. Then share your group's answers with the class. • Write two paragraphs about a fear or a phobia • Discuss in a small group a number of topics about psychology • Choose one of the topics and write a paragraph or two about it
• Use a chart listing categories to organize your study notes • Use a chain of reasoning to list the arguments marshaled by the author	• Express your opinions and support them with examples from a text or from your own experience and culture • Analyze and evaluate information • Infer information not explicit in a text • Draw conclusions • Evaluate an author's thesis and come up with arguments for and against it • Use a chart to compare the opinions of two authors • Make connections between ideas • Synthesize information and ideas	• Role-play an interview with Michael Pollan and Mark Bittman about American eating habits • Respond to a letter to the editor about food as though you were Pollan, Bittman, or Temple Grandin • Write one or two paragraphs to answer a question on an issue raised in the chapter • Discuss in a small group a number of issues about the way we eat • Choose one of the issues and write a paragraph or two about it

CHAPTER	READING	VOCABULARY
4 MEDICINE: Pioneers and Heroes **Theme:** Doctors whose discoveries helped mankind overcome terrible diseases **Reading One:** *The Hippocratic Oath — A Modern Version* (an online article) **Reading Two:** *The Invisible Enemy* (a textbook excerpt) **Reading Three:** *That Mothers Might Live* (a book excerpt)	• Understand and practice different reading strategies • Skim an oath to get an overview of its contents • Scan a text for dates to understand the sequence of events • Find the link between the title of a text and the first paragraph to focus on the most important idea • Identify the main ideas of a text • Understand the details that support the main ideas	• Understand and use synonyms and collocations • Recognize and learn the connotations of words • Understand the different usage of similar words • Categorize words • Use the Vocabulary list at the end of the chapter to review the words, phrases, and idioms learned in the chapter • Use this vocabulary in the After You Read speaking and writing activities
5 AMERICAN LITERATURE: Ernest Hemingway's "Indian Camp" **Theme:** A young boy's "coming of age" experience and how it is conveyed by the author **Reading One:** *Indian Camp — Part I* (a short story excerpt) **Reading Two:** *Indian Camp — Part II* (a short story excerpt) **Reading Three:** *Hemingway's Style* (a textbook excerpt)	• Understand and practice different reading strategies • Understand the elements of fiction: characters, setting, and plot • Identify the themes of a story • Scan a text for "compare and contrast" words to find essential information quickly • Complete charts about the sequence of events in a story • Understand the main ideas and the details that support the main ideas	• Guess the meaning of words from the context • Understand and use synonyms, phrasal verbs, and different word forms • Recognize words of varying intensity • Match "compare and contrast" words with their synonyms • Use the Vocabulary list at the end of the chapter to review the words, phrases, and idioms learned in the chapter • Use this vocabulary in the After You Read speaking and writing activities
6 ART HISTORY: The Life and Letters of Vincent Van Gogh **Theme:** An artist's life through his paintings and letters; the life of one of his paintings **Reading One:** *A Biography of Vincent Van Gogh (1853–1890)* (a book excerpt) **Reading Two:** *The Letters of Vincent Van Gogh* (a book excerpt) **Reading Three:** *Portrait of Dr. Gachet: A Timeline* (an online article)	• Understand and practice different reading strategies • Preview a text using visuals like paintings • Skim letters for a quick overview (names, places, dates) • Scan a text for dates to understand the sequence of events • Identify or complete the main ideas of a text • Understand the details that support the main ideas	• Guess the meaning of words from the context or from their Latin roots • Understand and use synonyms and connotations • Use dictionary entries to learn the meanings of words • Use the Vocabulary list at the end of the chapter to review the words, phrases, and idioms learned in the chapter • Use this vocabulary in the After You Read speaking and writing activities

NOTE-TAKING	CRITICAL THINKING	SPEAKING/WRITING
• Use a chart to categorize the main points of a text • Complete a short summary of the main points of a text • Create a timeline to understand the sequence of events	• In your reaction to certain situations, discuss how a doctor should behave in order to follow the Hippocratic Oath • Express your opinions and support them with examples from a text or from your own experience and culture • Analyze and evaluate information • Infer information not explicit in a text • Draw conclusions • Interpret quotes and how they relate to a text • Make connections between ideas • Synthesize information and ideas	• Role-play situations involving Jenner and Semmelweis • Write a portrait of someone you admire • Discuss in a small group a number of topics about medicine • Choose one of the topics and write a paragraph or two about it
• Use circling and margin notes to identify the themes of a story • Organize your study notes to compare and define a writer's style	• Answer questions based on information in a story or on your own experience and culture • Express your opinions and support them with examples from a story • Infer information not explicit in a story • Draw conclusions • Hypothesize about someone else's point of view • Find correlations between two texts • Analyze a writer's style • Make connections between ideas • Synthesize information and ideas	• In a small group, explain a point of style or theme with quotes and scenes from the story • Write two paragraphs to summarize the story and give your opinion • In a small group, discuss topics related to the story • Choose one of the topics and write a paragraph or two about it
• Fill in a chart to identify the events that occurred in Van Gogh's life in the different places where he lived • Fill in a chart to identify details that support the four main topics in Van Gogh's letters	• Interpret some of Van Gogh's paintings based on the information given in the text • Analyze and evaluate information • Infer information not explicit in a text • Draw conclusions • Hypothesize about someone else's point of view • Find correlations between two texts • Identify irony in a discussion of Van Gogh's life • Make connections between ideas • Synthesize information and ideas	• Debate in a group of four whether art should be censored by the government • Write two paragraphs about a painting by Vincent Van Gogh • Discuss in a small group topics related to Van Gogh's life, work, and art • Choose one of the topics and write a paragraph or two about it

CHAPTER	READING	VOCABULARY
7 **FORENSICS:** **Science and Fiction** **Theme:** What forensic science is and how its real-life practice differs from what is shown in popular TV series **Reading One:** *Basic Principles of Forensics* (a textbook excerpt) **Reading Two:** *The "CSI Effect" Is a Mixed Blessing for Real Crime Labs* (an online article) **Reading Three:** *The Forensic Use of DNA* (a book excerpt)	• Understand and practice different reading strategies • Skim a text by reading the topic sentence in each paragraph • Predict the content of a text from the title and subheadings • Read the last paragraph first to understand the point of a text • Get the main ideas of a text from the keywords in the topic sentences • Understand the details that support the main ideas	• Understand and use synonyms, idioms, and collocations • Recognize the different forms, meanings, and usage of a word • Match courtroom and legal vocabulary with their definitions • Use the Vocabulary list at the end of the chapter to review the words, phrases, and idioms learned in the chapter • Use this vocabulary in the After You Read speaking and writing activities
8 **PREHISTORY:** **From Wolf to Dog** **Theme:** When, where, why, and how wolves evolved into dogs and our best friends **Reading One:** *More Than Man's Best Friend* (a journal article) **Reading Two:** *Domesticating Wolves* (a book excerpt) **Reading Three:** *Frisky to the Rescue in Hurricane Katrina* (an online article)	• Understand and practice different reading strategies • Preview a text using visuals like drawings or photographs • Predict the type of text from the title • Use paraphrasing to identify the main ideas • Complete the main ideas of a text • Understand the details that support the main ideas	• Guess the meaning of words from the context or from their Greek or Latin roots • Understand and use synonyms, homonyms, and suffixes • Recognize idioms, phrasal verbs, and compound words • Use the Vocabulary list at the end of the chapter to review the words, phrases, and idioms learned in the chapter • Use this vocabulary in the After You Read speaking and writing activities

NOTE-TAKING	CRITICAL THINKING	SPEAKING/WRITING
• Use underlining and margin notes to identify who said what in a text • Organize study notes chronologically to clarify the sequence of events in a story	• Express your opinions and support them with examples from a text or from your own experience and culture • Analyze and evaluate information • Infer information not explicit in a text • Draw conclusions • Hypothesize about someone else's point of view • Relate broad themes to specific situations • Find correlations between two texts • Make connections between ideas • Synthesize information and ideas	• Role-play an interview: a professor interviewing a student applying to the forensic science program; OR a student reporter interviewing a lawyer from the Innocence Project • Write a letter to apply for a job as a crime scene investigator • Discuss in a small group topics related to forensics and career choice • Choose one of the topics and write a paragraph or two about it
• Fill in an organizer to review details to help you remember • Prepare for a test by filling in a list of questions and answers about each paragraph of a reading	• Recognize facts from opinions • Express your opinions and support them with examples from a text or from your own experience and culture • Analyze and evaluate information • Infer information not explicit in a text • Draw conclusions • Find correlations between two texts • Hypothesize about someone else's point of view • Make connections between ideas • Synthesize information and ideas	• Role-play a panel discussion about the evolution of dogs from wolves; the panel features the experts mentioned in the chapter • Write a two-paragraph anecdote about a family pet • Discuss in a small group topics related to dogs, wolves, and humans • Choose one of the topics and write a paragraph or two about it

CHAPTER	READING	VOCABULARY
9 EDUCATION STUDIES: Overcoming Inequalities **Theme:** How to overcome the inequalities in the American education system **Reading One:** *Savage Inequalities: Children in America's Schools* (a book excerpt) **Reading Two:** *The Autobiography of Malcolm X* (a book excerpt) **Reading Three:** *Where I Learned to Read* (a magazine article)	• Understand and practice different reading strategies • Identify the issues discussed in an essay by reading the first paragraph • Understand the most important idea of a text by reading the last paragraph first • Skim a text by reading the topic sentence in each paragraph • Identify or complete the main ideas of a text • Understand the details that support the main ideas	• Understand and use synonyms, antonyms, and different word forms • Guess the meaning of words from the context and use them in a new context • Use dictionary entries to learn the meanings of words • Use the Vocabulary list at the end of the chapter to review the words, phrases, and idioms learned in the chapter • Use this vocabulary in the After You Read speaking and writing activities
10 SOCIOLOGY: Crime and Punishment **Theme:** All aspects of crime: its types; where, how often, and why they occur; their effects on society, and what rehabilitation methods work best **Reading One:** *The Global Context* (a textbook excerpt) **Reading Two:** *Sociological Theories of Crime* (a textbook excerpt) **Reading Three:** *Prison Programs That Work* (a textbook excerpt)	• Understand and practice different reading strategies • Predict the content of a text from the first sentence or from the title and subheadings • Learn strategies for dealing with scientific names • Identify or complete the main ideas of a text • Understand the details that support the main ideas	• Guess the meaning of words from the context • Understand and use synonyms, suffixes, "scientific" verbs, different word forms, and words of different intensity • Use dictionary entries to learn the meanings of words • Use the Vocabulary list at the end of the chapter to review the words, phrases, and idioms learned in the chapter • Use this vocabulary in the After You Read speaking and writing activities

NOTE-TAKING	CRITICAL THINKING	SPEAKING/WRITING
• For each paragraph of the text, write a one-sentence summary of the author's argument (reasons for his point of view) • Fill in an organizer to identify important details about the three stages of the author's education (high school/college/post-college)	• Analyze the author's argument and respond to it with three reasons for or against • Express your opinions and support them with examples from a text or from your own experience and culture • Infer information not explicit in a text • Draw conclusions • Hypothesize about someone else's point of view • Find correlations between two texts • Make connections between ideas • Synthesize information and ideas	• Role-play an interview with Jonathan Kozol and Malcolm X about educational issues • In a small group, discuss the meaning of quotations from famous thinkers; decide how Kozol, Malcolm X, and Scibona would respond to each one • Write a report about a book you read or were forced to read • Discuss in a small group issues related to schools and teaching • Choose one of the topics and write a paragraph or two about it
• Use a map outline to remember the details of a text • Write a summary of a text to understand the main ideas and remember details	• Express your opinions and support them with examples from a text or from your own experience and culture • Analyze and evaluate information • Infer information not explicit in a text • Draw conclusions • Hypothesize about someone else's point of view • Relate specific situations to the perspectives or theories mentioned in a text • Find correlations between two texts • Make connections between ideas • Synthesize information and ideas	• In a small group, discuss rehabilitation programs and how their success can be linked to crime theories • Write a short essay to answer this question: "How can a society reduce crime?" • Discuss in a small group topics about crime theories and rehabilitation programs • Choose one of the topics and write a paragraph or two about it

ACKNOWLEDGMENTS

Our heartfelt thanks go first and foremost to Massimo Rubini. Without his vision, this project would never have gotten off the ground. Not only did we have the advantage of his insight and directives as a fellow "architect" of the series, but we also benefited from his warmth and kindness in every way.

We owe another great debt of gratitude to our editor *extraordinaire*, Françoise Leffler. We gained immeasurably from her broad understanding of the project, her professional expertise, and her keen sense of precision in all stages of the writing process. Having such a creative editor and patient collaborator was a great gift.

Our sincere thanks also go to Amy McCormick, for her support and executive decision-making during many trying moments; to Rosa Chapinal, for her patience and devoted efforts throughout the permissions process; to Jill Krupnik, for her work in negotiating complex permissions contracts; and to Jane Lieberth, for her very thorough and close reading of our manuscript in the production phase.

We thank our colleagues at the American Language Program at Columbia University and the Department of Language and Cognition at Eugenio María de Hostos Community College for their enduring professional support and friendship.

Finally, we remember our students, from whom we continue to learn every day and who remain in our hearts our true teachers.

Judy L. Miller and *Robert F. Cohen*

Reviewers

The publisher would like to thank the following reviewers for their many helpful comments.

Jeff Bette, Naugatuck Valley Community College, Waterbury, Connecticut; **Kevin Knight**, Japan; **Melissa Parisi**, Westchester Community College, Valhalla, New York; **Jason Tannenbaum**, Pace University, Bronx, New York; **Christine Tierney**, Houston Community College, Stafford, Texas; **Kerry Vrabel**, GateWay Community College, Phoenix, Arizona.

CHAPTER 1

BUSINESS: Steve Jobs, Innovator and CEO

BUSINESS: the academic study of economics and management

OBJECTIVES

To read academic texts, you need to master certain skills.

In this chapter, you will:

- Predict the author's point of view from the title of a text
- Predict the content of a text from the first paragraph
- Skim a text by reading the topic sentences
- Guess the meaning of words from the context
- Use dictionary entries to learn the meanings of words
- Understand and use synonyms and different word forms
- Use underlining, circling, and margin notes to identify important facts and people

A Consider These Questions

1 Which of these descriptions refer to Bill Gates (BG) of Microsoft, Steve Jobs (SJ) of Apple, Larry Page (LP) of Google, Sergey Brin (SB) of Google, or Mark Zuckerberg (MZ) of Facebook? Write their initials on the lines. See answers below.

_____ a. attended an expensive private high school

_____ b. completed a university education

_____ c. came from a middle-class background

_____ d. had family help in professional preparation

2 How easy do you think it would be for an adopted working-class dropout from a small college to become a hi-tech entrepreneur? Check (✓) the appropriate answer.

☐ **a.** very easy   ☐ **c.** difficult

☐ **b.** easy   ☐ **d.** very difficult

B The Personality of Innovators

1 Which personal qualities do you think would be most helpful for a business innovator, someone who invents new things? Check (✓) the appropriate qualities.

☐ **a.** takes risks   ☐ **e.** easily influenced by others

☐ **b.** independent   ☐ **f.** honest

☐ **c.** friendly   ☐ **g.** enthusiastic

☐ **d.** doesn't give up easily

2 What other qualities do you think would be useful? Write them on the lines.

_comfortable with change_____

_____

_____

A Warm-Up

Discuss the questions with a partner.

1. What career advice have you received from other people?

2. Has the advice been useful?

3. In your opinion, what is the best way to have a successful career in business?

B Reading Strategy

Predicting Author's Point of View from Title

The **title** of a text often helps us **predict (guess)** the **author's point of view** or **opinion** about the topic he or she is writing about.

Look at the title of the reading. What does the author probably think about the life of Steve Jobs? Circle one of the choices and discuss your answer with a partner.

a. a successful life

b. a failure in some ways

c. an unusual life

Now read the text to find out if your prediction was correct.

The Extraordinary Life of Steve Jobs

1   The man who shaped some of the greatest technological innovations of our time never graduated from college. Far from it: He **dropped out** of Reed College after only six months. Steve Jobs made this decision partly because he **spurned** the idea of "required" courses — courses he had to take even though he was not interested in the subject. All his life he resisted anyone or anything telling him what to do. But more fundamentally, his college tuition[1] was going to eat up all the money his parents had saved, and he didn't even know what he wanted to do with his life.

(continued on next page)

---

[1] *tuition:* school fees

2   Steven Paul Jobs was abandoned at birth and **adopted** by a working-class couple in California, Paul and Clara Jobs. His birth mother[2], an unmarried graduate student, wanted her baby to be given to college graduates. Paul and Clara Jobs were thrilled to get the baby, but Paul Jobs had never finished high school, and Clara had never completed college. Steve's birth mother refused to sign the adoption papers until the couple promised to make sure the child would go to college. The Jobs family honored this **vow**, recognizing Steve's abilities and doing everything in their power to give him a chance in life. At an early age, Jobs knew that he was adopted, but he never allowed people to refer to Paul and Clara as his "adoptive" parents if it implied that they were something less than "real" parents. As he said, "They *were* my parents, 1000%. They made me feel special."[3] But no one doubts that his early history made him feel different from others and very independent.

Steve Jobs (right) with Steve Wozniak and the Apple computer

3   Dropping out of college was a scary decision, but Jobs felt that he had to follow his interests and natural **intuition**. He stopped going to the classes he disliked and got permission to sit in on the classes he wanted. He went barefoot, slept on the floor in friends' rooms, and returned soda bottles for coins. On weekends, he walked miles to the Hare Krishna temple for a free meal. It was at this time that he discovered a lifelong interest in design, Eastern spirituality, and vegetarianism.

4   Eighteen months after dropping out, in that lucky time when working with computers was a limitless field of creativity, Jobs was in his family's garage working with his friend Steve Wozniak to invent Apple. Their passion and dedication met with success; by the time Jobs was 30, the company was worth $2 billion and had thousands of employees. Apple grew so large that it hired a businessman to help run the company. But things kept changing fast. Soon after the commercial **release** of a new product, the Macintosh, a power struggle within the board of directors ended with Steve Jobs being pushed out of his own company. It was a **devastating** moment for a man who had known only success.

5   In his speech to Stanford University graduates in 2005, Jobs said: "I didn't see it at the time but it turned out that getting fired from Apple was the best thing that could have happened to me." What changed in this period? Not his impatient and difficult personality. Not his obsessive attention to detail, nor his desire to connect technology with the arts and machines with beautiful design. Steve Jobs once again had an open field to experiment. During this period, he had some brilliant failures that turned into amazing successes. Against all odds, one of his new companies, named Pixar, became the most successful computer animation studio in the world. The technological **innovations** developed at his other company, NeXT, were at the heart of

---

[2] His birth mother, an American graduate student in speech pathology, and his birth father, a Syrian graduate student in political science, later married and had a daughter. "Closed" adoption procedures at that time made it impossible for them to find or claim their son.

[3] Quoted in *Steve Jobs* by Walter Isaacson (page 5)

the new ideas that Jobs eventually brought back to save Apple. And Steve Jobs got married and had a family. What happened after 2000 is iMac, iPod, iTunes, iPhone, and iPad history.

6 A great businessman, innovator, magician? A man of destiny gone too soon? History's final decision on the accomplishments of Steve Jobs is yet to be known. But his advice to young people was clear: Find what you love. Choose the work that satisfies you. He concludes his 2005 Stanford speech with this memory from the 1970s:

"When I was young, there was an amazing publication called *The Whole Earth Catalog*. On the back cover of their final issue was a photograph of an early morning country road, the kind you might find yourself hitchhiking on if you were so adventurous. Beneath it were the words: 'Stay Hungry, Stay Foolish.' I have always wished that for myself. And now, as you graduate to begin anew, I wish that for you.

Stay Hungry. Stay Foolish."

COMPREHENSION

🄐 Main Ideas

Check (✓) the statements that best express the main ideas in the reading. Discuss your answers with a partner.

☐ **1.** Children need college-educated parents in order to succeed.

☐ **2.** Having confidence in oneself and following one's interests and passions are the keys to success in life.

☐ **3.** Failure can be a motivating force for future successes.

☐ **4.** Giving up the work you love is the best way to be successful.

🄱 Close Reading

Read the quotes from the reading. Circle the statement that best explains each quote. Share your answers with a partner.

1. "The man who shaped some of the greatest technological innovations of our time never graduated from college." *(paragraph 1)*

   a. It is wrong that Jobs never graduated from college.

   b. It is unusual that Jobs never graduated from college.

2. "History's final decision on the accomplishments of Steve Jobs is yet to be known." *(paragraph 6)*

   a. It is too soon to make a final judgment on Steve Jobs's accomplishments.

   b. Steve Jobs's accomplishments are not that great.

3. "Stay Hungry, Stay Foolish." *(paragraph 6)*

   a. Want more. Don't be stupid.

   b. Be ambitious. Take risks.

VOCABULARY

 A **Guessing from Context**

> Looking up every unfamiliar word in the dictionary is not an effective way to read. It is much better to **guess the meaning of unfamiliar words from the rest of the sentence or paragraph (the context)** and keep reading. Some words in particular can help you guess. No one guesses correctly all the time. But practice makes all the difference. You can use the dictionary after you get the main idea of the reading.

Read each quote from the reading. Try to guess the meaning of the word in bold from other words in the context. Write the words that helped you guess. Then write your guess. Compare answers with a partner.

1. "The man who shaped some of the greatest technological innovations of our time never graduated from college. Far from it: He **dropped out** of Reed College after only six months." *(paragraph 1)*

   Words that helped you guess: _never graduated college / only six months_

   Your guess: _quit before the end_

2. "Steve Jobs made this decision partly because he **spurned** the idea of 'required' courses — courses he had to take even though he was not interested in the subject. All his life he resisted anyone or anything telling him what to do." *(paragraph 1)*

   Words that helped you guess: _____

   Your guess: _____

3. "Steven Paul Jobs was abandoned at birth and **adopted** by a working-class couple in California, Paul and Clara Jobs. His birth mother, an unmarried graduate student, wanted her baby to be given to college graduates." *(paragraph 2)*

   Words that helped you guess: _____

   Your guess: _____

4. "Steve's birth mother refused to sign the adoption papers until the couple promised to make sure the child would go to college. The Jobs family honored this **vow**, recognizing Steve's abilities and doing everything in their power to give him a chance in life." *(paragraph 2)*

   Words that helped you guess: _____

   Your guess: _____

5. "Dropping out of college was a scary decision, but Jobs felt that he had to follow his interests and natural **intuition**. He stopped going to the classes he disliked and got permission to sit in on the classes he wanted." *(paragraph 3)*

   Words that helped you guess: _____

   Your guess: _____

6. "Soon after the commercial **release** of a new product, the Macintosh, a power struggle within the board of directors ended with Steve Jobs being pushed out of his own company." *(paragraph 4)*

   Words that helped you guess: _____

   Your guess: _____

7. ". . . a power struggle within the board of directors ended with Steve Jobs being pushed out of his own company. It was a **devastating** moment for a man who had known only success." *(paragraph 4)*

   Words that helped you guess: _____

   Your guess: _____

8. "The technological **innovations** developed at his other company, NeXT, were at the heart of the new ideas that Jobs eventually brought back to save Apple." *(paragraph 5)*

   Words that helped you guess: _____

   Your guess: _____

B **Word Forms**

1 Fill in the chart with the correct word forms. Some categories can have more than one form. Use a dictionary if necessary. An *X* indicates there is no form in that category.

	NOUN	VERB	ADJECTIVE	ADVERB
1.	devastation	devastate	devastating	
2.	innovation / innovator			
3.		intuit	intuitive	
4.	adoption /		adopted / adoptive*	X

* Steve Jobs was an **adopted** child. Paul and Clara Jobs were his **adoptive** parents.

2 Complete the sentences with the correct form of the words. Choose from the two forms in parentheses.

1. Steve Jobs was an _____ thinker, but he admitted that
   (innovation / innovative)

   computer pioneers have been shameless about stealing some great ideas. He

   agreed with Picasso's statement: "Good artists copy, great artists steal."

2. It was a _____ feeling when Jobs lost his place at Apple,
   (devastate / devastating)

   but he later came back to the company in one of the most spectacular second acts

   in recent business history.

3. Steve Jobs had an _____ sister, with whom he grew up.
   (adopted / adoption)

   He also had a birth sister, the writer Mona Simpson.

4. Jobs said that sometimes we don't consciously know what to do, but we have an

   _____ about the direction our life should take.
   (intuit / intuition)

NOTE-TAKING: Underlining Important Facts and Writing Margin Notes

1 Go back to the reading. Underline important facts in Jobs's story. Then write notes in the margin that will help you remember these facts.

EXAMPLE:

The man who shaped some of the greatest technological innovations of our time never graduated from college. Far from it: He dropped out of Reed College after only six months. Steve Jobs made this decision partly because he spurned the idea of "required" courses — courses he had to take even though he was not interested in the subject. All his life he resisted anyone or anything telling him what to do. But more fundamentally, his college tuition was going to eat up all the money his parents had saved, and he didn't even know what he wanted to do with his life.	*no college education* *Why?* *didn't want to take* *required courses* *stubborn* *tuition too expensive* *no direction in life*

2 Complete each statement with the appropriate information from the box below.

1. Jobs _____*dropped out*_____ of college after six months.

2. Jobs's birth mother wanted the couple who adopted him to be

   _____.

3. Despite the many challenges he faced, Jobs found that following his

   _____ was essential to his future success.

4. At age 20, Jobs started to work in his parents' garage with Steve Wozniak

   _____.

5. At age 30, Jobs was fired from Apple because of a disagreement with the

   _____.

6. Jobs _____ to Apple when it bought NeXT, the company

   he developed after being fired from Apple.

7. According to Jobs, people can become successful in life when they are

   _____ and love what they do.

a. college graduates	**e.** returned
b. adventurous	**f.** board of directors
c. to develop Apple	**g.** interests and
d. dropped out	natural intuition

CRITICAL THINKING

Discuss the questions in a small group. Be prepared to share your answers with the class.

1. Look back at "Consider These Questions" at the beginning of the chapter. How did Steve Jobs's life fit this pattern?

2. What qualities did Jobs have that a business entrepreneur should have?

3. How did dropping out of college help Jobs? Is that a risk you would be willing to take? Why or why not?

4. "When I was young, there was an amazing publication called *The Whole Earth Catalog.* On the back cover of their final issue was a photograph of an early morning country road, the kind you might find yourself hitchhiking on if you were so adventurous." What do you think the road is a symbol for? Why is it early morning in the picture? What kind of life was Steve Jobs telling young people to live? What do you think of his advice?

A Warm-Up

Discuss the questions with a partner.

Cartoons today use CGI (Computer-Generated Imagery) because it saves money on drawing by hand. The science fiction movie *Jurassic Park* used CGI so that the dinosaurs would look more realistic.

1. Why do action movies use CGI?

2. Can you name some recent movies that used CGI to make things exciting?

B Reading Strategy

Predicting Content from First Paragraph

In newspaper articles, the **first paragraph often summarizes the main points** of the text. Reading the first paragraph of an article often allows you to predict (guess) the content of the article.

Read the first paragraph of "The Pixar Story." What do you think will be the main points of the article?

1. _____   4. _____

2. _____   5. _____

3. _____

Now read the text to find out if your predictions were correct.

The Pixar Story

1 The Pixar films *Toy Story, A Bug's Life, Monsters, Inc., Finding Nemo, Ratatouille, The Incredibles, Cars, WALL-E,* and *Up* made billions of dollars. But the story of Pixar is not just about money. It's a tale of technical innovation, teamwork, creativity, and business acumen.

2 The Pixar[1] team began in 1979, when George Lucas needed special effects for *Star Wars.* He enticed Edwin Catmull, a PhD in computer science, to Lucasfilm. Over the next few years, Catmull and his ensemble created innovative computer

---

[1] *Pixar* was chosen as a name related to "pixels." In digital imaging, a pixel is the smallest unit of a picture. The word *pixel* was formed from *picture* (*pix*) and *element* (*el*).

graphics programs and equipment. This included an imaging computer, the "Pixar," which could create high-resolution color images of anything from buildings and cars to tornadoes and aliens.

3   When Lucas had to sell the group in 1986, the only taker was Steve Jobs, who had just been fired from Apple. Jobs cashed in his Apple stock and reportedly paid $10 million to Lucas for the company he renamed Pixar.

4   Pixar began making animated TV commercials and short films like *Luxo Jr.,* which won an Academy Award. But Jobs was still pouring $50 million into a firm making no profits. Pixar's computer animation department, run by John Lasseter[2], had to keep fighting to survive.

5   In 1991, Jobs took an even more **drastic** step: He would keep paying for Pixar only if the employees gave all their stock shares to him, making him sole owner. Jobs began looking around for a buyer.

6   **Salvation** seemed to come from Disney Studios. Jobs made a deal with Disney to produce the first full-length feature film made entirely with computers. But Disney shut down Pixar's first film because the main character was unappealing. Technical **expertise**, they said, had to go along

Steve Jobs (right) with John Lasseter (center) and Michael Eisner, CEO of Disney

with being able to tell a good story. Lasseter went to screenwriting classes. Steve Jobs stayed home to play with his two-year-old son.

7   Very soon, however, the cutting-edge work of Pixar and NeXt, Jobs's other company, **paid off**. Steve Jobs became CEO of Apple again. Pixar's *Toy Story* became a **phenomenal** success.

8   In the first negotiation with Disney, Jobs had a **lack** of experience in the entertainment business and settled for a small percentage of the profits. In 2006, he threatened to withdraw from the partnership altogether. To keep Pixar, Walt Disney's nephew Roy staged a coup[3] inside the Disney board of directors, changed the leadership, and purchased Pixar. Catmull and Lasseter became heads at Disney. Steve Jobs became a billionaire.

9   When Steve Jobs died, Pixar issued a statement: "Steve saw the potential of what Pixar could be before the rest of us. . . . He took a chance and believed in our crazy dream of making animated films. The one thing he always said was 'make it great.'"

---

[2] *John Lasseter* began his career doing hand-drawn animation for Disney. He left to join the Computer Division in Lucasfilm's Industrial Light and Magic in 1984 in order to explore computer animation. He was one of the creative leaders of Pixar, winning several Academy Awards.

[3] *coup* (from French: *coup d'état*): a sudden overthrow of those in power

COMPREHENSION

A Main Ideas

Read each statement. Decide if it is *True* or *False* according to the reading. Check (✓) the appropriate box. If it is false, change it to make it true. Discuss your answers with a partner.

	TRUE	FALSE
1. The story about Pixar simply tells how money talks.	☐	☑
2. Catmull used his computer expertise to create the high-resolution images that the Pixar team is famous for.	☐	☐
3. Lucas found it easy to sell his company in 1986.	☐	☐
4. Jobs's idea to work with the entertainment industry eventually assured Pixar's success.	☐	☐
5. For Disney, knowing how to tell a good story was as important as having technical expertise.	☐	☐
6. Roy Disney was not a very good business leader.	☐	☐

B Close Reading

Read the quotes from the reading. Circle the statement that best explains each quote. Share your answers with a partner.

1. "Jobs cashed in his Apple stock and reportedly paid $10 million to Lucas for the company he renamed Pixar." (*paragraph 3*)

   a. It's not clear exactly how much was paid.

   b. Jobs reported that he paid $10 million.

2. "But Jobs was still pouring $50 million into a firm making no profits." (*paragraph 4*)

   a. Pixar lived on Jobs's credit.

   b. Pixar was earning no money.

3. "In 1991, Jobs took an even more drastic step: He would keep paying for Pixar only if the employees gave all their stock shares to him, making him sole owner." (*paragraph 5*)

   a. Jobs took a desperate measure.

   b. Jobs decided to invest more money.

4. "Steve Jobs stayed home to play with his two-year-old son." (*paragraph 6*)

   a. Jobs wanted to retire.

   b. Jobs was depressed and stopped working.

5. "Very soon, however, the cutting-edge work of Pixar paid off." (*paragraph 7*)

   a. The Pixar people were paid a salary.

   b. Pixar's efforts met with success.

6. "To keep Pixar, Walt Disney's nephew Roy staged a coup inside the Disney board of directors, changed the leadership, and purchased Pixar." (*paragraph 8*)

   a. Roy Disney thought Pixar was the way of the future.

   b. Roy Disney wanted to be the head of the studio.

VOCABULARY

A Synonyms

Cross out the word that is NOT a synonym (word with the same meaning) for the word in bold. Check your answers with a partner.

1. **acumen**	judgment	shrewdness	~~apprehension~~
2. **drastic**	necessary	~~desperate~~	extreme
3. **entice**	~~disgust~~	attract	invite
4. **expertise**	knowledge	~~inability~~	skill
5. **lack**	absence	shortage	sufficiency
6. **phenomenal**	astounding	~~unexceptional~~	extraordinary
7. **salvation**	~~waste~~	rescue	escape

B Using the Dictionary

Read the dictionary entry for the phrasal verb *pay off*.

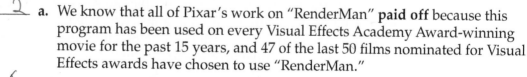

pay off *ph.v.* **1** to pay someone all the money you owe them **2** if something you do pays off, it brings success after a lot of effort or after a long time **3** to give someone money so they will keep quiet about something illegal or dishonest

Now read each sentence. Decide which meaning of the verb is being used. Write the number of the appropriate meaning.

__2__ a. We know that all of Pixar's work on "RenderMan" **paid off** because this program has been used on every Visual Effects Academy Award-winning movie for the past 15 years, and 47 of the last 50 films nominated for Visual Effects awards have chosen to use "RenderMan."

__1__ b. But not even the brilliance of the RenderMan program could **pay off** the company's debts and support its work.

__3__ c. Criminal organizations that counterfeit movies **pay off** their associates so that they won't talk about the piracy.

NOTE-TAKING: Circling Names and Writing Margin Notes

1 Go back to the reading. Circle the names of the important people in the Pixar story. Then write notes in the margin about the role of each person.

EXAMPLE:

The Pixar team began in 1979, when (George Lucas) needed special effects for *Star Wars*. He **enticed** (Edwin Catmull), a PhD in computer science, to Lucasfilm. Over the next few years, Catmull and his ensemble created innovative computer graphics programs and equipment. This included an imaging computer, the "Pixar," which could create high-resolution color images of anything from buildings and cars to tornadoes and aliens.

Filmmaker, needed special effects for "Star Wars" — hired Catmull

Computer scientist, created innovative imaging computer: the "Pixar"

2 Match the people in the Pixar story with their roles.

___d___ 1. George Lucas

___e___ 2. Edwin Catmull

___b___ 3. John Lasseter

___a___ 4. Roy Disney

___c___ 5. Steve Jobs

a. owner of Pixar as of 2006

b. head of Pixar's computer animation department

c. sole owner of Pixar in 1991

d. filmmaker, needed special effects for *Star Wars*

e. computer scientist, created the "Pixar," an innovative imaging computer

CRITICAL THINKING

Discuss the questions in a small group. Be prepared to share your answers with the class.

1. Apple was the first of the digital giants (before Amazon or Google) to make a wide-ranging deal with music companies, which led to iTunes. What in Steve Jobs's previous experience with Pixar helped him understand how to build bridges between creative people and "techies"?

2. Because Pixar wasn't making any profit, most management advisers would have told the owner to get rid of it. Why was Jobs the kind of person who would stick with Pixar?

3. Look up some information on the life of Steve Jobs. Try to answer the questions you might have had when you did the readings. Many people have said that Steve Jobs was a more complex and contradictory person than we think. Do you agree or disagree? Why or why not?

LINKING READINGS ONE AND TWO

Write a brief paragraph in answer to these questions. Share your writing with a partner.

1. How does the information in the biography of Steve Jobs help us understand his belief in a company like Pixar?

2. Jobs ended his Stanford commencement speech with the words: "Stay Hungry. Stay Foolish." Is that the advice he followed with Pixar? Why or why not?

READING THREE: The Map of Innovation

A **Warm-Up**

Discuss the questions with a partner.

1. If you were an entrepreneur in a new company, what kind of people would you hire to help you?

2. What would you be looking for in an employee?

B **Reading Strategy**

Skimming by Reading Topic Sentences

Skimming is a reading technique that is used to **get a quick "gist" of a text**. Reading the **topic sentence** (first sentence) of a paragraph and especially the **keyword** in it will help you get the gist, or main idea, of each paragraph in a text.

Look at the five topic sentences in the reading and circle the keywords that preview the main ideas. Then write these keywords on the lines.

PARAGRAPH 1: _teams_

PARAGRAPH 2: _____

PARAGRAPH 3: _____

PARAGRAPH 4: _____

PARAGRAPH 5: _____

Now read the text to find out more about its main ideas.

The Map of Innovation: Creating Something Out of Nothing

By Kevin O'Connor

1 I don't care how smart you are, or what you've **accomplished** in your life, or how revolutionary your product concept is, great companies are built by teams of people and not **solely** by their CEOs or founders. I want to talk about how to hire, organize, and **retain** great people because if you don't do all three of those things, **ultimately** nothing good is going to happen.

Team of business people at work

2 I always look for people who are way smarter than average. A lot of people confuse skills with intelligence.... Ideally you want to hire a person who is very smart and possesses the skills you need. If you are forced to choose between skills and smarts, smarts always wins. Intelligence is the most necessary trait when you're creating something that hasn't been done before. You need people who can figure out solutions to all the problems you are going to face.

3 Smart is good. But smart in and of itself isn't enough. That's why I also try to discover how competitive they are. The important thing is a continuous demonstration that they competed and won. If somebody has this **trait**, it will **manifest** itself somehow.

4 In sports, we call the limit of somebody's ability to endure everything his "pain threshold.[1]" The theory is that the greater the person's pain threshold, the longer he will go on fighting. The battle for a new market can be brutal. You need a **cohesive** team with a high pain threshold to wear your competition out, to make them quit. Find people who are "athletes," used to competing.

5 The boss's role is to make sure the organization is going in the right direction and to act with **integrity**, and to make sure the smart athletes she has hired have the resources they need to get the job done.

---

[1] *pain threshold:* the point at which a stimulus begins to produce a reaction

COMPREHENSION

A **Main Ideas**

Read each statement. Decide if it is *True* or *False* according to the reading. Check (✓) the appropriate box. If it is false, change it to make it true. Discuss your answers with a partner.

	TRUE	FALSE
1. Problem-solving skills and general intelligence are more important than specific skills.	☑	☐
2. CEOs build great companies.	☐	☑
3. Being competitive is all you need to succeed.	☐	☑
4. Smart employees also need to have a high pain threshold.	☐	☐
5. A good boss provides not only the general direction of the company but also the resources the employees need.	☑	☐

B **Close Reading**

Read the quotes from the reading. Circle the statement that best explains each quote. Share your answers with a partner.

1. "If you are forced to choose between skills and smarts, smarts always wins." (*paragraph 2*)

   a. Employees should always have the specific skills you need in your business.

   b. Intelligence should be the most important consideration when you hire.

2. "The theory is that the greater the person's pain threshold, the longer he will go on fighting." (*paragraph 4*)

   a. Employees should never want to give up.

   b. Employees should be able to avoid pain.

3. "The boss's role is to make sure the organization is going in the right direction and to act with integrity, and to make sure the smart athletes she has hired have the resources they need to get the job done." (*paragraph 5*)

   a. The boss should supervise what the employees are doing and make sure they are honest.

   b. The boss should make long-term decisions and make sure the employees have everything they need.

VOCABULARY

Synonyms

Complete each sentence with a word from the box. Use the synonym in parentheses to help you select the correct word. Compare answers with a partner.

accomplished	integrity	retains	traits
cohesive	manifests	solely	ultimately

1. At Zappos, the online shoe store, CEO Tony Hsieh (pronounced "Shay") believes that getting the corporate culture right will _____ultimately_____ lead to
(in the end)
better customer service and enthusiastic employees.

2. One of the many things Hsieh _accomplished_ before he came to
(achieved)
Zappos was building a multimillion-dollar Internet advertising company called LinkExchange, which he sold to Microsoft for $265 million.

3. At Zappos, employees get free health, dental, and eye care, free food in the cafeteria, and a workplace full of balloons, streamers, toys, parades, and costume parties. No wonder the company _retains_ its employees!
(keeps)

4. Each employee passes two job interviews to tell what _traits_
(qualities)
they can offer the company: One is a traditional interview, but the second asks them what superhero they would like to be in order to see what creative explanation they can offer.

5. After the training period, each employee is offered $3,000 to leave. Not many take the offer, which makes the company more _cohesive_ because
(unified)
everyone actually wants to be there.

6. Job satisfaction _manifests_ itself in the workers' careful
(shows)
attention to customer service.

7. Company _integrity_ can be seen in the fact that there are no
(honesty)
time limits on phone calls with customers, no prearranged scripts for employees to say, no hard sell, just problem solving for the customer.

8. Hsieh is not _solely_ interested in business; he has also
(only)
written a book titled *Delivering Happiness: A Path to Profits, Passion, and Purpose.*

CRITICAL THINKING

Discuss the questions in a small group. Be prepared to share your ideas with the class.

1. Many employers don't like to hire people who are smarter than they are. What would Kevin O'Connor say about this? Would Steve Jobs agree with O'Connor? Why or why not?

2. Why does O'Connor use "she," not "he," in paragraph 5?

3. Do you think that being competitive is one of the most important traits for new hires in a company? Should employees be competitive with each other? Explain your answer. Did Jobs follow this advice at Pixar?

4. According to O'Connor, the boss shouldn't micromanage every detail of everyday life in the company. She (or he) should take care of long-term perspectives and the task of getting adequate resources for her (or his) team. Do you agree with this assessment? Would Jobs qualify as a good boss of Pixar according to O'Connor? Why or why not?

AFTER YOU READ

BRINGING IT ALL TOGETHER

Work in groups of four. Role-play an interview with Steve Jobs and Kevin O'Connor about business. Two journalists ask the questions suggested below. Jobs and O'Connor can prepare their answers in advance. Use some of the vocabulary you studied in the chapter (for a complete list, go to page 21).

TOPIC: Business

ROLES:
- Journalist 1
- Journalist 2
- Steve Jobs
- Kevin O'Connor

QUESTIONS:
- Kevin O'Connor, do you think that Steve Jobs followed your rules?
- Steve Jobs, do you agree about what you should or shouldn't have done as CEO of Pixar? Did you act with integrity and fulfill a boss's role?
- Steve Jobs, do you agree that intelligence is one of the most important qualities for your employees? Did you employ the brightest people in your companies?
- Kevin O'Connor, do you think that the Apple board of directors was correct to invite Steve Jobs to come back?
- Steve Jobs, do you agree that being competitive (an athlete) is an important trait, or would you add other traits, too?

Add your own questions:
- _____
- _____

WRITING ACTIVITY

Write two paragraphs about business management.

- **First paragraph:** Summarize the information about business management discussed in this chapter.
- **Second paragraph:** Write about your reaction to this advice and experience.

Use at least five of the words you studied in the chapter.

DISCUSSION AND WRITING TOPICS

Discuss these topics in a small group. Choose one of them and write a paragraph or two about it. Use the vocabulary from the chapter.

1. Many people say that Apple products are both useful and elegant. Do you agree or disagree? Why or why not? Are there other products that combine these two aspects today?

2. What do you think of the corporate culture of Zappos, the online shoe company? Why would the boss bother to create such an environment for workers who receive only $11 an hour? Would you like to work there? How would you answer their question about a superhero? Do you think that's a good question? Why or why not?

3. Computer animation cuts down on the number of people a studio has to pay to make a cartoon. Like all kinds of automation, it is generally more cost-efficient, although it may use different kinds of workers. Why were people so suspicious at first of animated cartoons made only by computers?

4. In a CNN interview ("How Steve Jobs's Pixar Experience Helped Lead to Apple's iCloud") conducted by Mark Millan, Steve Jobs said the following:

   "One of the things I learned at Pixar is the technology industries and the content industries do not understand each other. In Silicon Valley and at most technology companies, I swear that most people still think the creative process is a bunch of guys in their early 30s, sitting on a couch, drinking beer and thinking of jokes. No, they really do. That's how television is made, they think; that's how movies are made. Likewise, record executives can't relate to technical people."

   When you think of the technology you enjoy today, do you also believe it is created by "a bunch of guys in their early 30s, sitting on a couch, drinking beer and thinking of jokes"? Why or why not?

SELF-ASSESSMENT

In this chapter you learned to:

O Predict the author's point of view from the title of a text

O Predict the content of a text from the first paragraph

O Skim a text by reading the topic sentences

O Guess the meaning of words from the context

O Use dictionary entries to learn the meanings of words

O Understand and use synonyms and different word forms

O Use underlining, circling, and margin notes to identify important facts and people

What can you do well? ✔

What do you need to practice more? ✔

CHAPTER 2

PSYCHOLOGY:
Fears and Phobias

PSYCHOLOGY: the study of the mind and how it works

OBJECTIVES

To read academic texts, you need to master certain skills.

In this chapter, you will:

- Scan a text to find specific information

- Preview a text using visuals

- Understand scholarly references

- Understand and use synonyms, collocations, and different word forms

- Guess the meaning of words from their Greek or Latin roots

- Use dictionary entries to learn the meanings of words

- Organize and categorize study notes

A Consider This Case

1 Read the letter to "Dear Speak Out" — an advice column in a student newspaper.

> Dear Speak Out,
>
> Whenever I tell people about my fear, they look at me like I'm crazy. Yet whenever I see the painted face of a clown, I break out in a cold sweat, and my heart feels like it's going to jump out of my chest. My stomach turns to jelly, and I'm afraid I'm going to throw up. That's why I don't go to circuses, fairs, festivals, or birthday parties for kids. I guess you can blame it all on my sister. She loved horror movies—the scarier, the better. I sneaked into the living room one night when she was watching a movie about a killer clown. When I saw what she was watching, I was so afraid I couldn't move. I was just a little boy, but since then, the fear has only gotten worse. Believe me, it's no laughing matter. What should I do?
>
> Worried in College

2 Discuss the questions with a partner.

1. What is this student afraid of? Why?

2. What advice would you give Worried in College? Check (✓) your answer.

☐ **a.** Calm down and act normally.   ☐ **d.** See a therapist.

☐ **b.** Talk with some clowns.   ☐ **e.** *Other*: _____

☑ **c.** Keep avoiding clowns.

B Think about Your Fears

All of us have fears, but they usually don't interfere with our daily lives. What are you afraid of?

1 Check (✓) the things or situations that make you uncomfortable or worried.

☐ snakes   ☐ speaking in public   ☐ social situations

☐ mice   ☑ very small places   ☐ air travel

☐ insects   ☐ the dark   ☐ seeing blood
(spiders, cockroaches)
        ☐ getting injections   ☐ clowns
☐ high places

2 Discuss the questions in a small group.

1. Some things or situations affect you but don't affect others. Why?

2. What do you do about fears you might have?

3. If you had a strong fear, would you ask anyone for help? Who?

A Warm-Up

You can prepare for a reading by looking at the title. The title of the reading is "When Does a Fear Become a Phobia?"

Check (✓) each possible answer.

1. From this title, you can tell that . . .

   ☐ **a.** a fear is not the same thing as a phobia

   ☐ **b.** a fear can turn into a phobia

   ☐ **c.** phobias only happen at certain times

2. What kind of information do you think this reading will give you?

   ☐ **a.** definitions

   ☐ **b.** examples

   ☐ **c.** professional opinions

B Reading Strategy

Scanning

Scanning a text means **looking at it quickly to find specific information**. This skill can be useful on standardized tests when you may not have time to read everything. You just look quickly to find the answer to the question. Scanning is also helpful when you have many pages to read. You can learn to look only for the essential information.

From the title of the reading, it is clear that the text is going to explain the difference between a simple fear and a phobia.

Scan the reading for the *definition* of a phobia. (Hint: Look for the words "A phobia is . . .") Underline it in the reading and write it on the lines.

_____

_____

_____

Now read the text to find out more about what a phobia is.

WHEN DOES A FEAR BECOME A PHOBIA?

By Rod Plotnik, from "Anxiety Disorders," in *Introduction to Psychology*

1   People are afraid of many things: snakes, bugs, getting injections, taking exams, flying in airplanes, meeting new people, speaking in public, and seeing blood. Sometimes our worries become so strong and **intense** that we cannot **function** normally in daily life. That's when these **fears** become **phobias**. A phobia is an **anxiety disorder** characterized by extreme irrational fear and heightened physiological arousal[1] that is out of proportion to the situation. The feared object or situation is met with great anxiety if it cannot be avoided.

[1] *physiological arousal:* a physical state characterized by a fast heartbeat, rapid breathing, sweating, confusion, and dizziness because stress hormones are flooding the body

2   Anxiety is a feeling of constant worry and **dread**. Anxiety conditions are characterized by constant worry or by self-defeating behavior aimed at preventing anxious situations from happening. People with a strong fear of elevators, for example, may be unable to work or live in buildings where elevators would be part of their everyday lives. They may refuse good jobs because they cannot ride in elevators. People with social phobias may be so afraid of speaking in public that they cannot function in school or at work.

3   Anxiety disorders represent the most common **psychological** disorders[2] in the United States, with approximately 30 to 40% [percent] of the population developing them at some point in their lives. Anxiety disorders can have a negative effect on work, social, and family functioning and they can lead to other **severe** disorders, such as **depression** and alcoholism.

[2] *psychological disorders:* also include depression, substance abuse (alcoholism and drug use), and schizophrenia (with hallucinations and disorganized behavior)

COMPREHENSION

A   Main Ideas

Read each statement. Decide if it is *True* or *False* according to the reading. Check (✓) the appropriate box. If it is false, change it to make it true. Discuss your answers with a partner.

	TRUE	FALSE
1. Everybody has phobias.	☐	☑
2. People with phobias have trouble living a normal life.	☑	☐
3. Phobias are much more extreme than ordinary fears.	☐	☑
4. Phobias are very unusual psychological problems.	☑	☐

B   Close Reading

Read the quotes from the reading. Circle the statement that best explains each quote. Share your answers with a partner.

1. "A phobia is . . . an . . . extreme irrational fear . . . out of proportion to the situation." (*paragraph 1*)

   a. This fear is something most people would feel.

   b. This fear is great because the situation is bad.

   c. This fear is not necessary in the circumstances.

2. "Anxiety conditions are characterized by constant worry or by self-defeating behavior aimed at preventing anxious situations from happening." (*paragraph 2*)

   a. Someone with an anxiety condition is able to deal with his or her fears effectively.

   b. Someone with an anxiety condition wants to avoid what he or she is afraid of.

   c. Someone with an anxiety condition will do anything to be anxious.

3. "Anxiety disorders . . . can lead to other severe disorders, such as depression and alcoholism." (*paragraph 3*)

   a. People with anxiety disorders sometimes become very depressed.

   b. People's phobias sometimes become too severe.

   c. People with depression are sometimes alcoholics.

VOCABULARY

A Synonyms

Work with a partner. Read "When Does a Fear Become a Phobia?" again and discuss the meanings of the words in bold. Then match each word with its synonym.

_e_ 1. fear   a. very serious

_c_ 2. anxiety   b. operate

_d_ 3. intense   c. illness

_b_ 4. function   d. overwhelming

_a_ 5. severe   e. worry

___ 6. disorder   f. dread

B Collocations

When **words** are **used together regularly**, they become a **pair** — not for grammatical reasons, but because of their association with each other.

For example, we "make a mistake," but we "do our homework." The reason for using "make" with "mistake" and "do" with "homework" is that these words always go together. "Make a mistake" and "do our homework" are **collocations**.

With a partner, decide whether the words in bold can be used together. Check (✓) *Yes* or *No*.

		YES	No
1. a.	Can we have a **severe disorder**?	☑	☐
b.	Can we have a **severe fear**?	☐	☑
2. a.	Can we have an **intense pain**?	☑	☐
b.	Can we have an **intense disorder**?	☐	☑
3. a.	Can we have **intense anxiety**?	☐	☑
b.	Can we have **severe anxiety**?	☑	☐

C Word Forms

1 Fill in the chart with the correct word forms. Some categories can have more than one form. Use a dictionary if necessary. An **X** indicates there is no form in that category.

	NOUN	VERB	ADJECTIVE	ADVERB
1.	anxiety	X	anxious	anxiously
2.		fear		fearful
3.			intense	intensely
4.	phobia	X	Phobic	X
5.		dread	dreadful /	dreaded
6.		X	psychological	
7.		X	severe	
8.	depression			X

2 Complete the summary of the main points of the reading with the correct form of the words. Choose from the forms in parentheses.

Many people are _____ anxious _____ about something, but this
1. (anxiety / anxious / anxiously)
_____ anxiety _____ does not prevent them from functioning normally
2. (anxiety / anxious / anxiously)
in everyday life. An anxiety of overwhelming _____ intensity _____ is
3. (intensity / intense / intensely)
called _____. People who are suffering from phobias
4. (a phobia / phobic / phobias)
_____ fear _____ being in certain situations, such as riding in elevators
5. (a fear / fear / fearful)
or making speeches. This makes it difficult for them to function in school or at work.

These anxiety disorders, which affect people _____ psychologically _____,
6. (psychology / psychological / psychologically)
undoubtedly have a _____ severe _____ impact on the quality of their
7. (severity / severe / severely)
lives. People with phobias live lives filled with _____ and are
8. (dread / dreadful / dreaded)
often very _____ depressed _____.
9. (depress / depression / depressed)

CRITICAL THINKING

Discuss the questions in a small group. Be prepared to share your ideas with the class.

1. How can a phobia affect a person's family life? Give examples.

2. In what ways can a phobia affect an individual's social life?

3. Why do you think a phobia might lead to a deep depression? To alcoholism?

A Warm-Up

What kinds of phobias do you think are most common in the United States? List them here. Share your answers with a partner.

Claustrophobia
Arachnophobia
Trypanophobia
Social phobia.

B Reading Strategy

Previewing Using Visuals

As the expression **"A picture is worth a thousand words"** suggests, readers of charts and graphs figure out the information given in the visual, or picture, without having to read long texts. **Looking at charts and graphs** will help you **prepare for the content** of the reading.

Look at this graph and at the graph on page 30. Discuss the questions with a partner.

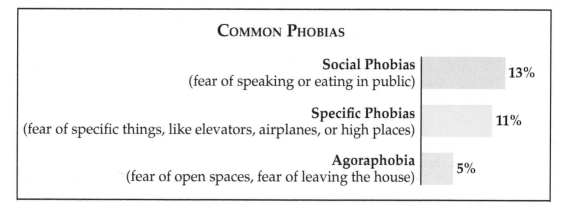

COMMON PHOBIAS

Social Phobias
(fear of speaking or eating in public) — 13%

Specific Phobias
(fear of specific things, like elevators, airplanes, or high places) — 11%

Agoraphobia
(fear of open spaces, fear of leaving the house) — 5%

1. What are the most common phobias? Which is the most common in this group?
2. What are some examples of specific phobias?
3. Which disorder do people who are afraid to leave their house have?

Now read the text to find out more about the different phobias featured in the graphs.

CASE STUDIES

By Rod Plotnik, from "Anxiety Disorders," in *Introduction to Psychology*

Social Phobias: Why Didn't Billy Say Anything in Class?

1   In junior high school Billy never ever spoke up in class or answered any questions. The school counselor said that Billy would become sick to his stomach the whole day if he knew he would be called on to speak. Billy began to hide in the restrooms to avoid going to class. Billy's fear of speaking up in class is an example of a social phobia. Social phobias **are characterized by irrational**, deep, and continuous fear of performing in social situations. The individuals fear that they will humiliate or embarrass themselves (American Psychiatric Association, 1994).

2   As a fearful social situation comes nearer, great anxiety builds up and may result in nausea, sweating, and other signs of heightened **physiological arousal**. Although a person with a social phobia realizes that the fear is **excessive** or irrational, he or she may not know how to deal with it except by avoiding the situation.

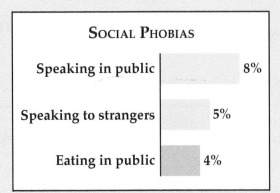

SOCIAL PHOBIAS

Speaking in public   8%

Speaking to strangers   5%

Eating in public   4%

Specific Phobias: Why Couldn't Kate Get On a Plane?

3   Kate's phobia of flying began in her childhood, when she **experienced** a very bumpy flight that left her scared and anxious. Later, as a young adult, her fear of flying was made worse by **traumatic** memories of a flight which killed several of her fellow-students from Syracuse University. Her phobia of flying kept her from visiting friends and family. She would make reservations to fly and try to go but would always cancel at the last minute. About 25 million Americans have an irrational and intense fear of flying. They refuse to get on a plane. Another 30 million have **moderate** to high degrees of anxiety when they fly. Kate is someone who has *aerophobia*, a specific phobia.

4   Specific phobias are characterized by severe and **persistent** fears that are unreasonable and brought on by a specific object or situation (flying, heights, spiders, seeing blood). Among the more common specific phobias are fear of animals (*zoophobia*), fear of heights (*acrophobia*), fear of closed spaces (*claustrophobia*), fear of injury or blood, and fear of flying.

5   The content and occurrence of specific phobias vary with cultures. For example, fear of ghosts is present in many cultures but becomes a specific phobia only if the fear turns excessive and irrational.

Agoraphobia: Why Couldn't Rose Leave Her House?

6   Fear trapped Rose in her house for years. If she thought about going outside to do her shopping, pain raced through her arms and chest. She grew hot and started sweating. Her heart beat rapidly and her legs felt like rubber. She said that thinking about leaving her house caused terror, sometimes lasting for days. This 39-year-old mother of two is one of many Americans suffering from an intense fear of being in public places, an anxiety disorder which is called *agoraphobia*.

7   Agoraphobia is characterized by anxiety about being in places or situations from which escape might be difficult or embarrassing if panic-like **symptoms** (sudden dizziness, for example) were to occur. These symptoms are extremely persistent and may continue for years if not treated.

COMPREHENSION

Ⓐ Main Ideas

Complete the sentences with information from the reading.

1. Unlike ordinary fears that come and go with time, phobias are severe,

   _____, and _____.

2. There are many different phobias including _Zoophobia_,

   agoraphobia, and _Claustrophobia_

3. People with phobias suffer from certain physical symptoms, such as

   _____, _____, and _____.

4. The nature of specific phobias depends on what _____

   a person is part of.

Ⓑ Close Reading

Read the quotes from the reading. Circle the statement that best explains the quote. Share your answers with a partner.

1. "Although a person with a social phobia realizes that the fear is excessive or irrational, he or she may not know how to deal with it except by avoiding the situation." (*paragraph 2*)

   a. A person with a social phobia knows how to overcome his or her fears.

   (b.) A person with a social phobia tries to escape from the situation he or she fears.

   c. A person with a social phobia isn't aware that he or she is being unreasonable.

2. "Specific phobias are characterized by severe and persistent fears that are unreasonable and brought on by a specific object or situation (flying, heights, spiders, seeing blood)." (*paragraph 4*)

   (a.) Specific phobias need something to trigger symptoms.

   b. Specific phobias occur in the absence of a specific object.

   c. Specific phobias do not occur in normal situations.

(continued on next page)

3. "Her heart beat rapidly and her legs felt like rubber." (*paragraph 6*)

    a. She couldn't feel her heart.

    b. She couldn't catch her breath.

    c. She felt like she couldn't stand up.

VOCABULARY

A Synonyms

Complete each paragraph with the words from the box. Use the synonym in parentheses to help you select the correct word. Compare answers with a partner.

arousal	experience	physiological	traumatic

Seventy-five percent of people who _____experience_____ phobias can
                                      1. (have)

trace the beginning of their symptoms to a specific _____traumatic_____
                                        2. (very frightening)

event. The _____Physiological_____ response to fear is to prepare for "fight
                    3. (bodily)

or flight" — for defense or escape. The heart beats faster; adrenaline, the stress

hormone, pumps through the body; and normal functions like digestion slow down

or stop. This state of _____arousal_____ is useful if you really have to
                    4. (readiness)

fight or run. If not, it will make you dizzy, sick to your stomach, and panicked. In

a phobia, the body is remembering something fearful or imagining it even though

there is no danger.

excessive	symptoms	irrational	moderate	persistent

Thus, most researchers believe that phobias are learned through bad experiences

or observation. An example of conditioning through a bad experience would

occur when a child almost drowns in a pool. Even after he or she is saved, the fear

produced by such an event will make the child show _____symptoms_____
                    5. (signs)

of the phobia when facing any water sport even if there is no danger. Other children

may show a slight or _____moderate_____ fear of the water, but a phobic
                    6. (medium)

child experiences a _____persistent_____ effect. Other children may laugh
                    7. (long-lasting)

and think the fear is _____excessive_____, and adults may tell the child
                    8. (too much)

that such a feeling is ___irrational___, but the conditioning remains.

9. (unreasonable)

In other cases, children may observe parents or other close adults who are deeply and permanently afraid of the water, and copy their reactions. Such phobias may diminish with patience and time. Yelling at children or punishing them will do no good.

B **Word Usage:** *be characterized by*

> In a **definition**, we often include a **description of the main characteristics** or qualities of the thing being defined, and we use the idiom **be characterized by**.
>
> **EXAMPLE:**
> * A phobia **is characterized by** intense and irrational fear.
>   *This means that the main characteristic of a phobia is a feeling of great fear.*

Work with a partner. Take turns describing the main characteristics of the phobias mentioned in the reading.

1. **Social phobia:** _A social phobia is characterized by . . ._____

2. **Specific phobia:** _____

3. **Claustrophobia:** _____

4. **Zoophobia:** _____

5. **Agoraphobia:** _____

6. **Aerophobia:** _____

C **Using the Dictionary**

Read the dictionary entry for *disorder*.

> **disorder** *n.* **1** [C] a mental or physical problem that can affect your health for a long time: *a serious heart disorder* | *After two years of therapy, Duane was able to conquer his eating disorder.* **2** [U] a situation in which many people disobey the law, especially in a violent way and are difficult to control: *Most urban areas were generally free of civil disorder.* **3** [U] a situation in which things are not organized at all: *The smallest problem can throw all their services into disorder.*

Now answer the questions. Share your answers with a partner.

1. Which definition of the word is used in this chapter?

2. How are the three definitions related? What do all "dis-orders" have in common? [*dis-* is a prefix meaning "not"]

3. Why do we refer to phobias as "disorders," and not "diseases"?

NOTE-TAKING: Filling Out an Organizer

We can use note-taking to study for a test. Take notes on the phobias and patients discussed in the readings. Use these organizers to fill in your study notes.

PHOBIAS

Definition of a phobia: _A phobia is . . ._ _____

_____

How to tell the difference between a phobia and a fear: _____

_____

Types of phobias: _____

_____

CASE STUDIES

Name: _Billy_ _____

Phobia: _Social Phobia_ _____

Characteristics: _never spoke in class_ _____

Physical Symptoms: _sick to his stomach, hiding in the restroom_ ___

***

Name: _____

Phobia: _____

Characteristics: _____

Physical Symptoms: _____

***

Name: _____

Phobia: _____

Characteristics: _____

Physical Symptoms: _____

CRITICAL THINKING

Ⓐ Drawing Conclusions

People's feelings are usually situated along a continuum going from ordinary fears to phobias. Look at this graph.

No fearful
symptoms   **Fears**   **Phobias**

Now decide whether these are examples of fears or phobias. Check (✓) the appropriate box. Discuss with a partner. Explain your answers based on the information in the readings.

	FEAR	PHOBIA
1. John is an actor who is nervous every time he has to go on stage. He has such "stage fright" that he usually throws up in the bathroom before he goes out to face the audience.	☐	☐
2. Janet almost fainted when her mother cut herself in a cooking accident. Seeing the blood made Janet feel shaky. She called an ambulance and went with her mother to the hospital.	☐	☐
3. David was driving across the George Washington Bridge when all of a sudden he couldn't drive any further. He was sure the bridge would collapse into the water, and he would die. The police had to come to drive him home.	☐	☐

Ⓑ Cultural Aspects

Phobias and their symptoms can be greatly influenced by culture. Read about a typically Japanese phobia.

> **TKS (*tajin kvofusho*)** is a common phobia in Japan. It is characterized by a fear of offending others: fear of making eye contact, fear of trembling, fear of blushing or producing offensive odors. It affects 20% of students, more males than females, usually in adolescence.
>
> Japanese society teaches people to pay attention to other people's needs without asking them directly, to avoid direct eye contact, and to conform to what others are doing and saying.

Discuss the questions in a small group. Be prepared to share your answers with the class.

1. What kinds of cultural influences make TKS fairly common in Japan?

2. What kinds of cultural influences and pressures make it common for many North Americans to be afraid to speak in public?

3. Are there any cultural influences in the country you come from or a country you are familiar with that can explain certain specific phobias?

Discuss the questions in a small group. Be prepared to share your answers with the class.

1. To do scientific study in psychology, we first need to define what we are talking about. Why do we need a definition of a disorder? Explain your answer using phobias as an example.

2. Scientific work in psychology also requires that students study examples of disorders. Why do we need examples?

3. What is your reaction when you read about people with phobias?

4. Studies have shown that most individuals with a mental disorder do not seek treatment. Why do you think they don't seek treatment?

5. If you had a problem, to whom would you go for help?

READING THREE: Treatments for Phobias

A Warm-Up

Discuss the questions with a partner.

1. Have you ever been afraid of something or someone?

2. How did you overcome this fear?

B Reading Strategy

Understanding Scholarly References

In-Text Citations:
References to the work of scholars and researchers are a vital part of academic texts. Citations are essential in order to give credit to other professionals and to assure readers that your study or article is following best professional practices.

- Researchers report that programs similar to the one above resulted in reduced social fears in about 30–80% of people who completed the program (Heimberg & Juster, 1994). *This means that the statistical data can be found in the 1994 report of researchers named Heimberg and Juster.*

- (Heimberg & Juster, 1994; Heimberg et al., 1990) *This means there are two different studies: one done by Heimberg and Juster in 1994 and another one done in 1990, which had several collaborators.* **Et al.** *is an abbreviation for* **et alii,** *"and others."*

Bibliography or References:
To find the exact names of the studies referred to and the names of the publications in which they appeared, you must look at the bibliography or references at the end of each chapter or in the back of the book. In that way, you can identify the sources of the facts and look up the publications to get further information.

Work with a partner. Find three different citations in the reading. Write them on the lines. Then explain each one.

1. _____

2. _____

3. _____

Now read the text to find out more about treatments for phobias according to different scholars and researchers.

TREATMENTS FOR PHOBIAS

By Rod Plotnik, from "Anxiety Disorders," in *Introduction to Psychology*

Cognitive-Behavioral Therapy

1   Many people are fearful and anxious about public speaking, but that doesn't mean that they have a social **phobia**. Individuals with social phobias have such intense, excessive, and irrational fears of doing something humiliating or embarrassing in public that they will go to any length to avoid speaking in public. However, there are a number of **cognitive**-behavioral[1] programs to treat social phobias. These programs usually include these four **components** (Heimberg et al., 1990).

1. **EXPLAIN**. Psychologists[2] *explain* to people that since the fears in social phobias are usually learned, there are methods to unlearn such fears. The person is told how certain thoughts can exaggerate the phobic feelings.

2. **LEARN AND SUBSTITUTE**. Psychologists found that some individuals needed to *learn* new social skills (starting a conversation, writing a speech) so

---

[1] *cognitive:* refers to the mind. *Cognitive-behavioral* programs use the mind to change habits.

[2] *psychologist:* someone who has received a doctoral degree (Ph.D. or Psy.D.) in psychology from a university. Some psychologists do clinical work and counseling; some do only research.

that they could function better in social situations. The individuals were asked to **record** their thoughts immediately after thinking about being in a feared situation. Then they were shown how to *substitute* positive and healthy thoughts for negative and frightened ones.

3. **EXPOSE**. Therapists first used *imaginary exposure*, during which a person **imagines** being in the situation that makes them fearful. For example, some people imagined presenting material to their coworkers, saying something in class, or starting a conversation with a stranger. After **exposing** people **to** these situations in the imagination, therapists used *real (in vivo) exposure*, in which the person gives his or her speech in front of a group of people or initiates a conversation with strangers.

4. **PRACTICE**. Therapists asked subjects to *practice* homework assignments. For instance, individuals were asked to imagine themselves in feared situations and then to eliminate negative thoughts by replacing them with positive ones. In addition, individuals were told to gradually get used to making longer and longer presentations or conversations.

(continued on next page)

2   Researchers report that programs similar to the one above resulted in reduced social fears in about 30 – 80% of people who completed the program (Heimberg & Juster, 1994; Heimberg et al., 1990).

Drug Therapy

3   Some individuals with social phobias may not be able to complete a program of cognitive-behavioral therapy or may choose not to. Instead, these individuals may choose to go to a psychiatrist[3] and receive drug therapy. Drug therapy involves taking medications, such as tranquilizers (benzodiazepines) and, less frequently, antidepressants (Davidson, 1994).

4   However, there are two problems with drug treatment. First, about 50 – 75% of individuals relapse[4] when they stop taking the drugs. The original intense phobic symptoms return. Second, long-term drug treatment can lead to serious side effects, such as loss of memory (Davidson, 1994).

5   Although the results of cognitive-behavioral therapy and drug therapy are similar, the advantage of cognitive-behavioral therapy is that there are no side effects.

[3] *psychiatrist:* someone who has received a medical degree (M.D.) from a medical school and specialized in psychological disorders

[4] *relapse:* to go back to your old habits or behaviors

REFERENCES

Davidson, J.R.T. (1994). International advances in the treatment of social phobia. *Journal of Clinical Psychiatry*, 55, 123–129.

Heimberg, R.G., Dodge, C.S., Hope, D.A., Kennedy, C.R., & Zollo, L.J. (1990). Cognitive-behavioral group treatment for social phobia: Comparison with a credible placebo control. *Cognitive Therapy and Research*, 14, 1–23.

Heimberg , R.G., & Juster, H.R. (1994) Treatment of social phobia in cognitive-behavioral groups. *Journal of Clinical Psychiatry*, 55, 38–46.

COMPREHENSION

Ⓐ Main Ideas

Read each statement. Decide if it is *True* or *False* according to the reading. Check (✓) the appropriate box. If it is false, change it to make it true. Discuss your answers with a partner.

	TRUE	FALSE
1. Fear can be a learned response.	☐	☐
2. Exposure therapy is a gradual process of becoming less sensitive to a specific fear.	☐	☐
3. The best approach is to do both drug therapy and cognitive-behavioral therapy.	☐	☐
4. Most people relapse after cognitive-behavioral therapy.	☐	☐

Read the quotes from the reading. Circle the statement that best explains each quote. Share your answers with a partner.

1. "Individuals with social phobias have such intense, excessive, and irrational fears of doing something humiliating or embarrassing in public that they will go to any length to avoid speaking in public." (*paragraph 1*)

   a. These people will travel to all four corners of the world to avoid speaking in public.

   b. These people will do whatever is necessary to avoid speaking in public.

   c. These people will evaluate the short- and long-term benefits of speaking in public.

2. "There are a number of cognitive-behavioral programs to treat social phobias. These programs usually include these four components." (*paragraph 1*)

   a. All cognitive-behavioral programs are the same.

   b. There aren't many cognitive-behavioral programs.

   c. Cognitive-behavioral programs all share certain points.

3. "About 50 – 75% of individuals relapse when they stop taking the drugs." (*paragraph 4*)

   a. It is safe to say that at least 49% of the people who take drug therapy do not relapse.

   b. It is safe to say that 25% of the people who take drug therapy will probably not relapse.

   c. It is safe to say that the majority of individuals who take drug therapy do not relapse.

VOCABULARY

A Greek and Latin Roots

In the past, most scholars in the West studied the Greek and Latin languages in school. When they discovered something new in the **sciences and social sciences**, they created **names using Greek and Latin roots**. In this way, the names could be easily understood by scientists in many different countries.

In vivo is an expression from the Latin meaning "in life," as opposed to *in vitro*, which means "in the laboratory."

Cogito is the Latin word for "think."

Phobos in Greek means "fear." It has given us the word *phobia*. Today we add Greek or Latin prefixes to define certain phobias. *Cynophobia*, for example, is a fear of dogs, from the Greek *kyon* for "dog."

1 Work with a partner. Answer the questions.

1. What do we mean when we talk about **in vivo** psychological exposure?

2. What is **in vitro** fertilization?

3. What are the **cognitive** effects of a disease?

2 Match these names of phobias with their meanings. Other names of phobias can be found on the Internet.

_____ 1. arachnophobia   a. fear of water

_____ 2. hematophobia   b. fear of technology

_____ 3. hydrophobia   c. fear of blood

_____ 4. technophobia   d. fear of spiders

B Synonyms

Complete each paragraph with the words or phrases from the box (from all three readings). Use the synonym in parentheses to help you select the correct word or phrase. Compare answers with a partner.

cognitive	experience	fearful	record
components	exposed to	physiological	

A specific brain area involved with remembering _____ _fearful_ _____

1. (scary)

experiences is the amygdala. The amygdala is one of the _____

2. (parts)

of the limbic system; this system controls some instinctive behavior and emotions.

Scientists used to believe that the amygdala had to work together with the cerebral

cortex (the part of the brain concerned with _____ behavior).

3. (thinking)

Now they know that the amygdala can _____ sensory

4. (register)

information directly from the nervous system without immediately connecting

to our "thinking" brain. In this way, a person's body can already be preparing

to run or fight without the conscious part of the brain totally aware of being

_____ danger. If phobics are shown pictures of spiders or

5. (faced with)

snakes very quickly, they are not even aware of seeing them. Yet their limbic systems

are already making _____ changes in the heart rate and sweat

6. (physical)

glands. This suggests that we can _____ an emotion before

7. (feel)

we know why.

| characterized by | functioning | persistent | traumatic |
| excessive | imagine | severe | |

People with antisocial personality disorder are often called psychopaths or sociopaths. Criminals with antisocial personality disorder, such as serial killers, show less activation in the _____ of the
8. (operation)
amygdala than normal criminals or noncriminals (Kiehl et al., 2001). They have a _____ and _____ emotional
9. (serious)   10. (lasting)
lack. Psychopaths have no regret for what they have done and no fear when they

_____ their punishment in the future. Antisocial personality
11. (think about)
disorder is _____ the inability to experience normal
12. (described as)
emotional responses such as shame, guilt, and fear, as well as the inability to feel empathy for others. It is possible that this inability to register emotion is genetic in origin and may be triggered by _____ events in childhood,
13. (very shocking)
such as abuse. People with phobias may show _____
14. (too much)
emotional responses, while serial killers don't have enough of a response: they appear "cold blooded." This label fits because we share hunger and sex instincts with cold-blooded reptiles, but we seem to share emotions only with other warm-blooded animals. Emotions are so essential to the human experience that we consider those who have no shame or fear to be inhuman. Only a very small portion of any population qualifies as psychopaths.

NOTE-TAKING: Organizing and Categorizing

1 Organize the material in the reading by first remembering the four stages of therapy. Then explain what happens at each stage.

Stage	What Happens
1. EXPLAIN	
2.	
3.	
4.	

2 Who would say these statements, the therapist or the individual, and at what stage? Write **T (therapist)** or **I (individual)** and **S (stage)** followed by the appropriate number.

a. "I've practiced what I'm going to say, and I'm not going to humiliate myself."   _____

b. "Fears can be unlearned with patience and practice."   _____

c. "Let's imagine standing up to speak at the meeting."   _____

d. "I need to keep doing this work at home."   _____

CRITICAL THINKING

Work in a small group. Substitute a "positive" thought for each of these "negative" thoughts and then identify the phobia.

	Negative Thought	Positive Thought	Phobia
1.	"The people on the street are going to crush me."	"The people on the street are friendly and wish me no harm."	
2.	"I will humiliate myself when I speak."		
3.	"The plane will crash as soon as it takes off."		
4.	"I'm going to fall off the balcony."		

BRINGING IT ALL TOGETHER

Discuss the questions in a small group. Then share your group's answers with the class. Use some of the vocabulary you studied in the chapter (for a complete list, go to page 44).

1. Why can't you tell people who have phobias to just "face their fears" and stop being silly? Why do some people need help?

2. Is it possible to know that your behavior is irrational and still not be able to stop? Explain some situations where this can occur even if you are not phobic. Why do you think this happens?

3. Do you think "Worried in College" (from the letter at the beginning of the chapter) has a phobia or just a fear of clowns? Would he be helped by therapy? Would you advise him to go?

4. If you had a phobia, what kind of treatment would you choose: cognitive-behavioral therapy or drug therapy? Explain. Which therapy might you choose if you didn't have health insurance?

5. A phobia is when you have too much fear. Why is being able to feel fear important to human beings as a species? How could feeling no fear be a handicap for humanity?

WRITING ACTIVITY

We wouldn't be human if we didn't have some fears or phobias. Write two paragraphs about either a fear or a phobia in your life.

- Your writing could be about a simple **fear**: fear about leaving home for the first time, going to a new school, or studying abroad. It could be about facing a bully or taking an exam or going to a horror movie.
  OR
- Your writing could be about aspects of any **phobia** we studied.

Write one paragraph about the problem and the other about any solution you found or are looking for. Did anyone help you? Use at least five of the words and idioms you studied in the chapter.

DISCUSSION AND WRITING TOPICS

Discuss these topics in a small group. Choose one of them and write a paragraph or two about it. Use the vocabulary from the chapter.

1. How does learning about psychology help you understand yourself and others? Can you learn as much through experience and common sense?

2. How was being afraid of spiders and snakes probably beneficial for humans in evolutionary history? Why do you think we have phobias about snakes but not about guns?

3. What kind of personality do you think a person would have to have if he or she wanted to be a therapist?

VOCABULARY

Nouns	Verbs	Adjectives	Phrases and Idioms
anxiety	experience	cognitive	be characterized by
arousal	function *	excessive	expose sb to
component *	imagine *	intense *	in vivo
depression *	record	irrational	
disorder		moderate	
dread		persistent *	
fear		physiological	
phobia		psychological *	
symptom		severe	
		traumatic	

* = AWL (Academic Word List) item

SELF-ASSESSMENT

In this chapter you learned to:

- ○ Scan a text to find specific information
- ○ Preview a text using visuals
- ○ Understand scholarly references
- ○ Understand and use synonyms, collocations, and different word forms
- ○ Guess the meaning of words from their Greek or Latin roots
- ○ Use dictionary entries to learn the meanings of words
- ○ Organize and categorize study notes

What can you do well? ☑

What do you need to practice more? ☑

CHAPTER 3

NUTRITION STUDIES:
Food Rules

OBJECTIVES

To read academic texts, you need to master certain skills.

In this chapter, you will:

- Skim an interview and scan a text for specific answers

- Understand the tone of a text and identify the author's point of view

- Guess the meaning of words from the context

- Use dictionary entries to learn the meanings of words

- Understand and use synonyms, prefixes, and antonyms

- Organize and categorize study notes to identify important ideas

- Create a chain of reasoning to understand the author's arguments

A **Consider These Questions**

Discuss the questions with a partner.

1. What kinds of foods do you think will keep you healthy?

2. Where do you get most of your information about food? Do you watch cooking programs on TV? Do you like to cook?

3. What are your favorite foods?

4. Do you like to eat at home? In restaurants? Do you usually eat with others or alone?

B **Your Opinion**

1 According to surveys, Americans are getting fatter and fatter. What do you think are some of the reasons? Rank these reasons in order of importance: *1* is the most important, and *5* is the least important. Compare answers with a partner.

_____ a. lack of exercise

_____ b. too many sugary sodas

_____ c. restaurant portions that are too large

_____ d. companies making food with too much fat, sugar, and salt

_____ e. not enough fresh fruits and vegetables available

2 What do you think are the consequences of the obesity epidemic for developed countries like the United States? Check (✓) the answers you think are probable.

☐ a. more heart disease

☐ b. more cancer

☐ c. more flu

☐ d. more diabetes

☐ e. higher health care costs

A Warm-Up

These words are often used to discuss *nutrition*. Match the words with their definitions.

_____ 1. carbohydrates

_____ 2. pesticides

_____ 3. organic

_____ 4. obesity

_____ 5. saturated fat

a. body weight greater than what is healthy

b. type of fat from meat and milk products

c. produced by farming methods that do not use chemicals

d. chemical substances used to kill insects that destroy crops

e. sugar and starches that release energy in the body

B Reading Strategy

Skimming an Interview

Before you read an interview, you can skim it or **get a quick general idea** of what will be discussed by **looking at the questions** asked by the interviewer.

The reading is an interview with Michael Pollan, the author of *Food Rules* and *The Omnivore's Dilemma*. To get a general idea of what Pollan will discuss, skim the interview.

Look at the questions asked by the interviewer and write the keyword(s) for each question on the lines.

Question 1: _rules_____

Question 2: _____

Question 3: _____

Question 4: _____

Question 5: _____

Question 6: _____

Now read the interview to find out Michael Pollan's answers to these questions.

An Interview With Michael Pollan

1 **AMY GOODMAN (INTERVIEWER):** OK? *Food Rules: An Eater's Manual.* What are the rules?

2 **POLLAN:** Well, there are 64 of them, and they're very simple. . . . They all come down to the big, main message, which is: eat food, not too much, mostly plants. I mean, the whole **edifice** of nutritional science, when you really look at it, that's all you need to know. It's a little easier said than done.

3 **AMY GOODMAN:** What is it that you mean by the "nutritional-industrial complex"?[1]

4 **POLLAN:** Whenever nutritionists come out with a new finding, the industry uses it to sell more food to people. The great example in our own time is the low-fat campaign begun by the government in the 1970s under Senator George McGovern's leadership. They thought they were doing something really good, which was telling people to eat less meat and cut down on saturated fat. But the industry took what had been a **critique** of their actions and turned it into a very clever new way to sell new food. They reengineered the whole food supply to have less fat, but with more carbohydrates. And so, people **binged** on carbohydrates. Since the low-fat campaign started, we have gotten an average of eighteen pounds heavier!

5 If you want to take back control of your diet from this nutritional-industrial complex, from the corporations who want to cook for you and don't cook very well, because they use cheap raw **ingredients**, too much salt, sugar and fat to cover that up, you're going to have to cook yourself. I mean, food you cook yourself is healthier food. We know this. So the challenge is finding the time in the day to do it.

6 **AMY GOODMAN:** Explain how agriculture fits in with the whole issue of food and diet.

7 **POLLAN:** We basically redesigned government **subsidies** in a way that forced prices down. And that leads to this overproduction of corn and soy which I think is one of the causes of the obesity epidemic. You know, I mean, we're eating 500 more calories per person per day since this period. And that's because they're really cheap, and attractively packaged.

8 **AMY GOODMAN:** What about pesticides?

9 **POLLAN:** The thing to understand about pesticides is that they don't **afflict** all foods equally. And, you know, there's a wonderful list called the Dirty Dozen online that lists the ones that have the most pesticide **residue**. I don't think spinach is one of them. I might be wrong. I would urge you to check it. But broccoli isn't that bad. Strawberries are really bad. Apples are really bad. So it helps to know when it's worth the money to buy organic to know that, because sometimes it's not. If you're spreading a limited budget over, you know, organic food, there are better places to spend than others.

---

[1] *nutritional-industrial complex:* Dwight D. Eisenhower, the 34th president of the United States (1953 – 1961), warned against the "military-industrial complex" and its potentially harmful influence on the government decisions of a democracy. Pollan uses the "nutritional-industrial complex" to warn against its harmful influence on our food supply.

10 **AMY GOODMAN:** And do you think that we can revolutionize the American diet?

11 **POLLAN:** Yeah, reform it. You see the growth of farmers' markets, which has been stunning. I mean, the number of farmers' markets for locally grown fruits and vegetables has doubled twice in ten years. We don't know how much money is spent at farmers' markets, but it's big right now.

12 **AMY GOODMAN:** What about your Rule 58, do all your eating at a table, and Rule 59, try not to eat alone?

13 **POLLAN:** Well, we're doing a lot of eating on the run. We're eating in the car. Eating at tables is a very civilizing act, and you eat more mindfully at a table. Basically, restoring food to its social dimension, I think, is really, really important. When we eat alone, we tend to eat more. Eating at a table, you eat a little more slowly, because you're talking, and you're putting down your fork to engage in conversation. And you realize at the table that food is not just fuel. It's communion, too. One of the seedbeds of civil society is table manners. You learn generosity. You learn sharing. You learn manners.

COMPREHENSION

Ⓐ Main Ideas

Read each statement. Decide if it is *True* or *False* according to Michael Pollan. Check (✓) the appropriate box. If it is false, change it to make it true. Discuss your answers with a partner.

	TRUE	FALSE
1. The blame for obesity lies with each individual person, not the food industry.	☐	☐
2. It would be important to buy organic spinach but not necessarily organic apples or strawberries.	☐	☐
3. We eat less when we don't pay attention to what we're doing.	☐	☐
4. Government subsidies make high-calorie food cheaper than low-calorie food.	☐	☐
5. Meals cooked at home are not as healthy as commercially prepared food.	☐	☐
6. Farmers' markets are not always organic, but the food is fresher.	☐	☐
7. The food companies manipulate data in order to sell more food.	☐	☐

Read the quotes from the reading. Circle the statement that best explains each quote. Share your answers with a partner.

1. "We basically redesigned government subsidies in a way that forced prices down. And that leads to this overproduction of corn and soy." (*paragraph 7*)

   a. Government gives money to farmers to produce corn and soy. Prices go down, and farmers produce more and more.

   b. Government gives money to farmers to produce corn and soy. Prices go down, and farmers produce less and less.

   c. Government gives money to farmers to produce corn and soy. Prices rise, and farmers produce more and more.

2. "I mean, the number of farmers' markets for locally-grown fruits and vegetables has doubled twice in ten years." (*paragraph 11*)

   a. This shows that people want cheap food.

   b. This shows that people want fresher food.

   c. This shows that people want organic food.

3. "And you realize at the table that food is not just fuel. It's communion, too." (*paragraph 13*)

   a. Eating is essential for energy.

   b. Eating is a social act.

   c. Eating is both of the above.

VOCABULARY

A Guessing from Context

Read each sentence and guess the meaning of the word in bold from the context. Then match the word with its meaning from the box below. Compare answers with a partner.

__d__ 1. Potato chips are a trigger food for me. When I start to eat them, I can't stop, and I **binge**.

____ 2. The whole **edifice** of nutritional science is very complex, so people need some simple rules.

____ 3. It's not a good idea to eat in front of the TV because you're not paying attention to what you do. It's better to eat **mindfully**.

____ 4. We eat not only to satisfy our hunger for food but also for companionship and sharing. This social **dimension** of food is often forgotten because we are so rushed and busy.

____ 5. This garden is **afflicted** with fungus and weeds.

____ 6. Vegetables should be the main **ingredients** of a good meal, not salt, sugar, or fat.

_____ 7. Government **subsidies** support farmers financially so that they do not suffer from changes in market prices for their produce.

_____ 8. Although the pesticide DDT kills malaria mosquitoes, it leaves long-lasting toxic **residue** in the food chain and was banned from use in the U.S. in 1972.

_____ 9. People shouldn't **engage** in activities that endanger their health.

_____ 10. Because of the time pressures of modern life, many people these days eat **on the run**: while driving, walking, and working on the Internet.

a. remains	**f.** components
b. aspect	**g.** participate
c. consciously	**h.** structure
d. overeat	**i.** while doing something else
e. made sick	**j.** sums of money

B Using the Dictionary

Read the dictionary entries for *critic, critical, criticize* and *critique*.

> **critic** *n.* **1** someone whose job is to give his/her judgment about whether a movie, book, etc. is good or bad: *a film critic; a literary critic* **2** someone who tends to make harsh judgments
>
> **critical** *adj.* **1** making harsh judgments **2** making careful and fair judgments **3** very important **4** very serious or dangerous
>
> **criticize** *v.* to say what faults you think someone or something has
>
> **critique** *n.* a piece of writing describing the good and bad qualities of a film, book, etc.
>
> **critique** *v.* to judge whether someone or something is good or bad

Now complete the sentences with the correct word form. Write the number of the appropriate definition in parentheses.

a. Michael Pollan is a severe _____ of the food industry in the United States.

b. He believes that our food supply is in _____ condition, and places some of the blame on government farm policies.

c. Pollan is very _____ of the food industry; he particularly

_____ its use of too much salt and sugar.

d. One of the aims of his work is to develop a _____ spirit in people so that they will not just accept everything the advertisers and food companies say.

e. Like all published authors, Pollan shows his books to an editor, who reviews his

writing and _____ it.

NOTE-TAKING: Categorizing

Go back to the reading and read it again. Underline the keywords and write notes in the margin. Then use the following categories to organize your notes. Share your notes with a partner.

Rules	• *main message: don't eat too much, eat mostly plants*
Food Industry	•
Agricultural Policy	•
Pesticides	•
Change	•
Social Dimension	•

CRITICAL THINKING

Discuss the questions in a small group. Be prepared to share your opinions with the class.

1. Michael Pollan writes books in order to convince people to change their eating habits. How else could we convince people to change? Is there a role for schools? For TV?

2. Blaming fast-food restaurants for their obesity, several people have tried to sue these chain stores in court and collect legal damages. Do you think fast-food restaurants should be legally responsible for obesity? What is the role of individual responsibility in obesity, in your opinion?

3. Michael Pollan says: "My basic philosophy of eating is that if your great-grandmother wasn't familiar with it, you probably want to stay away from it."

   Do you agree with Pollan about eating only traditional food that your great-grandmother would recognize? Why or why not?

   Do you think that all traditional things are better than modern ones? Why or why not?

A Warm-Up

Discuss the questions with a partner.

1. Should government play a role in helping people eat better? Why or why not?
2. Should people be *forced* to eat healthier food?

B Reading Strategy

Scanning

Scanning a text means **reading it quickly to find specific or essential information.** For example, you can scan a text to find the answer to a question.

The title of the reading begins with a question: **Bad Food**? Scan the text to find what these bad foods are. Underline the answer in the text and write the names of these unhealthy foods on the lines. Write the number of the paragraph in parentheses.

_____

_____

Now read the text to find out more about bad food and what to do about it.

Bad Food? Tax It, and Subsidize Vegetables

By Mark Bittman

Mark Bittman writes about food for the opinion section of the New York Times.

1   What will it take to get us Americans to change our eating habits? The need is **indisputable**, since heart disease, diabetes and cancer are all in large part caused by the Standard American Diet. (Yes, it's SAD.) Though experts increasingly recommend a diet high in plants and low in animal products and processed foods, ours is quite the opposite, and there's little disagreement that changing it could improve our health and save tens of millions of lives. And — not unimportant during the current struggle over budgets and spending — a **sane** diet could save tens if not hundreds of billions of dollars in health care costs.

2   Yet the food industry appears incapable of marketing healthier foods. And whether its leaders are confused or just **stalling** doesn't matter, because the fixes are not really their problem. Their **mission** is not public health but profit, so they'll continue to sell the health-damaging food that's most

(continued on next page)

profitable, until the market or another force makes them do otherwise. That "other force" should be the federal government, fulfilling its role as an agent of the public good.

3   Rather than subsidizing the production of unhealthful foods, we should do the opposite and tax things like soda, French fries, doughnuts, and hyper-processed snacks. The resulting income should be given to a program that encourages a good diet for Americans by making healthy food more **affordable** and widely available.

4   The average American consumes 44.7 gallons of soft drinks annually. (Although that includes diet sodas, it does not include noncarbonated sweetened beverages, which add up to at least 17 gallons a person per year.) Sweetened drinks could be taxed at 2 cents per ounce, so a six-pack of Pepsi would cost $1.44 more than it does now. An equivalent tax on fries might be 50 cents per serving; a quarter extra for a doughnut. (We have experts who can figure out how "bad" a food should be to qualify, and what the rate should be. Diet sodas would not be taxed.)

5   Simply put: Taxes would reduce consumption of unhealthful foods and **generate** billions of dollars annually. That money could be used to subsidize the purchase of staple foods[1] like seasonal greens, vegetables, whole grains, dried legumes, and fruit. We could sell those staples cheap — let's say for 50 cents a pound — and almost everywhere: drugstores, street corners, convenience stores, bodegas, supermarkets, liquor stores, even schools, libraries and other community centers.

6   Right now it's harder for many people to buy fruit than Froot Loops; chips and Coke are a common breakfast. And since the rate of diabetes continues to **soar** — one-third of all Americans either have diabetes or are pre-diabetic, most with Type 2 diabetes, the kind associated with bad eating habits — and because our health care bills are about to become truly **insurmountable**, this is urgent for economic sanity as well as national health.

_____

[1] *staple food:* a food that is needed and used all the time

COMPREHENSION

A Main Ideas

Complete the sentences based on the main ideas of the reading.

1. Experts argue that a major cause of heart disease, cancer, and diabetes

    in the United States is the ___Diet___

    because it is high in ___animal products___ and low in

    ___vegetables.___

2. The food industry has contributed to the food problem in the U.S. because it

    _____.

3. To solve the problem, the author wants the government to tax

    _____ and use the money to

    _____.

B Close Reading

Read the quotes from the reading. Circle the statement that best explains each quote. Share your answers with a partner.

1. "Though experts increasingly recommend a diet high in plants and low in animal products and processed foods, ours is quite the opposite, and there's little disagreement that changing it could improve our health and save tens of millions of lives." (*paragraph 1*)

   a. Almost everyone agrees that we need more fruits and vegetables and less dairy and meat.

   b. Experts disagree about more vegetables and less dairy and meat.

   c. Experts agree that we need less meat and more dairy.

2. "[The] mission [of food companies] is not public health but profit, so they'll continue to sell the health-damaging food that's most profitable, until the market or another force makes them do otherwise." (*paragraph 2*)

   a. Trying to persuade food companies with words is hopeless.

   b. Only the market can change the food companies.

   c. Only the government can change the food companies.

3. "That 'other force' should be the federal government, fulfilling its role as an agent of the public good." (*paragraph 2*)

   a. The food industry should cooperate with the public.

   b. The free market should protect the public from the food industry.

   c. The government should protect the public from the food industry.

4. "Right now it's harder for many people to buy fruit than Froot Loops; chips and Coke are a common breakfast." (*paragraph 6*)

   a. The author is just giving information.

   b. The author does not agree with this situation.

   c. The author is seeking to entertain.

VOCABULARY

Ⓐ Synonyms

Cross out the word that is NOT a synonym for the word in bold. Compare answers with a partner.

1. **affordable**	economical	moderate	~~economic~~
2. **generate**	bring about	destroy	create
3. **indisputable**	questionable	certain	undeniable
4. **insurmountable**	possible	hopeless	unbeatable
5. **mission**	agenda	training	objective
6. **sane**	reasonable	sensitive	sensible
7. **soar**	rise	flow	increase
8. **stalling**	waiting	delaying	refusing

Ⓑ Prefixes *in-*, *im-*, *il-*, *ir-* and Antonyms

In- is one of the prefixes meaning "not" or "the opposite of."
- **inevitable** = cannot be avoided
- **indisputable** = not in dispute, not argued with

We use *im-*, *il-*, or *ir-* instead of *in-* in words beginning with: *

- *m*: **moral**   →   im**moral** = not moral
- *p*: **patient**   →   im**patient** = not patient
- *l*: **logical**   →   il**logical** = not logical
- *r*: **responsible**   →   ir**responsible** = not responsible

_____

*There are always some exceptions, such as "unmitigated," "unlabeled," and "unreasonable." To be sure, you need to check in the dictionary.

1 Look at the list of words beginning with the prefix *in-*, *im-*, *il-*, or *ir-*. What is the meaning of each word? Write it on the line.

MEANING

1. insurmountable   _not able to be overcome_____

2. incapable   _____

3. irrational   _____

4. insane   _____

5. immoderate   _____

6. illegal   _____

2 Fill in the chart with the *antonym* (opposite) of each word (using prefixes) and the meaning of the antonym. Compare answers with a partner.

	ANTONYM	MEANING OF THE ANTONYM
1. mobile	immobile	not moving; unable to move
2. relevant		
3. dependent		
4. practical		
5. significant		
6. mortal		
7. conclusive		
8. curable		

NOTE-TAKING: Chain of Reasoning

Go back to the reading and read it again. Take notes. Use your notes to fill each box of the chain with the argument given by Mark Bittman in the corresponding paragraph of the reading.

1		2	
heart disease, cancer, diabetes caused by diet	→		→

3		4	
	→		→

5		6
	→	

CRITICAL THINKING

Discuss the questions in a small group. Be prepared to share your answers with the class.

1. Mark Bittman believes that government should tax unhealthy foods because the community has to pay for the health care costs that unhealthy lifestyles create. Do you think this is a convincing argument? The government taxes cigarettes to make people stop smoking. Is eating unhealthy food similar to the case of smoking? Give reasons for your answer.

2. Bittman gives an argument for taxing unhealthy foods so people will not buy these foods as much. But what about the people who really like French fries and soda? Give the arguments **against** Bittman's idea of involving the government in healthy eating. What do you think the soda companies said in their campaign against the proposed soda tax?

3. What other arguments could you give **in favor** of Bittman's solution? Do you think his campaign can become as popular as the "Don't Drink and Drive" campaign?

4. Some school districts want to ban soda in schools. They want students to drink milk, juice, or water. Should the government exercise its authority over schools in this way? What would people think about this in your school? What kind of educational work would have to be done in schools on this subject?

5. Can you think of any other potentially unhealthy foods that should be taxed? What would people think about this? When it is a question of people's health, should it really matter "what people think," or should actions to protect people be taken without their input? Why or why not?

LINKING READINGS ONE AND TWO

1 Fill in the chart with the main ideas from Readings One and Two.

Name	Problem With U.S. Food & Diet	Solution For U.S. Consumers
Michael Pollan	• Too much salt, too much sugar, too much fat in food made by the food industry • • •	• Cook for yourself, eat more plants • • •
Mark Bittman	• SAD is unhealthy because high in animal products and low in plants •	• Change your eating habits: eat less meat and dairy, eat more fruits and vegetables •

2 Work in groups of four. Role-play an interview with Michael Pollan and Mark Bittman. Two journalists want to find out what Pollan and Bittman think about American eating habits.

TOPIC: American eating habits

ROLES:

- Journalist 1
- Journalist 2
- Michael Pollan
- Mark Bittman

EXAMPLE:

J 1: Michael Pollan and Mark Bittman, you both criticize the food corporations, or "the nutritional-industrial complex." Tell us what you think of the corporations. What are they doing wrong?

MP: The big food companies make food that contains too much salt, too much fat, and too much sugar. Americans are getting too fat.

MB: Yes, I agree. The obesity epidemic is making us sick, and it costs us a lot of money in medical treatment.

J 2: ...

READING THREE: Humane Treatment for the Animals We Eat

Ⓐ Warm-Up

Discuss the questions with a partner.

1. Do animals have rights? What rights do they have?
2. Do we owe anything to the animals we eat? Give examples.

Ⓑ Reading Strategy

Understanding Tone and Identifying Point of View

Tone is the general **feeling or attitude** expressed in a piece of writing. In some texts it is important to understand the tone used by the author, since it will help you identify the **author's point of view about the topic** he or she is writing about.

Look at the title of the reading. Do you expect the author to be objective about the issue, providing ideas both in favor of humane treatment and against it? Circle your answer.

a. objective
b. not objective

Now read the article to find out if your guess was correct.

Humane Treatment for the Animals We Eat

Rudy Henler

1   In the 16th century, Sir Thomas More described an imaginary ideal society in his book *Utopia*. His Utopians would allow only slaves to kill animals because they did not want free citizens to experience the cruelty associated with killing living things. In modern slaughterhouses, cattle have often been killed with a lot of unnecessary suffering: animals stressed by **abject** fear and pain.

2   Temple Grandin,[1] a **renowned** animal behavioral scientist, is a leading authority on improving conditions at processing plants, advising the United States government on the federal **Humane** Slaughter Act (calling for painless killing), and writing guidelines for the American Meat Institute. An example of her practical designs: slaughterhouse ramps where cattle walk single file, able to see only three animals ahead, with the walkway turning in 180-degree curves so the cattle cannot see anything unexpected that will make them **balk**. When there are high walls, no shadows, no loud noises, no hitting, no slippages underfoot, the animals proceed without fear, and industry efficiency improves. Although many animal welfare advocates say we should avoid eating meat entirely, livestock animals[2] serve a **human** purpose, and Grandin believes humans should recognize their caretaking role toward these animals.

3   Animal activists have also **alerted** people **to** the cruel conditions of the veal industry. **Deprived of** their mothers at birth, male veal calves are put in tiny pens alone, chained at the neck, unable to walk — all in order to keep their meat very tender. Raised on a liquid diet **deficient** in iron and fiber, full of chemicals, antibiotics, and hormones, the calves are literally dragged to the slaughter at about 4 months old. Such conditions are now banned in Britain, and many consumers and chefs in the U.S. resist buying or preparing veal raised in this way.

---

[1] *Temple Grandin* (b. 1947) is a scientist and best-selling author. She was one of the first people with high-functioning autism to speak out about how people with the disorder feel and react. She says that she uses her autistic sensitivity to understand animals and advocate for them.

---

[2] *livestock animals:* About 40 billion pounds of cattle and pigs are slaughtered for human consumption every year in the U.S.

4   There is also a growing switch from red meat to poultry. But chickens tightly confined in battery cages in huge factory-like warehouses are also fed antibiotics and hormones. Transportation and slaughter conditions are often **appalling**. Consequently, consumers have become interested in stores like Whole Foods, up-scale hotel chains like Omni, cafeterias at universities and companies like Google, as well as Burger King, and Ben and Jerry's Ice Cream, which all use only "cage-free" eggs and "organic" chickens.[3] Despite the added cost, this trend is growing, fed by consumer disgust with the treatment of animals and worries over the industrialization of the food supply.

---

[3] Less than 10% of the eggs and chickens consumed are certified organic, free-range, or cage-free, and they are more expensive than the factory-bred ones. Labels like "cage-free" may not necessarily translate into better conditions for chickens. Some large companies use the Humane Society to check on the chickens and eggs they buy just to make sure. "Organically fed" chickens are more adequately checked by government inspection.

Now that you've read the article, decide whether you think the author's arguments are convincing. What other information would you want to have? Write it on the line.

_____

COMPREHENSION

Ⓐ Main Ideas

Read each statement. Decide if it is *True* or *False* according to the reading. Check (✓) the appropriate box. If it is false, change it to make it true. Discuss your answers with a partner.

	TRUE	FALSE
1. Temple Grandin wants us to stop eating animals.	☐	☐
2. Her inventions allow animals to avoid slaughter.	☐	☐
3. Grandin believes that we owe animals a decent life and a peaceful death.	☐	☐
4. Organic foods are growing in popularity despite their higher price.	☐	☐
5. The United States has laws regulating the killing of animals.	☐	☐
6. U.S. laws forbid the killing of veal calves.	☐	☐
7. People are making choices that show they don't care about how animals are treated.	☐	☐

B Close Reading

Read the quotes from the reading. Circle the statement that best explains each quote. Share your answers with a partner.

1. "[More's] Utopians would allow only slaves to kill animals because they did not want free citizens to experience the cruelty associated with killing living things." (*paragraph 1*)

   a. Killing animals is too dirty a job for free people.

   b. Free people should not become hardened by indifference to suffering.

   c. Slaves could kill animals with greater efficiency than free men.

2. "When there are high walls, no shadows, no loud noises, no hitting, no slippages underfoot, the animals proceed without fear and industry efficiency improves." (*paragraph 2*)

   a. Many corporations approve of Grandin's designs.

   b. Grandin's designs are not profit oriented.

   c. No animals ever get hurt on Grandin's equipment.

3. "Animal activists have also alerted people to the cruel conditions of the veal industry." (*paragraph 3*)

   a. Animal activists advertise for donations to help their cause.

   b. Animal activists warn people before they attack them.

   c. Without campaigns in the press and the Internet, people would not know what happens on farms.

4. "... many consumers and chefs in the U.S. resist buying or preparing veal raised in this way." (*paragraph 3*)

   a. People use their buying power to show their disapproval.

   b. People have no way of expressing their opposition.

   c. People are losing their taste for veal.

VOCABULARY

A Synonyms

Read the paragraph about Temple Grandin. Match each word or phrase in bold with its synonym in the box below. Compare answers with a partner.

Temple Grandin is a __renowned__ __advocate__ of the rights of people with
              1.   2.
autism, a disorder that involves changes in the way the brain processes information.

Grandin insists that parents of children as young as two years old and even

younger be __alerted to__ the possibility of autism in their children so that they can
         3.

provide special teachers and speech therapy very early. Grandin was helped very early in life and was not **deprived of** an education. Some people think autistic
4.
children are **deficient** in intelligence, but this is not necessarily true. There
5.
has been **appalling** prejudice against autistic people in the past, and Grandin
6.
herself was teased as a child. She describes her hypersensitivity to sound and how this has helped her understand some of the reasons animals **balk** during
7.
transportation. She also says that she is a visual thinker, able to play back visual memories in great detail. This has helped her design livestock equipment effectively to avoid the **abject** terror animals can feel when facing death.
8.

———	**a.** refuse to continue	———	**e.** shocking
———	**b.** lacking	———	**f.** warned about
_1_	**c.** famous	———	**g.** extreme
———	**d.** prevented from having	———	**h.** supporter

B Using the Dictionary

Read the dictionary entries for *human* and *humane* and for *inhuman* and *inhumane*.

> **human** *adj.* belonging to or relating to people, especially as opposed to animals or machines
>
> **humane** *adj.* treating people or animals in a way that is kind, not cruel
>
> **inhuman** *adj.* very cruel, without any normal feelings of pity
>
> **inhumane** *adj.* treating people or animals in a cruel and unacceptable way

Now complete each sentence with the appropriate word.

1. This accident was the result of _____ error.

2. Animals should be raised in more _____ conditions.

3. _____ rights include the right to be treated in a _____ way by our governments.

4. Charlotte Brontë and Charles Dickens wrote about the alarmingly _____ conditions in charity schools and other institutions for the poor in 19th-century Britain.

5. Slaughtering animals in fear and pain is cruel and _____.

CRITICAL THINKING

Discuss the questions in a small group. Be prepared to share your opinions with the class.

1. In the reading, there are many arguments **in favor** of humane treatment for animals. What are the arguments **against** humane treatment for animals? What would the corporations that don't go along with Temple Grandin say?

2. Would it surprise you to know that McDonald's is one of the biggest supporters of Temple Grandin's equipment? Why would this company want to be seen as a supporter of humane treatment for animals? Why is it easier for big companies to change than for smaller companies and farms?

3. In modern society, people enjoy human rights: the right to enjoy free speech, to choose their leaders, to practice their beliefs and customs. Do animals have rights? Why or why not, in your opinion? Jeremy Bentham, a 19th-century philosopher, wrote: "The question is not whether animals can think but whether they can suffer." Which side was he on? What do you think about this issue?

AFTER YOU READ

BRINGING IT ALL TOGETHER

Choose one of the Letters to the Editor and respond as though you were Michael Pollan, Mark Bittman, or Temple Grandin. Use some of the vocabulary you studied in the chapter (for a complete list, go to page 66). Read your letter to a partner.

LETTER TO THE EDITOR ONE: FROM BROOKLYN, NEW YORK

All of this agitation about organic food is just a class thing: rich people have it, and poor people don't.

In the upper-class private schools on New York's Upper East Side, each school has its own chef who cooks fresh food every day for the school cafeteria with only organic ingredients. Back where I live, public school lunches are potatoes, corn, pizza, hot dogs, and soda. Ketchup counts as a vegetable.

In the supermarket in my neighborhood, there's no organic beef or chicken or eggs, and even if there were, it would be three times more expensive than the other choices. The government subsidizes farmers to grow corn but not organic vegetables.

I'm fed up.

Angry

LETTER TO THE EDITOR TWO: FROM BALTIMORE, MARYLAND

I have a simple solution to the problems described by food critics. Everyone should become a vegetarian!

We wouldn't have to slaughter animals in appalling conditions. We wouldn't have to ingest all the hormones, antibiotics, and chemicals pumped into animals. Our eating habits would be healthier, and our behavior more humane. Obesity would no longer be a problem. The whole edifice of American agriculture would change.

I can't think of one logical argument against eating only vegetables, fruits, legumes, and grains.

A Proud Vegan

WRITING ACTIVITY

Choose one question and write one or two paragraphs to answer it. Use at least five of the words and idioms you studied in the chapter.

1. What rights, if any, do animals have?

2. What foods should we eat?

3. Why don't we eat the foods we're supposed to eat?

4. Is it ethical to eat animals?

DISCUSSION AND WRITING TOPICS

Discuss these topics in a small group. Choose one of them and write a paragraph or two about it. Use the vocabulary from the chapter.

1. Would you want to be a vegetarian? Why or why not? What are the advantages and disadvantages of such a choice? Would you eat some eggs and dairy but no meat? Would you eat fish? Or would you be a complete vegan and eat only plants?

2. Should people be *forced* to change unhealthy food habits? Or should education play a role? How?

3. Michael Pollan has said: "Don't buy any food advertised on TV." Why would he say this? Do you think he is correct or not?

4. Some animal activists are extremists. They favor destroying farms or laboratories that mistreat animals. What do you think of these tactics? What tactics would you encourage if you wanted to ensure that animals have "a decent life"?

5. What is the role of government, if any, in regulating the meat industry and agriculture both domestically and internationally?

VOCABULARY

Nouns	Verbs	Adjectives	Adverb
advocate *	afflict	abject	mindfully
carbohydrates	balk	affordable	
critique	binge	appalling	**Phrases and Idioms**
dimension *	generate	deficient	alert sb to
edifice	soar	human	on the run
ingredient	stall	humane	
mission		indisputable	
obesity	**Phrasal Verbs**	insurmountable	
pesticide	deprive of	organic	
residue	engage in	renowned	
saturated fat		sane	
subsidy *			

* = AWL (Academic Word List) item

SELF-ASSESSMENT

In this chapter you learned to:

○ Skim an interview and scan a text for specific answers

○ Understand the tone of a text and identify the author's point of view

○ Guess the meaning of words from the context

○ Use dictionary entries to learn the meanings of words

○ Understand and use synonyms, prefixes, and antonyms

○ Organize and categorize study notes to identify important ideas

○ Create a chain of reasoning to understand the author's arguments

What can you do well? ☑

What do you need to practice more? ☑

MEDICINE:
Pioneers and Heroes

MEDICINE: the science or practice of the diagnosis, treatment, and prevention of disease

OBJECTIVES

To read academic texts, you need to master certain skills.

In this chapter, you will:

- Skim an oath and scan a text for dates

- Find the link between the title of a text and the first paragraph

- Understand and use synonyms, collocations, and connotations

- Understand the different usage of similar words

- Categorize words

- Categorize and summarize study notes

- Create a timeline to understand the sequence of events

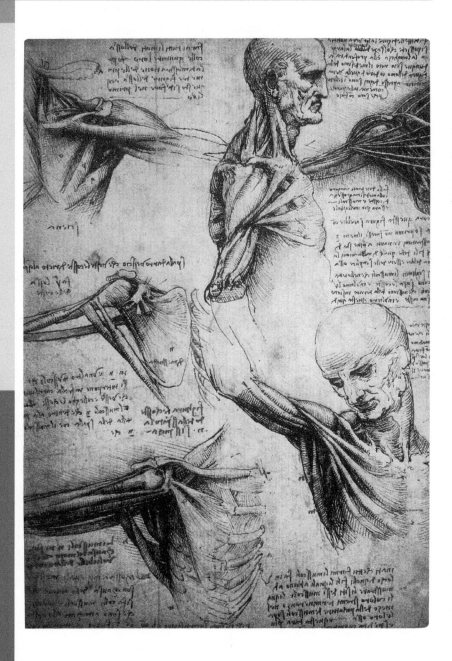

Consider These Questions

1 What are the characteristics of a good doctor?

If you were choosing a doctor, how would you rate these considerations from *most important* (1) to *least important* (6)? Compare answers with a partner.

_____ friendly

_____ graduated from a famous medical school

_____ experienced

_____ inexpensive

_____ situated in a convenient location

_____ willing to take the time to talk about patients' problems

Are there any other important considerations that may be missing from the list? Write them on the lines.

_____

_____

_____

2 What are the reasons for improved life expectancy since 1900?

In 1900, the average life expectancy in the United States was 45 years old. Today it is almost 80. What explains this increase?

Look at the list of factors. In a small group, discuss how each factor has contributed to greater life expectancy. Are there any other important factors? Write them on the lines.

1. clean water supplies

2. vaccines against many diseases

3. universal primary and secondary education

4. plentiful food

5. more machines to help with hard work

6. antibiotics

7. better communication and transportation

8. stricter housing codes

9. better health care

Others:

_____

_____

A **Warm-Up**

When doctors graduate from medical school, they make a promise to serve the community by taking an oath. This promise or oath is named after **Hippocrates**, a doctor who lived in ancient Greece (ca. 460–370 B.C.) and is considered the father of Western medicine.

What do you think this oath should make doctors promise? Make a list of the four things you consider most important. Share your answers with a partner.

1. _____

2. _____

3. _____

4. _____

B **Reading Strategy**

Skimming an Oath

An **oath**, or a **pledge (promise)** to do something a certain way, is usually written in the first person singular ("I") or plural ("We"). Because **each point of the oath starts with the first person pronoun**, it is easy to skim for an overview of its contents.

Look over the sentence pattern of the *Hippocratic Oath*. Circle the "I" introducing each main point of the oath and underline the keyword(s) identifying its topic.

Now read the oath to find out more about what doctors promise to do when they take it.

The Hippocratic Oath – A Modern Version

This modern version of the Hippocratic Oath *was written in 1964 by Louis Lasagna, Academic Dean of the School of Medicine at Tufts University. It is used in many medical schools today.*

1   I swear[1] to fulfill, to the best of my ability and judgment, this covenant:[2]

2   I will respect the **hard-won** scientific gains of those physicians[3] in whose steps I walk, and gladly share such knowledge as is mine with those who are to follow.

3   I will apply, for the benefit of the sick, all **measures** [that] are required, avoiding those twin traps of over-treatment or neglect.

4   I will remember that there is art to medicine as well as science, and that warmth, sympathy, and understanding may **outweigh** the surgeon's knife or the chemist's drug.

5   I will not be ashamed to say "I do not know," nor will I fail to call in my **colleagues** when the skills of another are needed for a patient's **recovery**.

6   I will respect the privacy of my patients because their problems are not told to me so that the world may know.

7   Most especially I will act with great care in matters of life and death. If it is given me to save a life, all thanks. Above all, I must not play at God.

8   I will remember that I do not treat a fever chart, a cancerous growth, but a sick human being, whose illness may **affect** the person's family and economic stability. My responsibility includes these related problems, if I am to care **adequately** for the sick.

9   I will **prevent** disease whenever I can because prevention is preferable to a cure.

10   I will remember that I remain a member of society, with special obligations to all my fellow human beings, those who are well in mind and body as well as those who are **infirm**.

11   If I do not **violate** this oath, may I enjoy life and art, respected while I live and remembered with affection thereafter. May I always act so as to preserve the finest traditions of my calling[4] and may I long experience the joy of healing those who seek my help.

---

[1] *swear:* to make a public promise

[2] *covenant:* a formal agreement

[3] *physician:* a medical doctor

[4] *calling:* someone's profession or trade

COMPREHENSION

A Main Ideas

1 Check (✓) the areas covered in the Oath.

☐ **1.** showing sympathetic attitudes

☐ **2.** respecting doctor-patient privilege

☐ **3.** sharing knowledge

☐ **4.** making money

☐ **5.** preventing disease

☐ **6.** making sure to know all the answers

☐ **7.** having a social conscience

2 Choose one of the main ideas in the *Hippocratic Oath* and give your opinion about it. Discuss your answers to the questions with a partner.

1. How should a doctor behave in regard to this point?

2. Has a doctor ever disappointed you or your family on this point?

3. What would you do if you were a doctor?

B Close Reading

Read the quotes from the reading. Circle the statement that best explains each quote. Share your answers with a partner.

1. "I will respect the hard-won scientific gains of those physicians in whose steps I walk, and gladly share such knowledge as is mine with those who are to follow." (*paragraph 2*)

    a. A good doctor shares the past and the present.

    b. Scientific discoveries do not come easily and must be shared.

    c. A good doctor builds on the past and shares his or her knowledge to help the future.

2. "[W]armth, sympathy, and understanding may outweigh the surgeon's knife or the chemist's drug." (*paragraph 4*)

    a. Technical procedures are the most important thing in the medical profession.

    b. Sometimes the best medicine is a doctor's kind and compassionate approach.

    c. A surgeon's lack of compassion cuts deeper than a knife.

3. "I will not be ashamed to say 'I do not know.'" (*paragraph 5*)

    a. A good doctor must be honest even when it makes him or her look bad.

    b. Shame can sometimes come from seeming to know too much.

    c. Shame often comes from a lack of knowledge.

(continued on next page)

4. "I will remember that I do not treat a fever chart, a cancerous growth, but a sick human being, whose illness may affect the person's family and economic stability." (*paragraph 8*)

    a. Paying the doctor can cost a lot of money.

    b. A doctor should not ignore social reality.

    c. For a doctor, the family comes first.

VOCABULARY

 ## Synonyms

Complete the summary of the main points of the *Hippocratic Oath* with the words from the box. Use the synonym in parentheses to help you select the correct word. Compare answers with a partner.

adequately	colleagues	infirm	outweigh	recovery
affect	hard-won	measures	prevent	violate

First and foremost, according to Hippocrates, doctors should help their patients

find ways to _____prevent_____ illnesses. But in all stages of care, doctors
    1. (avoid)

must not _____ the bonds of privacy and confidentiality that
    2. (disregard)

should exist between doctors and patients. Moreover, it is expected that doctors will

take care of all individuals in need, no matter how _____ they
    3. (weak)

are. Compassion should _____ any financial considerations.
    4. (be far stronger than)

Doctors who take care of their patients _____ should
    5. (sufficiently)

consider not only their patients' illnesses but also how their treatment plans will

_____ their patients' family life and economic welfare. Doctors
    6. (have an impact on)

should not regard themselves as superheroes, acting alone without asking the advice of

their _____. To make sure that their patients enjoy the benefits
    7. (fellow professionals)

of a smooth and healthy _____, doctors should ask for help
    8. (recuperation)

when it is needed. In addition, doctors should keep up with the progress made in their

field by taking advantage of research scientists' _____ medical
    9. (attained with great difficulty)

discoveries. With such knowledge, doctors can be fully aware of the appropriate

actions required in each patient's case. Taking all these _____
    10. (necessary actions)

will assure the best medical care for each patient.

B Word Usage: *affect* vs. *effect*

Use the verb **affect** to talk about something that produces changes.
- The disease **affects** the central nervous system.

Use the noun **effect** to talk about the results of those changes.
- The disease has harmful **effects** on the central nervous system.

Effect can be used as a verb to mean "to make something happen." However, this use is formal and not often used.
- The president's policy will **effect** positive changes in our lives.

Complete the paragraph with the correct form of the words. Choose from the two forms in parentheses. Compare answers with a partner.

Advances in scientific research have _____
1. (affected / effected)
medical care all over the world. Knowing more about disease has had an

_____ not only on the medical profession but also on
2. (affect / effect)
ordinary families. The discovery of penicillin and other antibiotics has had a

great _____ on global childhood mortality by lowering
3. (affect / effect)
the death rate considerably. Today, fewer children are suffering from the

_____ of yesterday's traditional childhood diseases. It is
4. (affects / effects)
hard to realize exactly how much we have been _____ by
5. (affected / effected)
breakthroughs in medical science. We owe our lives to them.

NOTE-TAKING: Categorizing and Summarizing

1   Go back to the reading and read it again. Note the main points in the margin.

EXAMPLE:

I will respect the hard-won scientific gains of those physicians in whose steps I walk,	*learn from the past*
and gladly share such knowledge as is mine with those who are to follow.	*help younger colleagues*

(continued on next page)

Now put the main points in categories.

Duty to the Profession	• Learn from the past • Help younger colleagues
Duty of Care	• • • • •
Social Context	• • •

2 Using the categories above, complete this short summary of the main points of the *Hippocratic Oath*.

"The Hippocratic Oath" deals with doctors' duty to their profession. Doctors must have full knowledge of the research findings of the past in order to be able to give their patients adequate care. Doctors must also share their knowledge with younger colleagues. In this way, they will be able to contribute to the quality of medical care in the future. In addition,

CRITICAL THINKING

Work in a small group. Discuss what people who believe in the *Hippocratic Oath* would say about these situations. Be prepared to share your ideas with the class.

1. Doctors who agree to use the drugs of certain pharmaceutical companies in the treatment of their patients receive money and other personal favors from these companies.

2. News stories about some celebrities have been made more interesting for the public because their doctors have shared information about the celebrities' medical care with the press.

3. Some patients want their doctors to help them end their lives because the pain they suffer without the benefit of a good quality of life is unbearable.

4. In some health plans, doctors are given only a limited amount of time to meet with a patient and often receive monetary punishments when they refer too many of their patients to specialists.

5. To avoid dealing with the bureaucratic demands of health plans, some doctors accept only wealthy patients who can afford to pay them privately.

READING TWO: The Invisible Enemy

A Warm-Up

Discuss the question with a partner.

Most people are vaccinated against certain diseases when they are young. Without certain vaccinations, students cannot attend American universities. Do you think this is fair? Why or why not?

B Reading Strategy

Scanning for Dates to Understand Sequence

Some texts are **organized by dates, years, or time periods,** and the respective events associated with them. Scanning such a text for dates helps you **understand the sequence (order) of events** it describes.

Scan the reading for dates and time periods. Circle them. Then write them on the lines.

_____

_____

_____

_____

_____

_____

_____

_____

_____

This story begins very long ago in history. What time span does it cover? When does it end? Compare answers with a partner.

Now read the text to find out more about the events and people that marked the history of "The Invisible Enemy."

THE INVISIBLE ENEMY

"No man dared count his children as his own until they had had the disease."
—*Charles-Marie de la Condamine, French scientist and explorer, 1701–1774*

"The most terrible of all the ministers of death."
—*T. B. Macaulay, British poet, historian, and politician, 1800–1859*

1   An ancient and deadly enemy for almost 10,000 years, smallpox killed millions of human beings all over the world. During epidemics, from 50 to 60% of the population would **contract** the disease, and 20 to 30% of its victims would die.

2   In the 16th century, Spanish conquerors brought smallpox to the Americas, **decimating** most of the native populations because they had never been exposed to the disease before and had no **immunity**. More Native Americans died of smallpox than died in battle with white settlers. In the 18th century, the British deliberately **infected** Native Americans with smallpox during the French and Indian War.[1] In London, death claimed 80% of the children under five years old who caught the disease; in Berlin, 98%. One-third of those who survived smallpox went blind. Spread by contact through the air, the disease **ravaged** every class of society. It caused a rash and blisters on the skin that left its survivors scarred for life. Queen Elizabeth I, Mozart, and George Washington all knew the suffering it brought.

3   Over the centuries, human beings gained knowledge of "the speckled monster." For one thing, they learned that survivors never caught the disease again. From this observation of natural immunity came the practice of variolation. Variolation probably began in China and India. In the early 18th century, Lady Mary Wortley Montagu[2] observed its use in Turkey, where her husband was ambassador. She brought the practice to England in 1721. Through a small cut, the pus from a smallpox blister is placed under the skin. This causes a low-grade smallpox infection. If the disease does

---

[1] **French and Indian War:** the war between Great Britain and France in North America that took place between 1754 and 1763

---

[2] **Lady Mary Wortley Montagu:** an English writer and aristocrat who lived between 1669 and 1762. Today she is chiefly remembered for her letters, particularly those from Turkey, as wife to the British ambassador.

not develop any further, the person will get well and be immune ever after. It was a dangerous **procedure** because the virus was not always weak enough and those who were variolated could start epidemics. Nevertheless, the process was usually successful, probably because in variolation the disease entered the body through the skin rather than through the lungs, and was thus less **virulent**. Although only about 2% of variolation patients died, it was still too many.

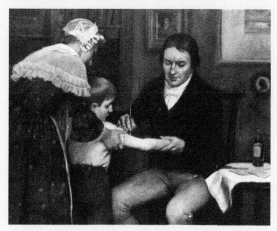

Edward Jenner vaccinating a child

4   Edward Jenner,[3] an English country doctor, heard stories about farmworkers who had contracted cowpox (a mild infection of animals) and then never got smallpox. Jenner became known not because he discovered the cowpox/smallpox connection — many farmers knew this from observation — but because he investigated it scientifically and proved it, showing the world how to benefit from it. Following the **principles** of his teacher, who said, "Don't think, try," he set up experiments with various children, including eventually his own

son. He inoculated them with cowpox and then proved that they no longer reacted when variolated with smallpox. The children had **acquired** cross-immunity. He called his prevention method a "vaccine" from the Latin for "cow." He sent his findings to the British Medical Association in 1797, but they refused to publish his revolutionary views without more proof. Variolators, who were afraid to lose their **livelihoods**, argued against him. Cartoonists showed patients growing cows' heads after getting vaccinated. But when other doctors and scientists repeated his experiments and found that he was right, Jenner became a hero. In France, Jenner was so **revered** that on his request the French emperor Napoleon freed some British prisoners of war, saying: "Ah, Jenner. I can refuse him nothing."[4]

5   In 1840, variolation was **banned** in Britain, and in 1853 universal vaccination became **compulsory** in England and Wales. More than a century later, however, 15 million people in the world were still getting the disease every year, and 2 million were dying from it. In 1967, the United Nations' World Health Organization began a global campaign to **eradicate** smallpox with free vaccines. The last known natural case of smallpox was in Somalia in 1977. In 1980, thanks to Edward Jenner's work and to all the "microbe hunters" fighting humanity's invisible enemies, the World Health Assembly officially declared "the world and its peoples" free from smallpox. Today, the smallpox virus exists only in laboratories. These discoveries of the past remain the hope of the future for other diseases that **plague** mankind.

---

[3] *Edward Jenner:* a British doctor who lived from 1749 to 1823

[4] Napoleon vaccinated all his troops in 1805 and French civilians a year later.

COMPREHENSION

A Main Ideas

Read each statement. Decide if it is *True* or *False* according to the reading. Check (✓) the appropriate box. If it is false, change it to make it true. Discuss your answers with a partner.

	TRUE	FALSE
1. It is clear in the reading that observation is an important scientific tool.	☐	☐
2. Jenner's development of the smallpox vaccine came from his knowledge of the concept of natural immunity.	☐	☐
3. Jenner's ideas were immediately accepted by the people of his time.	☐	☐
4. Human beings still face the danger of catching smallpox.	☐	☐

B Close Reading

Read the quotes from the reading. Circle the statement that best explains each quote. Share your answers with a partner.

1. "During epidemics, from 50 to 60% of the population would contract the disease, and 20 to 30% of its victims would die." (*paragraph 1*)

   What would happen in a population of 1,000?

   a. 400 to 500 people would not get smallpox.

   b. Up to 700 people would die.

2. "The British deliberately infected Native Americans with smallpox during the French and Indian War." (*paragraph 2*)

   a. The British used smallpox as a weapon.

   b. The British passed smallpox to the Native Americans without realizing it.

3. "Over the centuries, human beings gained knowledge of 'the speckled monster.'" (*paragraph 3*)

   a. Over time people gradually found a way to cure the disease.

   b. Observation over time made people familiar with the disease.

4. "Cartoonists showed patients growing cows' heads after getting vaccinated." (*paragraph 4*)

   a. The cartoonists made fun of Jenner's method.

   b. The cartoonists supported Jenner's method.

VOCABULARY

(continued on next page)

A Categorizing Words

Work with a partner. Put the words from the box into the categories listed below. There can be several answers. Discuss your choices with a partner.

acquire	compulsory	eradicate	livelihood	procedure
ban	contract	immunity	plague	ravage
be revered	decimate	infect	principles	virulent

CATCHING A DISEASE	FOLLOWING RULES AND METHODS
acquire	

CAUSING A LOT OF DESTRUCTION	PRACTICING THE MEDICAL PROFESSION

B Collocations

Work with a partner. Read the dictionary entries for *destroy*, *eliminate*, and *eradicate*.

destroy *v.* **1** to damage something so badly that it does not exist anymore or cannot be used or repaired **2** to ruin someone's life completely, so that they have no hope for the future

eliminate *v.* **1** to get rid of something completely **2** to kill someone in order to prevent them from causing trouble

eradicate *v.* to completely get rid of or destroy something

(continued on next page)

Now decide which verb or verbs can be paired with these words or phrases to make collocations.

> Remember that **collocations** are "word partners." They are words or phrases that are paired together frequently.

1. _eliminate/eradicate_ a disease

2. _____ the threat of a disease

3. _____ smallpox

4. _____ human life

5. _____ people's chances of survival

6. _____ the danger of the approaching enemy

7. _____ people's hopes

C Synonyms

Complete each sentence with a word from the box. Use the synonym in parentheses to help you select the correct word. Compare answers with a partner.

acquired	contracted	immunity	plagued	procedures	virulent
compulsory	eradicated	infected	principle	ravaged	

1. For thousands of years, smallpox (or variola) was one of the most terrible diseases

   that had ever _____ plagued _____ mankind.
   (tortured)

2. "Smallpox was always present, filling the churchyards with corpses, tormenting

   with constant fear all whom it had not yet _____."
   (contaminated)

   — *T. B. Macaulay,* History of England, *1848*

3. Even when it did not kill, the disease was so _____ that it
   (strong)
   turned loved ones into objects of horror with scars and blindness.

4. The first humans are believed to have _____ the disease at
   (caught)
   the time of the first agricultural settlements in Africa 10,000 years ago.

5. The earliest proof of smallpox skin blisters dates back to around 1780 B.C.,

   preserved by the _____ used to mummify remains in
   (methods)
   ancient Egypt.

6. An epidemic of smallpox in 180 B.C. killed the Roman emperor Marcus Aurelius and _____ the Roman Empire: between 3.5 and 7 million
   (damaged)
   people lost their lives.

7. From a population of 25 million people when the Spanish soldiers first arrived in Mexico, not even 2 million remained in 1620 because none of the natives had any natural _____ against smallpox.
   (protection)

8. In rural areas of England, Germany, France, and Italy, many farmers knew that cowpox gave a(n) _____ immunity to smallpox, and
   (obtained and not inborn)
   several farmers had actually tried to use this knowledge.

9. Jenner demonstrated that this folk medicine could be elevated to a scientific

   _____ when the scientific method was used.
   (basic rule)

10. Fifty years ago, it was still _____ for Americans traveling
    (required)
    abroad to carry a World Health Organization smallpox vaccination certificate.

11. "Future generations will know only by history that the terrible smallpox ever

    existed and was _____ by you."
    (eliminated)
    — *Thomas Jefferson* writing to Edward Jenner

NOTE-TAKING: Creating a Timeline

1 Go back to the reading, where you circled the important dates and time periods. Underline the words that refer to what happened at different times. Create a timeline that reflects all the relevant dates and events mentioned in the reading.

8000 B.C.: Start of smallpox

16th c.: Smallpox spreads to the Americas, ravaging Native American peoples

2 Match the items on the left with the explanations on the right. Discuss your answers with a partner.

_c_ 1. thousands of years ago

____ 2. rash and blisters

____ 3. variolation

____ 4. Turkey

____ 5. Edward Jenner

____ 6. vaccine

____ 7. Napoleon

____ 8. 15 million

____ 9. global campaign

a. doctor who discovered the best way to immunize against smallpox

b. modern smallpox prevention method

c. period when smallpox became deadly

d. number of people still getting smallpox every year in the 1950s

e. cause of smallpox scars on the face

f. country where Lady Wortley Montagu learned about variolation

g. admirer of Jenner

h. 1967 World Health Organization effort to rid the world completely of smallpox

i. first immunity procedure for smallpox, with pus from a smallpox blister

CRITICAL THINKING

Discuss the questions in a small group. Be prepared to share your conclusions with the class.

1. The title of the reading is "The Invisible Enemy." Why is this a good title for this reading?

2. Jenner's teacher was attempting to explain the scientific method when he told his students: "Don't think, try." What did he mean by that?

3. Edward Jenner included his own son in his later experiments with the vaccine. Why do you think he did that? Would you have done the same?

4. Napoleon was born an ordinary person and became emperor of France; he carried the ideas of the French Revolution all over Europe with his conquests. What is similar about Napoleon and Jenner? Why do you think Napoleon said: "Ah, Jenner, I can refuse him nothing"?

5. Why did the United Nations decide to launch a global campaign against smallpox? Should this be the role of the United Nations? Why is some smallpox bacteria still kept in labs in certain places in the world?

6. Go back to the quotes from La Condamine and Macaulay on page 76. How do these quotes relate to the reading? Explain their meaning.

Discuss the questions in a small group. Take notes. Then write a summary of the ideas that the members of your group shared with each other.

1. Did Jenner respect the principles of the Hippocratic Oath?

2. Which promises from the oath did he keep, and how did he keep them?

3. Do you think Jenner felt "the joy of healing" as the oath describes it? Why is healing "a joy"?

READING THREE: That Mothers Might Live

A Warm-Up

Review the statistics and discuss the question with a partner.

In the past, the biggest killer of women was childbirth.

- In the 1800s, 40% of women giving birth died in the process.
- In 2005, according to the World Health Organization, the global mortality rate for women during childbirth was less than 1%.

Why do you think this change occurred?

B Reading Strategy

Finding Link between Title and First Paragraph

There is often a **direct link** between the title of a text and the contents of its **introductory paragraph**. Understanding this **link helps the reader focus** with more confidence on the rest of the text.

"That Mothers Might Live" is the title of the reading. Read the first paragraph. Answer the questions.

1. Why were the mothers dying?

_____

2. What is the name of the ward that needed improvement?

_____

Now read the whole text to find out what happened and who made it possible that "mothers might live."

That Mothers Might Live[1]

1   In 1844 in Vienna (Austria), the General Hospital had two wards[2] where poor women could have their babies. Both wards saw an equal number of births. In the First Division, attended by doctors, 600 to 800 mothers died each year from what was called childbed fever.[3] In the Second Division, where women were helped only by midwives, there were 60 deaths, one-tenth as many. Women would beg on their knees not to be sent to the First Division and often arranged to give birth in the streets rather than be sent to the "death house."

2   The difference between the wards was common knowledge among ordinary people, but only Dr. Ignaz Semmelweis (1818–1865) cared enough to **seek** a solution. He found it only after a colleague died with the same symptoms as childbed fever. The colleague had been dissecting cadavers to practice surgery and accidentally cut himself with the knife. Semmelweis made the connection: Doctors, using cadavers to teach anatomy lessons in the morning, were carrying disease to their pregnant patients in the afternoon. Midwives, on the other hand, were women and were not allowed to do dissection. Thus, they did not infect the mothers in the Second Division. Semmelweis made all the doctors under him wash their hands with chlorinated limewater[4] before examining pregnant patients and also when going from patient to patient. This hand washing immediately lowered the mortality rate

from 18% to less than 2%. Semmelweis's results were extraordinary. Countless women and babies owed him their lives.

Ignaz Semmelweis with a patient

3   The story of Ignaz Semmelweis should have ended in glory, but it didn't. He and his theories were rejected by the **rigid**, all-male medical **authorities** of the time. His observations went against accepted **notions**, which blamed disease on an imbalance in the "basic humors" (or fluids) of each person's body. Doctors didn't understand Semmelweis's idea that childbed fever was **transmitted** from one person to another, carried by dirty hands. No one at that time realized that bacteria could cause disease. This would only become clear more than 15 years later when Louis Pasteur did his **pioneering** work on germ theory in France. Semmelweis had the **empirical** data on his side — his **statistics** told the story — but no one listened because he had no theoretical explanation. In reality, doctors didn't want to accept the idea that their practices were responsible for so many deaths. Semmelweis was

---

[1] *"That Mothers Might Live"*: title of a Hollywood short film about Ignaz Semmelweis directed by Fred Zinnemann; it won the Academy Award in 1939

[2] *ward*: In the past, hospital beds for people who needed medical treatment were located in large rooms called wards.

[3] *childbed fever:* a severe bacterial infection spreading through the blood

[4] *limewater:* a disinfectant similar to bleach

laughed at and attacked. They said he was too young, a Hungarian outsider, a young man with **radical** ideas who insulted "gentlemen" doctors for having dirty hands! He was dismissed from the hospital.

4   Continuing to practice medicine back in Hungary, Semmelweis spent many years developing his ideas before he wrote his book in 1861. The book received poor reviews, and Semmelweis accused his opponents of murdering women through their stubbornness and **ignorance**. He eventually suffered a nervous breakdown and was taken to a mental hospital. He died there two weeks later — probably the result of being beaten by the guards — a poor reward for a tireless struggle to save women's lives.

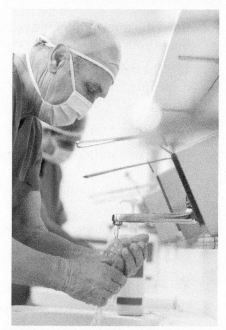

Modern-day surgeons always scrub their hands before operating.

COMPREHENSION

Ⓐ Main Ideas

Read each statement. Decide if it is *True* or *False* according to the reading. Check (✓) the appropriate box. If it is false, change it to make it true. Discuss your answers with a partner.

	TRUE	FALSE
1. Semmelweis succeeded in discovering that doctors infected their patients.	☐	☐
2. The fact that women were forbidden to do dissections in the hospital is not an important part of this story.	☐	☐
3. With Semmelweis's discovery, the mortality rate of childbearing women in his hospital went down considerably.	☐	☐
4. The medical establishment of the time had a clear idea about how disease was transmitted.	☐	☐
5. The Viennese doctors were offended that Semmelweis blamed them for women's deaths, and he was fired from his position.	☐	☐
6. Semmelweis died in Hungary with full recognition for his accomplishments.	☐	☐

B Close Reading

Read the quotes from the reading. Circle the statement that explains each quote. Share your answers with a partner.

1. "The difference between the wards was common knowledge among ordinary people, but only Dr. Ignaz Semmelweis (1818 – 1865) cared enough to seek a solution."(*paragraph 2*)

   a. Except for Semmelweis, doctors didn't worry about the problem.

   b. The solution was common knowledge to most people.

2. "The story of Ignaz Semmelweis should have ended in glory, but it didn't." (*paragraph 3*)

   a. Semmelweis should have been a better person.

   b. Semmelweis should have been recognized for his great service.

3. "Doctors didn't understand Semmelweis's idea that childbed fever was transmitted from one person to another, carried by dirty hands." (*paragraph 3*)

   a. Exactly how diseases spread was a mystery at that time.

   b. Doctors were unaware of what Semmelweis was saying.

VOCABULARY

A Synonyms

Complete the essay with the words from the box. Use the synonym in parentheses to help you select the correct word. Compare answers with a partner.

authorities	ignorance	pioneered	rigid	statistics
empirical	notions	radical	seek	transmitted

*Louis Pasteur
in his laboratory*

Louis Pasteur (1822 – 1895) was a French chemist and microbiologist who

_____pioneered_____ the germ theory of disease. Along with a colleague,
1. (first developed)

Robert Koch, Pasteur disproved the _____ held for a
2. (beliefs)

long time by the _____ in the medical field. At that time,
3. (powerful people)

doctors did not know that infection causes disease. This prevented doctors from

understanding that many diseases are, in fact, spread from one person to another by

tiny microorganisms called bacteria and viruses. The _____
4. (based on practical testing)

data from Pasteur's important laboratory work and the _____
5. (numbers and measurements)

from his experiments allowed him to _____ an explanation
6. (search for)

for many interrelated biological, chemical, and physical questions. Scientists were

eventually forced to accept Pasteur's _____ germ theory of
7. (revolutionary)

disease, which held that micro-organisms infect human beings and animals, causing

illnesses that are _____ from one organism to another.
8. (communicated)

   Pasteur was one of the great benefactors of humanity. We remember him

for the proof of the germ theory and for many discoveries, including the

pasteurization of milk, wine, and beer, as well as the first vaccines for rabies and

anthrax. In a speech to the Faculty of Letters in Douai, Pasteur said: "In the field

of observation, chance favors only the prepared mind." He warned against the

_____ thinking and _____ that
9. (inflexible)   10. (lack of knowledge)

prevent us from accepting new ideas, and asked that we be prepared for even greater

insights into the secrets of our natural world.

B **Word Usage: *the authorities* vs. *the authority***

> Use **the authorities** (*noun plural*) to talk about the people or organizations
> that are in charge of a particular country or area:
> - Semmelweis's theories were viciously attacked by **the** rigid, all-male medical
>   **authorities** of the time.
>
> Use **the authority** (*noun singular*) to talk about the power someone has
> because of an official position:
> - The medical authorities who were opposed to Semmelweis's ideas had **the**
>   **authority** to make life difficult for him.

Complete the sentences with either *authority* or *authorities*. Compare answers with a partner.

1. Semmelweis struggled to get his ideas about hand washing accepted by the medical _____ of his time.

2. Based on the empirical evidence he had collected, he believed that he had the _____ to make certain recommendations.

3. But the _____ of Vienna took offense as the young doctor raised serious questions about their long-held professional practices.

4. Despite the positive results of his changes, Semmelweis did not have the _____ to overrule those doctors who had an interest in maintaining things as they were.

C Connotations

> A **connotation** is a **feeling** or **idea** that a word makes you think of. This feeling can be **positive or negative**.

1   Look at each word. Decide if it generally has mainly *Positive*, *Negative*, or *Neutral* connotations. Check (✓) the appropriate box. Discuss your answers with a partner.

	POSITIVE	NEGATIVE	NEUTRAL
1. spread	☐	☐	☑
2. ravage	☐	☑	☐
3. rigid	☐	☑	☐
4. rigorous	☐	☐	☑
5. stubborn	☐	☑	☐
6. persistent	☐	☑	☐
7. radical	☐	☐	☐
8. extreme	☐	☐	☐

2   Complete the sentences with the appropriate words. Choose from the two words in parentheses. Compare answers with a partner.

1. The doctors who refused to change their habits even in the face of Semmelweis's positive results were _____ stubborn _____ and resistant to change
   (persistent / stubborn)
   because Semmelweis's criticism was an attack on their professional privileges.

2. Semmelweis never gave up his struggle; he was _____ in

(persistent / stubborn)

defense of using new methods, although to his opponents his attitude was mere

_____.

(persistence / stubbornness)

3. Pasteur's germ theory was a(n) _____ departure from

(extreme / radical)

previous theories.

4. Dismissing Dr. Semmelweis from his job was a(n) _____

(extreme / radical)

reaction to his request for better practices in the hospital.

5. Antiseptic procedures _____ the world after Lister's work

(spread across / ravaged)

became well known.

6. In our time, AIDS has _____ many African countries.

(spread across / ravaged)

7. Edward Jenner was _____ in his use of the scientific

(rigid / rigorous)

method, but he was not so _____ as to exclude the insights

(rigid / rigorous)

of folk medicine.

CRITICAL THINKING

Discuss the questions in a small group. Be prepared to share your ideas with the class.

1. Go back to the first paragraph of the reading. Based on the statistics given, what was the approximate total number of births each year for the two wards combined?

2. Despite his statistics, doctors said they couldn't take Semmelweis seriously because he did not yet have a theory to explain his findings. Do you need a theory if what you do works? Why or why not? What was probably the real reason they didn't want to listen to him?

3. What did the variolators who opposed Jenner and the Viennese authorities who opposed Semmelweis have in common?

4. Did Semmelweis obey the pledge of the Hippocratic Oath? Could his opponents have used part of the oath against him?

5. Was Semmelweis correct to call those who wouldn't listen to him "murderers"? Were his "tireless efforts" worth it? Why do you think he had a nervous breakdown?

BRINGING IT ALL TOGETHER

Work in groups of three. Role-play one of the two situations. Follow the instructions for each one. Use some of the vocabulary you studied in the chapter (for a complete list, go to page 91).

SITUATION ONE: **Jenner and the variolators**

1. Review the reasons a variolator might give for opposing Jenner's vaccine. What might Jenner answer? How would each of them discuss the Hippocratic Oath?

2. One student will play Jenner, the second a variolator, and the third will be the discussion organizer, who introduces the problem and asks questions.

SITUATION TWO: **Semmelweis and his opponents**

1. Discuss what Semmelweis's opponents might say against his recommendations. What might Semmelweis answer? How would each of them discuss the Hippocratic Oath?

2. One student will play Semmelweis, the second an opponent, and the third will be the discussion organizer, who introduces the problem and asks questions.

After the role-plays, discuss the results. Were the arguments convincing? Were you able to use some of the vocabulary words?

WRITING ACTIVITY

Write a portrait of someone you admire or revere. Explain your reasons. Describe how the person's behavior reflects the principles you believe are important. Write two or three paragraphs and use at least five of the words and idioms you studied in the chapter.

DISCUSSION AND WRITING TOPICS

Discuss these topics in a small group. Choose one of them and write a paragraph or two about it. Use the vocabulary from the chapter.

1. "In the field of observation, chance favors only the prepared mind." How does Pasteur's quote relate to Jenner and Semmelweis and their accomplishmments? How does Pasteur's work relate to their efforts?

2. Karl Marx dedicated his book *Capital* to Charles Darwin, whom he considered the greatest revolutionary thinker of his age. Could a case be made to add Pasteur to the list of the great revolutionary thinkers of the 19th century? Why or why not?

3. Jenner kept an open mind about farmers' beliefs about cowpox. Do you know any other "folk remedies" or aspects of traditional medicine that can be of use in today's world?

4. Doctors are held to a high moral standard in the Hippocratic Oath, more than other professions. Is this fair? Is it justified? Why or why not?

VOCABULARY

Nouns	Verbs	Adjectives	Adverb
authorities *	acquire *	compulsory	adequately
colleague *	affect *	empirical *	
ignorance *	ban	infirm	**Idiom**
immunity	contract *	radical *	hard-won
livelihood	decimate	rigid	
measure	eradicate	virulent	
notion *	infect		
principle *	outweigh		
procedure *	pioneer		
recovery *	plague		
statistics *	prevent		
	ravage		
	revere		
	seek *		
	transmit		
	violate *		

* = AWL (Academic Word List) item

SELF-ASSESSMENT

In this chapter you learned to:

○ Skim an oath and scan a text for dates

○ Find the link between the title of a text and the first paragraph

○ Understand and use synonyms, collocations, and connotations

○ Understand the different usage of similar words

○ Categorize words

○ Categorize and summarize stud·

○ Create a timeline to understar sequence of events

What can you do well? ✓

What do you need to prac·

CHAPTER 5

AMERICAN LITERATURE: Ernest Hemingway's "Indian Camp"

AMERICAN LITERATURE: the study of written works of lasting artistic merit by authors from the United States

OBJECTIVES

To read academic texts, you need to master certain skills.

In this chapter, you will:

- Identify and understand the elements of fiction: characters, setting, plot, themes

- Scan a text for "compare and contrast" words

- Guess the meaning of words from the context

- Understand and use synonyms, phrasal verbs, and different word forms

- Recognize words of varying intensity

- Use circling and margin notes to identify themes

- Organize study notes to compare and define a writer's style

Hemingway and one of his sons

Consider These Questions

Discuss the questions in a small group.

1. Did you have a close relationship with your father when you were growing up? Has the relationship changed over the years? What are the qualities of a good father?

2. Did you ever go to work with your parents? Have you ever seen them at work? What did you learn from the experience?

3. All great novels, all great movies, all great short stories,[1] are just works of fiction invented by writers. How can stories that are not real tell us important truths about ourselves and our feelings?

READING ONE: Indian Camp (Part I)

A Warm-Up

"Indian Camp" is one of the first short stories Ernest Hemingway (1899–1961) wrote. The main character is Nick Adams, a child who, like Hemingway, loved to go hunting and fishing with his father in the woods of northern Michigan. Nick's father, like Hemingway's father, was a doctor.

Discuss the questions with a partner.

1. What do you think this short story is going to be about?

2. Literary critics call this "a semi-autobiographical" story (semi- means "half"). What does this say about the story?

B Reading Strategy

Understanding the Elements of Fiction

When reading literature, it is important to keep in mind some of the elements of fiction: **characters**, **setting**, and **plot**.
As you read:
   – Circle the names of the main **characters** (people in the story).
   – Underline the **setting** (where and when the story takes place).
   – Write notes in the margin about the **plot** (main events that take place).

Read the beginning of the story. Notice the circled names, the underlined information, and the note in the margin.

As you read the rest of the story, circle the names of other characters and underline more information about the setting. Then read the story again and write other notes about the plot.

---

[1] *short story*: a story that is longer than a personal anecdote and shorter than a novel; usually a narrative (telling about a series of events) that contains a fully developed theme

Indian Camp[1]

by Ernest Hemingway

PART I

1　　At the lake shore there was another rowboat drawn up. The two Indians stood waiting.

　　Nick and his father got into the stern (back) of the boat and the Indians **shoved** it **off** and
5　one of them got in to **row**. Uncle George sat in the back of the camp rowboat. The young Indian shoved the camp boat and got in to row Uncle George.

　　The two boats started off in the dark. Nick lay back with his father's
10　arm around him. It was cold on the water. The Indian who was rowing them was working very hard, but the other boat moved further ahead in the mist all the time.

　　"Where are we going, Dad?" Nick asked.

　　"Over to the Indian camp. There is an Indian lady very sick."
15　"Oh," said Nick.

Nick, his father, and his uncle George are taken across a lake, at night, to an Indian camp.

　　Across the bay they found the other boat **beached**. Uncle George was smoking a cigar in the dark. The young Indian pulled the boat way up on the beach. Uncle George gave both the Indians cigars.

　　They walked up from the beach through a meadow following the
20　young Indian who carried a **lantern**. Then they went into the woods and followed a trail that led to the logging road that ran back into the hills. It was much lighter on the logging road as the timber was cut away on both sides. The young Indian stopped and blew out his lantern and they all walked on along the road.

25　　They came around a bend and a dog came out barking. Ahead were the lights of the shanties[2] where the Indian bark-peelers[3] lived. More dogs rushed out at them. The two Indians sent them back to the shanties. In the shanty nearest the road there was a light in the window. An old woman stood in the doorway holding a lamp.

30　　Inside on a wooden bunk lay a young Indian woman. She had been trying to have her baby for two days. All the old women in the camp had been helping her. The men had moved off up the road to sit in the dark and smoke out of range of the noise she made. She **screamed** just as Nick and the two Indians followed his father and Uncle George into the shanty.
35　She lay on the lower bunk, very big under a **quilt**. Her head was turned to one side. In the upper bunk was her husband. He had cut his foot very badly with an ax three days before. He was smoking a pipe. The room smelled very bad.

---

[1] This story was written almost 100 years ago and does not reflect how Native Americans live in the United States today.

[2] *shanty:* a roughly built house where very poor people live

[3] *bark-peeler:* someone who takes off the outer covering of a tree

Nick's father ordered some water to be put on the stove, and while it
40 was heating he spoke to Nick.

"This lady is going to have a baby, Nick," he said.

"I know," said Nick.

"You don't know," said his father. "Listen to me. What she is going
through is called being in labor. The baby wants to be born and she wants
45 it to be born. All her muscles are trying to get the baby born. That is what
is happening when she screams."

"I see," Nick said.

Just then the woman cried out.

"Oh, Daddy, can't you give her something to make her stop screaming?"
50 asked Nick.

"No. I haven't any **anesthetic**," his father said. "But her screams are not
important. I don't hear them because they are not important."

The husband in the upper bunk rolled over against the wall.

The woman in the kitchen motioned to the doctor that the water was
55 hot. Nick's father went into the kitchen and poured about half the water
out of the big kettle into a basin. Into the water left in the kettle he put
several things he unwrapped from a handkerchief.

"These must boil," he said, and began to **scrub** his hands in the basin
of hot water with a cake of soap he had brought from the camp. Nick
60 watched his father's hands scrubbing each other with the soap. While his
father washed his hands very carefully and **thoroughly**, he talked.

"You see, Nick, babies are supposed to be born head first but sometimes
they're not. When they're not, they make a lot of trouble for everybody.
Maybe I'll have to operate on this lady. We'll know in a little while."
65 When he was satisfied with his hands he went in and went to work.

"Pull back that quilt, will you George?" he said. "I'd rather not touch it."

Later when he started to operate, Uncle George and three Indian men
held the woman still. She bit Uncle George on the arm and Uncle George
said, "Damn squaw!"[4] and the young Indian who had rowed Uncle George
70 over laughed at him. Nick held the basin for his father. It all took a
long time.

His father picked the baby up and slapped it to make it breathe and
handed it to the old woman.

"See, it's a boy, Nick," he said. How do you like being an **intern**?"
75 Nick said, "All right." He was looking away so as not to see what his
father was doing.

"There. That gets it," said his father and put something into the basin.
Nick didn't look at it.

"Now," his father said, "there's some stitches to put in. You can watch
80 this or not, Nick, just as you like. I'm going to sew up the **incision** I made."

Nick did not watch. His curiosity had been gone for a long time.

------
[4] *squaw:* a word for a Native American woman, now considered offensive

COMPREHENSION

A Main Ideas

1 The Characters

Identify the main characters who appear in this part of the story. What are their relationships to one another? Write down the names that are made known to us.

Nick (the main character)   _____

_____   _____

_____   _____

2 The Setting

Describe where and when the story takes place. Refer to the natural environment and the kind of community where the action occurs. Indicate the time of day.

1. Where: _____

2. When: _____

3 The Plot

Work with a partner. Complete the sentences to show the sequence of the main events in this part of the story.

1	2
Nick, his father, and his Uncle George are taken across a lake at night to an Indian camp.	A young Indian woman _____ _____ _____

3	4
Nick's father is a doctor. He prepares _____ _____	He operates on _____ without _____. She bites _____

5	6
The baby _____ _____ _____	Nick's father _____ _____ _____

Read the quotes from the reading. Circle the statement that best explains each quote. Share your answers with a partner.

1. "Nick and his father got into the stern (back) of the boat and the Indians shoved it off and one of them got in to row. Uncle George sat in the back of the camp rowboat. The young Indian shoved the camp boat and got in to row Uncle George." (*lines 3–8*)

   a. The Indians did all the work.

   b. All the men shared the work.

2. "They walked up from the beach through a meadow following the young Indian who carried a lantern. Then they went into the woods and followed a trail that led to the logging road that ran back into the hills." (*lines 19–21*)

   a. The Indians lived among the other people in Michigan.

   b. The Indians lived isolated from the rest of society.

3. "They came around a bend and a dog came out barking. Ahead were the lights of the shanties where the Indian bark-peelers lived. More dogs rushed out to them. The two Indians sent them back to the shanties." (*lines 25–27*)

   a. The dogs were protecting the Indian camp against intruders.

   b. The dogs were there to greet the friendly Indians.

4. "This lady is going to have a baby, Nick," he said.
   "I know," said Nick.
   "You don't know," said his father. (*lines 41–43*)

   a. The father wanted his son to listen to what he would tell him.

   b. The father understood that his son was too young to see all this.

5. "Later when he started to operate, Uncle George and three Indian men held the woman still." (*lines 67–68*)

   a. Uncle George and the other men were afraid the woman would bite them.

   b. There was no painkiller for the woman, and the doctor was going to cut her.

VOCABULARY

 Guessing from Context

> In some cases, you may not be able to understand the exact meaning of a word, but **context clues** (other words in the rest of the sentence or paragraph) will give you the **general idea**.
>
> **EXAMPLE:** "screamed"
>> Inside on a wooden bunk lay a young Indian woman. She had been trying to have her baby for two days. . . . The men had moved off up the road to sit in the dark and smoke out of range of the noise she made. She **screamed** just as Nick and the two Indians followed his father and Uncle George into the shanty.
>
> **Clues:** trying to have her baby for two days / the noise she made
> **Guess:** probably a loud sound expressing pain
> **Dictionary:** to make a loud high noise with your voice because you are hurt, frightened, excited

Look at the list of words from the reading. Locate each word in the reading and try to guess its meaning from the context clues. Write down the clues, your guess, and then the dictionary meaning. Was your guess correct?

1. **shove off**
   (line 4)

   Clues: _"a row boat was drawn up" on the shore and it was_
   "shoved off" and "one of [the Indians] got in to row"

   Guess: _to push a boat to get it into the water_

   Dictionary: _to push a boat away from the land, usually with a pole_

2. **beached**
   (line 16)

   Clues: _____

   Guess: _____

   Dictionary: _____

3. **lantern**
   (line 20)

   Clues: _____

   Guess: _____

   Dictionary: _____

4. **quilt**
   (line 35)

   Clues: _____

   Guess: _____

   Dictionary: _____

5. **anesthetic**
   (line 51)

   Clues: _____

   Guess: _____

   Dictionary: _____

6. scrub
(line 58)

Clues: _____

Guess: _____

Dictionary: _____

7. thoroughly
(line 61)

Clues: _____

Guess: _____

Dictionary: _____

8. incision
(line 80)

Clues: _____

Guess: _____

Dictionary: _____

Ⓑ Synonyms

Complete the text with the words or phrases from the box. Use the synonym or meaning in parentheses to help you select the correct word or phrase. Compare answers with a partner.

anesthetic	incision	lantern	rowed	scrubbed	thoroughly
beached	intern	quilt	screamed	shoved . . . off	

To get the two rowboats into the water, the Indians ___*shoved*___ them ___*off*___
                                                1. (pushed . . . off)

from the land. After they _____ to the other
                      2. (used oars to make the boat move across the water)

shore, the Indians _____ the boats. The men followed a
                    3. (pulled onto the land)

young Indian whose _____ permitted them all to see their
                  4. (lamp that you can carry)

way in the dark. They knew which shanty to go to because an old woman met them

at the door.

Overcome by the pain of labor, the pregnant woman _____.
                                                  5. (cried out)

She was lying under a _____ to keep warm. The boy asked his
                    6. (thick bed cover)

father if he had a(n) _____ for her. Did he feel sorry for her, or
                  7. (painkiller)

was he merely unhappy to hear the noise?

In preparation for the surgery, the father _____ his hands
                                  8. (cleaned by rubbing)

_____, using the soap that he had brought with him. The
9. (completely and carefully)

(continued on next page)

father wanted his son to be a(n) _____ and made him assist

10. (doctor-in-training)

during the operation. After the baby was born, the father needed to sew up the area

where he had made a(n) _____ in the mother's body.

11. (deep cut)

C Gradations of Intensity

The words in the list refer to sounds coming from a person's mouth. How intense is each sound? Give a number to each, with *1* being the least intense and *4* being the most intense. Discuss with a partner. Some disagreement is possible.

_____ speak

_____ yell

_____ scream

_____ shout

CRITICAL THINKING

A Making Inferences

Discuss the questions in a small group. Be prepared to share your answers with the class.

1. We know Nick, the father (Dad), and Uncle George by their names. Why don't we know any of the Indians by their names?

2. Why do the Indians live in shanties? Why do you think the author repeats this word three times *(lines 25–28)* instead of using a synonym? What does he want to say about the kind of life the Indians live?

3. Why didn't Nick watch what his father was doing near the end? Why had "his curiosity" already "been gone for a long time"? How has he lost his innocence?

4. The story is full of images appealing to the senses. What does the reader see, hear, and smell through Hemingway's words?

5. Giving birth is usually a "woman's" story, but here it seems to have been taken over by men. How?

6. From whose point of view is the story told: the women? the Indians? the doctor? Nick? How does this point of view add to the appeal of the story?

B Drawing Conclusions

Also consider these questions about the woman's labor (*lines 43–71*).

1. When Nick says, "I see," (*line 47*) do you think he really understands what his father is saying? Why does he say it?

2. Why does Nick ask his father to give the woman some pain medication and call him "Daddy" (*line 49*)? Is he sorry for the woman? Or does he want her to be quiet? Why does he use a child's "Daddy" this time and not "Dad"?

3. Why does Nick's father say to him that the woman's screams "are not important" (*line 51*)? Would he have said that about his own wife or a woman of his world? Or is this what any doctor would say, concentrating more at the moment on the job he needs to do than on the patient's suffering?

4. Why does the Indian woman's husband turn his face to the wall when he hears the doctor say his wife's screams are unimportant (*line 53*)?

READING TWO: Indian Camp (Part II)

A Warm-Up

Discuss the questions with a partner.

1. What do you think will be Nick's reaction to all the things he saw that night?

2. What questions do you think he'll ask his father when it's all over?

B Reading Strategy

Identifying Themes

The **themes** of a story are its **unifying ideas**. The themes contain the **message** the author wishes to communicate to the reader. As you read, you need to think not only about the words but also about the emotions and ideas of the story.

As you read Part II of "Indian Camp," check (✓) some of the themes.

☐ 1. sons learning about life from their fathers

☐ 2. children not being ready for certain life lessons

☐ 3. negative treatment of Indians in American society

☐ 4. indifference toward suffering

Indian Camp

by Ernest Hemingway

PART II

1   His father finished and **stood up**. Uncle George and the three Indian men stood up. Nick put the basin out in the kitchen.

Uncle George looked at his arm. The young
5   Indian smiled **reminiscently**.

"I'll put some peroxide on that, George," the doctor said.

He bent over the Indian woman. She was quiet now and her eyes were closed. She looked very **pale**. She did not
10   know what had become of the baby or anything.

"I'll be back in the morning," the doctor said, standing up.

"The nurse should be here from St. Ignace by noon and she'll bring everything we need."

He was feeling **exalted** and **talkative** as football players are in the
15   dressing room after a game.

"That's one for the medical journals, George," he said. "Doing a cesarean[1] with a jack-knife[2] and sewing it up with nine-foot tapered gut leaders."[3]

Uncle George was standing against the wall, looking at his arm.

"Oh, you're a great man, all right," he said.

20   "Ought to have a look at the proud father. They're usually the worst sufferers in these little affairs," the doctor said. "I must say he took it all pretty quietly."

He pulled back the blanket from the Indian's head. His hand came away wet. He mounted on the edge of the lower bunk with the lamp in
25   one hand and looked in. The Indian lay with his face toward the wall. His throat had been cut from ear to ear. The blood had **flowed** down into a pool where his body sagged the bunk. His head rested on his left arm. The open razor lay, edge up, in the blankets.

"Take Nick out of the shanty, George," the doctor said.

30   There was no need of that. Nick, standing in the door of the kitchen, had a good view of the upper bunk when his father, the lamp in one hand, tipped the Indian's head back.

It was just beginning to be daylight when they walked along the logging road back toward the lake.

35   "I'm terribly sorry I brought you along, Nickie," said his father, all of his post-operative **exhilaration** gone. "It was an awful **mess** to put you through."

"Do ladies always have such a hard time having babies?" Nick asked.

"No, that was very **exceptional**."

40   "Why did he kill himself, Daddy?"

---

[1] *cesarean:* a surgical procedure to deliver a baby through a cut in the mother's abdomen

[2] *jack-knife:* a folding knife

[3] *gut leader:* a fishing line

"I don't know, Nick. He couldn't **stand** things, I guess."

"Do many men kill themselves, Daddy?"

"Not very many, Nick."

"Do many women?"

45   "**Hardly ever.**"

"Don't they ever?"

"Oh, yes. They do sometimes."

"Daddy?"

"Yes?"

50   "Where did Uncle George go?"

"He'll turn up all right."

"Is dying hard, Daddy?"

"No, I think it's pretty easy, Nick. It all depends."

They were seated in the boat. Nick in the stern, his father rowing. The

55 sun was coming up over the hills. A bass⁴ jumped, making a circle in the
water. Nick trailed his hand in the water. It felt warm in the sharp **chill**
of the morning.

In the early morning on the lake sitting in the stern of the boat with his
father rowing, he felt quite sure that he would never die.

---

⁴ **bass:** a fish

COMPREHENSION

 Main Ideas: The Plot

Work with a partner. Complete the sentences to show the sequence of the main
events in this part of the story.

1	**2**
Nick's father cleans _____ _____.	Nick's father talks proudly about _____.

3	**4**
He discovers that the baby's father _____ _____.	George disappears _____ _____.

5	**6**
Nick and his father leave _____ _____.	Father and son discuss _____ _____.

B Close Reading

Read the quotes from the reading. Circle the statement that best explains each quote. Share your answers with a partner.

1. "He was feeling exalted and talkative as football players are in the dressing room after a game." (*lines 14–15*)

   a. The father was thinking about how well he did his job.

   b. The father was thinking about his patient's suffering.

2. "Oh, you're a great man, all right," he said. (*line 19*)

   a. Uncle George was being ironic.

   b. Uncle George agreed with his brother.

3. "'Take Nick out of the shanty, George,' the doctor said." (*line 29*)

   a. The father wanted his son to leave so that he could do his job.

   b. The father realized the situation was too much for a young child.

4. "There was no need of that." (*line 30*)

   a. The boy didn't notice what was happening.

   b. It was too late; the boy had already seen everything.

5. "In the early morning on the lake sitting in the stern of the boat with his father rowing, he felt quite sure he would never die." (*lines 58–59*)

   a. He felt that he would never grow up.

   b. He wanted to feel safe and unafraid.

VOCABULARY

A Synonyms

1   Work with a partner. Read the reading again and discuss the meanings of the words or phrases in bold. Then match each word or phrase with its synonym.

__f__ 1. chill	a. almost never
_____ 2. exalted	b. remembering the past
_____ 3. exceptional	c. great happiness
_____ 4. exhilaration	d. communicative
_____ 5. flow	e. unusual
_____ 6. hardly ever	f. cold air
_____ 7. mess	g. sickly looking
_____ 8. pale	h. extremely happy
_____ 9. reminiscently	i. difficult situation
_____ 10. talkative	j. leak out

2 Complete the paragraph with some of the words and phrases from Exercise 1. Use the synonym in parentheses to help you select the correct word or phrase. Compare answers with a partner.

Nick's father enjoyed a feeling of _____ when
                                                        1. (great happiness)
his operation was a success. He had to use very primitive tools, and

doctors _____ succeeded in such circumstances. It
                    2. (almost never)
was truly an _____ case. The Indian woman was
                        3. (unusual)
_____, but she and the baby were alive. Nick's father became
        4. (sickly looking)
very _____ as he put antiseptic on his brother's bitten arm.
          5. (communicative)
At the same time, one of the Indian men smiled _____ as he
                                                                    6. (remembering the past)
watched the uncle's pain.

B Phrasal Verbs with *stand*

> A **phrasal verb** is a combination of a **verb** and a **particle** (or two). The combination has a special meaning, different from the meaning of the verb alone.
>
> Stand is a verb with many different meanings, including the meaning used in the reading: "to accept a situation."
> - The Native American husband couldn't **stand** his life and decided to end it.
>
> Stand is also used with different particles, like **up**, **for**, **in**, and **out**. The resulting phrasal verbs have many different meanings.

Read these sentences with phrasal verbs with *stand*. Guess the meaning of each phrasal verb and write it on the line. Check the dictionary for the correct meaning.

1. What does that candidate **stand for**? He's running for president, but I don't know what his ideas are.

   to support certain ideas

2. I would **stand against** racial discrimination if I ran for office.

   _____

3. The doctor was very sick and needed a replacement to **stand in for** him.

   _____

4. The person who is different from all the others will always **stand out** in a crowd.

   _____

(continued on next page)

5. Good friends will **stand by** one another in times of crisis.

_____

6. The husband was ashamed because he couldn't **stand up to** his wife's lover.

_____

7. Sometimes people have to **stand up for** what they believe in.

_____

NOTE-TAKING: Circling Themes and Writing Margin Notes

Here are some of the themes in "Indian Camp."

1. growing up and learning about life

2. seeing the world through a child's eyes

3. sadness and death

4. the relationship between a father and a son

5. the humiliation and isolation of people who are "different"

Read the story again (Parts I and II) and circle the sections that refer to the different themes. Write notes in the margin to identify the theme each section represents. Share your notes with a partner.

CRITICAL THINKING

Discuss the questions in a small group. Be prepared to share your ideas with the class.

1. For the first time in this part of the story, the father is referred to as "the doctor." Why?

2. After the birth, the doctor is feeling exalted and exhilarated. He is proud of his professional expertise. Does he deserve to be proud? What has he done?

3. When does the father call his son "Nickie" instead of Nick? Why? What has the father realized?

4. Why does Nick say that he will never die?

5. Do you think Nick is going to want to become a doctor when he grows up?

6. How do you think Nick feels about his father?

7. Do you agree with what Nick's father tells him at the end of the story?

LINKING READINGS ONE AND TWO

Work in a small group. You are detectives trying to find out the truth of this story. Answer the questions. Be prepared to explain your clues to the class.

> **ANALYSIS:** According to some literary critics, this story is about a white man named George, who made a Native American woman pregnant. When she had trouble giving birth, George called his brother, a doctor, to come help. The doctor was on vacation with his son and brought his young son along. The Native American woman's husband was so upset about the baby's true father and about how the white men treated his wife that he killed himself.

1. What evidence or clues can you find in the story to support this view?

   In the United States at that time, fathers gave out cigars to other men to
   celebrate the birth of their child.
   _____
   _____
   _____

2. Can the evidence be explained in any other way?

   George always smoked cigars. He offered some to the Indian men because that
   was the polite thing to do, and he knew Indian men like to smoke.
   _____
   _____
   _____

3. What is your group's conclusion?

   _____
   _____
   _____
   _____
   _____

Ⓐ Warm-Up

Discuss the questions with a partner.

1. What kinds of books do you like to read: action, mystery, horror, romance?

2. Who is your favorite author? Why?

Ⓑ Reading Strategy

Scanning for "Compare and Contrast" Words

Some texts focus on comparing and contrasting two things. Scanning such a text for "compare and contrast" words (*like, unlike, as,* etc.) helps you find essential information quickly.

Scan the first paragraph of the reading for words that will tell you whether the author is going to talk only about Hemingway or will compare Hemingway to other writers. Circle the words in the reading. Then answer the question.

Is the author going to compare Hemingway to other writers?

Yes ☐   **No** ☐

Now read the whole text to find out if your guess was correct.

Hemingway's Style

1   Hemingway pioneered a new style of writing. Unlike 19th-century writers, who wrote long descriptive passages with overly complicated prose,[1] Hemingway wrote sentences with plain grammar and easy words, concentrating on nouns and verbs, not adjectives. Rather than telling the reader what his characters were thinking and feeling, Hemingway focused on dialogue and action. He wanted us to read between the lines and discover the truth by ourselves, as we do in real life. He called this the "iceberg principle" or the "theory of omission." Like an iceberg, most of the story and particularly the emotions remain below the surface.

2   Sometimes what we say is not as important as what we leave unsaid. In Hemingway's characters' silences, we hear their inner conflicts. In his focus on action, we are given the speed and economy[2] of words of contemporary storytelling. This style was well suited to the author's themes of courage in the face of disillusionment and death.

---

[1] *prose:* writing in normal continuous form; not poetry

[2] *economy:* an efficient or controlled use of something

COMPREHENSION

Ⓐ Main Ideas

Check (✓) the main aspects of Hemingway's style according to the reading. Discuss your answers with a partner.

☐ **1.** simple sentences

☐ **2.** beautiful descriptions of nature

☐ **3.** more action than description of characters' feelings

☐ **4.** more nouns and verbs than adjectives

☐ **5.** everything not explained to the reader

Ⓑ Close Reading

Read the quotes from the reading. Circle the statement that best explains each quote. Share your answers with a partner.

1. "Unlike 19th-century writers, who wrote long descriptive passages with overly complicated prose, Hemingway wrote sentences with plain grammar and easy words, concentrating on nouns and verbs, not adjectives." (*paragraph 1*)

    a. 19th-century authors had more adjectives in their writing than Hemingway.

    b. 19th-century authors had fewer nouns and verbs in their writing than Hemingway.

2. "Rather than telling the reader what his characters were thinking and feeling, Hemingway focused on dialogue and action." (*paragraph 1*)

    a. Hemingway wanted his stories to be like real life, where you don't always know what people are thinking.

    b. Hemingway was not interested in the emotions and motivations of the characters in his stories.

3. "In Hemingway's characters' silences, we hear their inner conflicts." (*paragraph 2*)

    a. The reader will feel a lot of internal conflicts when thinking about the characters.

    b. The reader has to discover the characters' feelings by drawing conclusions from their actions.

4. "This style was well suited to the author's themes of courage in the face of disillusionment and death." (*paragraph 2*)

    a. These themes are better expressed indirectly and in simple language because they are very painful.

    b. These themes do not usually go along with a lot of action and dialogue.

VOCABULARY

A Word Forms

1 Fill in the chart with the correct word forms. Use a dictionary if necessary.

	Noun	Verb	Adjective
1.			complicated
2.	disillusionment		
3.	omission		

2 Complete the paragraph with the words or phrases from the box.

below the surface	contemporary	omit
complicated	disillusioned	suited to

In his new way of writing prose, Hemingway was an early pioneer of modern style. Hemingway avoided _____*complicated*_____

1.

sentences in order to communicate more clearly with the reader. He chose to

_____ internal monologues and write only what people

2.

say to each other, not what is _____. He felt this was more

3.

_____ the themes he was interested in exploring. His

4.

imperfect, _____ yet courageous characters continue to

5.

please readers in today's _____ society.

6.

B "Compare and Contrast" Words

1 Match the words or phrases with their synonyms (also "compare and contrast" words).

_____ 1. like   a. despite (the fact that)

_____ 2. rather than   b. while

_____ 3. although   c. just as

_____ 4. however   d. but

_____ 5. even though   e. instead of

2 Complete this biography of Hemingway with "compare and contrast" words. Choose the correct one from the words or phrases in parentheses.

Ernest Hemingway was born in a middle-class suburb of Chicago in the last year of the 19th century. _____ _While_ _____ his father liked
1. (However / While)
manly pursuits such as hunting, his mother loved music. She hoped her son would develop his artistic side, _____ as a child,
2. (but / like)
Hemingway was more interested in fishing and hunting trips with his father in the north woods of Michigan. He began his career as a newspaper reporter, and _____ staying home during World War I, he became
3. (even though / rather than)
an ambulance driver for the Allies in Italy. He was wounded and sent home; _____ , he set his novel *A Farewell to Arms* in the Italy
4. (just as / however)
he remembered. _____ many artists of his generation,
5. (Instead of / Like)
Hemingway went to Paris after the war because it was the center of creative innovation in the arts. In Paris, he wrote *The Sun Also Rises*, a novel about the fate of the "lost generation" of men and women who had become hopelessly disillusioned by the horrors of World War I . _____ his horror of war,
6. (Despite / Like)
Hemingway went to Spain in the 1930s, where he supported the Spanish republic in its losing fight against fascism. *For Whom the Bell Tolls* is a novel about that country's struggle just before World War II. _____ Hemingway spent
7. (Although / However)
the war years in London, he returned to the United States in the 1950s to write one of his most beloved novels, *The Old Man and the Sea.*

_____ Hemingway was pleased about winning the
8. (Even though / However)
Nobel Prize in Literature in 1954, he was depressed and in pain for most of the last years of his life as a result of a plane crash. In 1961, Hemingway used a gun to kill himself _____ his father had done many years before. Ernest
9. (just as / rather than)
Hemingway was married four times and had three sons.

NOTE-TAKING: Organizing to Compare and Define Style

1 Go back to the reading and read it again. Use the organizer to take notes on Hemingway's style as opposed to the style of 19th-century writers.

HEMINGWAY'S STYLE	19TH-CENTURY WRITERS' STYLE
1. dialogue	1.
2.	2.
3.	3.
4.	4.

2 Write the keywords that define the "iceberg principle."

_____

_____

_____

CRITICAL THINKING

Discuss the questions in a small group. Be prepared to share your answers with the class.

1. Why do literary critics have to explain Hemingway's style? Do some people think it is "too simple" or "too easy"? What do you think?

2. Most of Hemingway's stories are about men rather than women. How could this relate to the "iceberg principle"?

3. Why do you think many critics think of Hemingway as very "American" in his style?

BRINGING IT ALL TOGETHER

Work in small groups. Choose one of the points regarding Hemingway's style or choice of themes. Each group will explain the point it chose and present quotes and scenes from "Indian Camp" related to it. Use some of the vocabulary you studied in the chapter (for a complete list, go to page 114).

STYLE
- use of simple sentences; lack of adjectives
- revealing character through dialogue and action
- silences and conflicts — indirect reference to emotions
- the "iceberg principle"

THEMES
- fathers and sons
- the powerful and the powerless
- shame
- life and death

WRITING ACTIVITY

"Indian Camp" is a very complex story with many layers of meaning. What is your opinion of the story? Did you like it? Why or why not?

Write two paragraphs to summarize the story and give your opinion.
- **First paragraph:** Summarize the story.
- **Second paragraph:** Give your opinion. After you give your overall opinion, develop one point in particular that you liked or didn't like (such as the relationship between father and son or "the iceberg principle").

Use at least five of the words and idioms you studied in the chapter.

DISCUSSION AND WRITING TOPICS

Discuss these topics in a small group. Choose one of them and write a paragraph or two about it. Use the vocabulary from the chapter.

1. This story begins at night and ends in the morning. Does this journey from darkness to light have a particular significance?

2. What do you think Nick has learned from his experience?

3. What are the advantages and disadvantages of introducing a child to the realities of life at an early age?

4. Do you have an example of a "coming of age" episode in your life?

VOCABULARY

Nouns	Verbs	Adjectives	Adverbs
anesthetic	beach	complicated	reminiscently
chill	flow	contemporary *	thoroughly
disillusionment	row	exalted	
exhilaration	scream	exceptional	hardly ever
incision	scrub	pale	rather than
intern	stand	talkative	
lantern			**Phrases and**
mess	**Phrasal Verbs**		**Idioms**
omission	shove off		below the surface
quilt	stand up		suited to
			Prepositions
			like / unlike

* = AWL (Academic Word List) item

SELF-ASSESSMENT

In this chapter you learned to:

○ Identify and understand the elements of fiction: characters, setting, plot, themes

○ Scan a text for "compare and contrast" words

○ Guess the meaning of words from the context

○ Understand and use synonyms, phrasal verbs, and different word forms

○ Recognize words of varying intensity

○ Use circling and margin notes to identify themes

○ Organize study notes to compare and define a writer's style

What can you do well? ☑

What do you need to practice more? ☑

ART HISTORY: The Life and Letters of Vincent Van Gogh

ART HISTORY: the academic study of the historical development of the visual arts

OBJECTIVES

To read academic texts, you need to master certain skills.

In this chapter, you will:

- Preview a text using visuals

- Skim letters for a quick overview: names, places, dates

- Scan a text for dates to understand the sequence of events

- Guess the meaning of words from the context or from their Latin roots

- Understand and use synonyms and connotations

- Use dictionary entries to learn the meanings of words

- Take notes to identify supporting details

Self-Portrait in Front of the Easel

A **Consider These Questions**

What is art? Check (✓) the things you consider art.

☐ a painting

☐ a comic book/graphic novel

☐ a movie

☐ a fashion advertisement

☐ a building

☐ a photograph

☐ a piece of furniture

Now answer the questions. Discuss your answers with a partner.

1. How do we know something is "art"?

2. Does everyone have to agree?

3. Do you have a favorite movie, painting, or work of visual art?

   What do you like about it?

B **Art Requirements in College**

In many colleges in the United States, all undergraduates must study music and art appreciation[1] as part of their required courses. Discuss the questions with your classmates.

1. Why do many colleges make art appreciation a requirement even for science students?

2. How do you think instructors get students to "appreciate" art and recognize a masterpiece?

3. What does art bring to our lives? To your life?

---

[1] *music and art appreciation courses:* Learning about music or art, rather than participating in the creative process itself, is the focus of these courses.

Ⓐ Warm-Up

Discuss the questions with a partner.

1. In your opinion, what is a "successful" life?

2. Can a person who is poor be successful? A person without a spouse or children? A person who is not well known in his or her lifetime?

Ⓑ Reading Strategy

Previewing Using Visuals

As the expression **"A picture is worth a thousand words"** suggests, the paintings, drawings, or photographs that illustrate a text "show" readers information. Looking at these visuals will help you prepare for the content of the reading.

Look at the three paintings that illustrate the reading on pages 118 and 119. For each one, write short answers to these questions. Share your answers with a partner.

1. What is the subject of this painting?

2. What stands out in the painting? The shapes? The lines? The colors?

3. Does the subject seem "real" or "imaginary" to you?

4. What mood do you think the artist was in when he painted it?

The Potato Eaters	*Sunflowers*	*The Starry Night*
1. _____	_____	_____
2. _____	_____	_____
3. _____	_____	_____
4. _____	_____	_____

Now read the text to find out if the paintings gave you the right ideas about Van Gogh and his art.

A Biography of Vincent Van Gogh

(1853-1890)

1   Vincent Van Gogh was one of history's greatest painters, although he met only **rejection** and failure during his lifetime. Van Gogh was born in the Netherlands. The son of a Protestant minister,[1] he was well educated in French and English but was shy and **introverted** as a child, lacking **self-confidence**. His greatest friend was his younger brother Theo, who supported him emotionally and financially all his life.

2   At 16, Van Gogh began working for an art dealer, but he soon turned to religion because he wanted to do good in the world. He became a preacher[2] in the **impoverished** mining district of Belgium called the Borinage. **Dismissed** by his church after six months, Van Gogh stayed without pay, because he was concerned about the suffering of the poor miners.

The Potato Eaters

3   After his failure as a preacher, Van Gogh decided to devote his life to art. Although he had been drawing since childhood, his first major painting, "Potato Eaters," was completed when he was in his late twenties. In 1886, Van Gogh briefly attended formal art school

Sunflowers

in Antwerp, where he was put in the beginners' class. He discovered Japanese art, which **inspired** him to use bright, **vibrant** colors. For Van Gogh, color was the key to communicating his emotions.

---

[1] *minister:* a religious leader in some Christian churches

[2] *preacher:* someone who talks about religion but may not be officially ordained

[3] *the Impressionists:* artists who practiced a style of painting that uses color to produce effects of light or movement. Van Gogh met some of the Impressionists, including Degas, Pissarro, Toulouse-Lautrec, and Gauguin.

4   In 1887, Van Gogh visited Theo in Paris, where he met the Impressionists;[3] he liked their use of natural light and color, although he regretted their lack of **commitment** to social causes. Van Gogh wanted his artwork to hang in poor people's homes to bring them happiness through beauty. Unlike the Impressionists, Van Gogh painted not what he saw but what he felt. His style of Expressionism opened the way to the modern, abstract art of the 20th century.

The Starry Night

5   In 1888, Van Gogh moved to Arles, in the South of France. There, he spent most of the money Theo sent him on painting supplies, neglecting his health. Feeling lonely as a foreigner and an artist, he invited other painters to **found** an artists' colony. Only Paul Gauguin accepted, but the two soon **quarreled**. Suffering from severe depression,[4] Van Gogh asked to be taken to a mental hospital, where he continued painting. In Auvers, near Paris, Van Gogh shot himself. He was 37. His last words were, "The sadness will never end." Theo died six months later and was buried next to his brother.

---

[4] *depression:* a feeling of sadness that makes you believe there is no hope for the future. Van Gogh may have had *epilepsy* because he suffered from seizures. He also heard voices, which may explain why he cut off a part of his ear during a mental breakdown.

COMPREHENSION

A Main Ideas

Match the sentence beginnings with the sentence endings in the box below to make true statements about the reading. There is one choice that does not belong. Compare answers with a partner.

_____ 1. In describing Van Gogh's personality, one could say that

_____ 2. Van Gogh must have been lonely in his life because

_____ 3. Van Gogh was different from other painters at the time because

_____ 4. It is apparent that Van Gogh had a deep social conscience because

_____ 5. Van Gogh's life was undoubtedly very sad and painful because

> **a.** he killed himself.
> **b.** he wanted his paintings to express his emotions.
> **c.** he was shy, introverted, and uncomfortable in most social situations.
> **d.** he wanted his paintings to beautify poor people's homes.
> **e.** his use of vibrant colors distinguished him from other artists of his time.
> **f.** his only real friend was his younger brother Theo.

B Close Reading

Read the quotes from the reading. Circle the statement that best explains each quote. Share your answers with a partner.

1. "Dismissed by his church after six months, Van Gogh stayed without pay, because he was concerned about the suffering of the poor miners." (*paragraph 2*)

   a. Van Gogh was rejected by the miners.

   b. Van Gogh was passionately concerned about the poor.

   c. Van Gogh didn't need money at this time.

2. "In 1886, Van Gogh briefly attended formal art school in Antwerp, where he was put in the beginners' class." (*paragraph 3*)

   a. Van Gogh's talent was not recognized.

   b. Van Gogh attended the school as a treasured student.

   c. Van Gogh needed to leave school early.

3. "[He] met the Impressionists; he liked their use of natural light and color, although he regretted their lack of commitment to social causes." (*paragraph 4*)

   a. Van Gogh copied the Impressionists' style.

   b. Van Gogh and the Impressionists shared an interest in helping the poor.

   c. Van Gogh admired the Impressionists' work with outdoor light.

4. "There, he spent most of the money Theo sent him on painting supplies, neglecting his health." (*paragraph 5*)

   a. Buying art supplies was more important than buying food.

   b. Van Gogh sacrificed his art to health.

   c. Van Gogh realized he could not succeed unless he was healthy.

VOCABULARY

A Guessing from Context

> When you are not sure of the meaning of a word, try to **find other words in the context (context clues)** that bring you close to its meaning.
>
> • Van Gogh became a preacher in the **impoverished** mining district of the Borinage. He stayed without pay, concerned about the suffering of the poor miners.
>
> From the context, it is likely that *impoverished* is close in meaning to *poor* (context clue).

1   Guess the meaning of each word in bold by finding a word in the sentence that is close to its meaning. Underline the word that gives you the clue. Then match the words in bold with their meanings in the box below.

_____   1. Vincent Van Gogh was one of history's greatest painters, although he met only **rejection** and failure during his lifetime.

_____   2. He was shy and **introverted** as a child, lacking self-confidence.

_____   3. Van Gogh discovered Japanese art, which inspired him to use bright, **vibrant** colors.

_____   4. Unfortunately, the two artists didn't get along, and they soon **quarreled**.

a. dazzling	**c.** argued
b. reserved, quiet	**d.** lack of acceptance

2   Complete each sentence with a word from the box. Use the synonym in parentheses to help you select the correct word. There are two extra words. Compare answers with a partner.

commitment	impoverished	introverted	rejection
dismissed	inspired	quarrel	vibrant

1. In the ten years during which he created over 900 paintings, Van Gogh sold only

    one and lived in _____impoverished_____ conditions, surviving only on the
    (very poor)
    money his brother sent him.

2. In his religious preaching and at art school Van Gogh was _____
    (forced out)
    with very little consideration because he was too passionate and unusual.

3. In his time, Van Gogh's paintings met with criticism and _____
    (disapproval)
    because he wanted to free the artist from simply "representing" reality.

4. Van Gogh was _____ to paint things not as he saw them
    (motivated)
    but as he felt them.

5. His paintings were not polished: his drawing was rough, and he put many layers

    of paint on the canvas to show bright, _____ colors in a
    (vivid)
    personal perspective.

6. Van Gogh wanted his artwork to express his _____ to
    (devotion)
    compassion and social justice.

B Using the Dictionary

Read the dictionary entries for two verbs: *find* and *found*.

> **find** *v.* past tense and past participle **found**
> **1** to discover or see something either by searching for it or by chance
> **2** to discover or learn something by study, tests, or thinking about a problem
> **3** to learn or know something by experience
>
> **found** *v.* past tense and past participle **founded**
> **1** to start something such as an organization, institution, company, or city
> **2** to base your ideas, beliefs, etc. on something

Now read each sentence. Decide which verb is being used and what its specific meaning is. Write the base form of the verb and the number of the appropriate definition in its dictionary entry.

_____find (2)_____ a. After experimenting with many styles, Van Gogh finally **found** his own mature style when he went to the South of France.

_____ b. Vincent Van Gogh wanted to **found** an artists' collective that would pool resources to help artists live and that would take control of the sale of their art away from the art dealers.

_____ c. In the end, Van Gogh **found** that he and Gauguin could not get along: they were both depressed and disagreed about painting styles.

_____ d. Gauguin began to disagree with Van Gogh: he no longer wanted to **found** his style on Impressionism.

C Connotations

> As you have already learned in Chapter 4, page 88, a **connotation** is a feeling or idea that a word generally makes you think of. This feeling can be **positive** or **negative**.

Read the dictionary entries for *self-confident* and *self-satisfied*.

> **self-confident** *adj.* sure that you can do things well; not shy or nervous in social situations
>
> **self-satisfied** *adj.* too pleased with yourself and what you have done

Discuss the questions with a partner.

1. Which of these words has a negative meaning?

2. Was Van Gogh self-confident? Self-satisfied? Why or why not?

3. Would you say that you are self-confident? Self-satisfied? Why or why not? Do you know people who fit these descriptions?

NOTE-TAKING: Identifying Supporting Details

Go back to the reading and read it again. Van Gogh lived in many places. What happened to him in these places? Fill in the chart with the appropriate events. Use your own words; do not copy the text.

PLACE	EVENTS
The Netherlands	**Background:** • Born into religious family • Received good education • Worked for art dealer • Decided to use his faith to help people
The Borinage (Belgium)	**Job and concerns:** • • •
Antwerp (Belgium)	**Art school and inspiration:** • • •
Paris (France)	**Meeting other artists:** • • •
Arles (South of France)	**Gauguin:** • • **Health:** • •
Auvers (near Paris)	**Death:** • •

CRITICAL THINKING

Discuss the questions in a small group. Refer to the paintings that are shown in the chapter. Be prepared to share your opinions with the class.

1. How would you describe Van Gogh's *Self-Portrait in Front of the Easel* (page 115)? How did he see himself? Does this portrait show his character as described in the biography? How does a visual portrait compare to a portrait in words?

2. How does *The Potato Eaters* (page 118) show how Van Gogh felt during this period of his life?

3. When Van Gogh finished the *Portrait of Dr. Gachet* (page 133), he wrote to Theo: "I have finished a portrait with the heartbroken expression of our time." What do you think he meant?

4. Van Gogh's first mental breakdown came when Gauguin left. Why might Gauguin's departure have been very difficult for Van Gogh?

5. *The Starry Night* (page 119) is full of swirling movement in the heavens. What does this painting communicate to you?

6. In *Wheatfield with Crows* (page 130), one of Van Gogh's last paintings, black birds swoop down from a cloudy sky to a landscape of wind-swept wheat. What mood does the painting communicate?

7. Van Gogh's last words were "La tristesse durera toujours." ("The sadness will never end.") How would you explain their meaning?

READING TWO: The Letters of Vincent Van Gogh

 Warm-Up

> In academic work, a **primary source** is material written or created by people during the historical period being studied. A **secondary source** interprets and analyzes primary sources.
>
> **EXAMPLES:**
> - Reading One, a biography of Van Gogh written today, is a **secondary source**.
> - Reading Two, letters written by Van Gogh himself, is a **primary source**.

Check (✓) possible primary source material. Compare answers with a partner.

☐ diaries

☐ pottery

☐ encyclopedia

☐ songs

☐ high school textbook

☐ speeches

Skimming Letters

When you have letters to read, it is helpful to look at their "**physical landscape**" first in order to get an idea about the **names of the addressees** (the people the letters were written to), the **dates** when the letters were written, and the **places** where they were written. This **overview** will allow you to begin the reading with more confidence.

Skim the reading and answer these questions. Share your answers with a partner.

1. Who are the two people Van Gogh writes to? _____

2. How does Van Gogh address the two people? What relationship exists between

   Van Gogh and his addressees? _____

3. When were these letters written? _____

4. Where did Van Gogh write these letters? _____

Now read the letters to learn more about Van Gogh.

The Letters of Vincent Van Gogh

1

The Borinage, 1880

Dear Theo,

My only anxiety is: How can I be of use in the world? Can't I serve some purpose and be of any good? I feel imprisoned by **poverty**, **excluded** and alone, and certain necessities are beyond my reach. For the moment it seems that things are going badly for me, but perhaps a time will come when they will go right.

I feel a great **sympathy** for the miners and the weavers.[1] I would be very happy if someday I could draw them so that they would be brought before the eyes of the world. I have been living among them for two years, and I find something touching and almost sad in these workers, who are generally represented as a class of criminals and thieves by a very false and unjust public opinion.

Self-Portrait Without a Beard

(continued on next page)

---

[1] *weaver:* someone who makes cloth out of cotton, silk, or wool thread

The Netherlands, July 1882

Dear Brother,

I want you to understand clearly my **conception** of art. I want to do drawings that touch people. I want to express not sentimental feeling but serious sorrow. I want people to say of my work, "He feels deeply, he feels tenderly" — in spite of my roughness, perhaps even because of it.

What am I now in most people's eyes? A nobody, an **eccentric** and disagreeable man — someone who has no position in society and never will have — in short, the lowest of the low. Well, then, even if this were true, then I would want my work to show the heart of such a nobody. And art demands persistent work and continuous observation. You must not mind if I write you again — it is only to tell you that painting is such a joy to me.

3

Arles, August 11, 1888

Dear Theo,

No matter what I do, life is pretty expensive here, almost like Paris. I live three weeks out of four on bread with milk and eggs. It is the blessed warmth that is bringing back my strength, and I was certainly right in going at once to the South. You must be able to live on a piece of bread while you work all day, and have enough strength to smoke and drink your glass in the evening. And feel the stars and the infinite sky high and clear above you. Then life is almost **enchanted** after all. Oh, those who don't believe in this sun down here are fools.

Arles, September 29, 1888

My Dear Gauguin,[2]

Once again my brother and I are trying to make it possible for you to join me here. I must tell you that even when I am working, I keep thinking all the time about that plan to start a studio, which would have you and me as permanent residents. The two of us would turn it into a **refuge** and a place of shelter for comrades at moments when they are struggling with their art.

After you left Paris, my brother and I stayed together for a while. It was a time that will remain forever unforgettable to me! We often talked about the problems that are so very close to our hearts — measures to protect the artist's ability to make a living, to guarantee access to the tools of art (paints, canvases) and to keep for the artists a share in the price their paintings may bring a long time after they sell them for the first time.

When you come, we can go over all these discussions.

---

[2] *Paul Gauguin* (1848–1903): the son of a French journalist and the grandson of Flora Tristan, a French-Peruvian socialist and feminist. Gauguin's style evolved from Impressionism to a deep interest in primitive art in Tahiti, where he died.

Arles, January 28, 1889

My Dear Theo,

Only a few words to tell you that my health and work are not too bad. I'm surprised when I compare my condition today with what it was a month ago. I knew well enough that you could fracture your legs and arms and **recover** afterward, but I didn't know that you could fracture your brain and recover from that, too.

I still have a sort of "what's the use of getting better" feeling about me, even in my surprise at getting well, which I hadn't dared hope for.

Since it is still winter, let me go quietly on with my work. If it is the work of a madman, well, too bad. I can't help it. However, the **unbearable** hallucinations[3] have stopped and are now reduced to a simple nightmare.

6   Arles, April 22, 1889

My Dear Theo,

At the end of the month, I would like to go to the hospital at St. Remy.

Let's just say that I cannot live alone in a studio any more. I would be afraid of losing the power to work, which is coming back to me now. Temporarily, I wish to remain shut up as much for my own peace of mind as for others.[4]

7 (*Van Gogh's last letter*)   Auvers, July 23, 1890

My Dear Brother,

Thanks for your kind letter and for the 50-franc bill it contained.

There are many things I would like to write to you about, but I feel writing is useless. The truth is we can only make our pictures speak.

I have always told you, and I repeat it once again, I will always consider you to be more than just an art dealer. Through me, you have a role in the actual production of paintings, which will retain their calm even in the **catastrophe**.

For my work, I have risked my life and my reason.

That's all right. What can we do?

---

[3] *hallucinations*: voices or images that people hear or see in their own minds even though they are not real

[4] Some people in Arles, as well as Van Gogh's own father, asked the local authorities to lock Van Gogh up. Van Gogh preferred to go voluntarily and choose a hospital where he could continue to paint.

COMPREHENSION

A Main Ideas

Read each statement. Decide if it is *True* or *False* according to the reading. Check (✓) the appropriate box. If it is false, change it to make it true. Discuss your answers with a partner.

	TRUE	FALSE
1. Van Gogh was too self-absorbed to care about the suffering of others.	☐	☐
2. Despite his simple lifestyle, Van Gogh always found it difficult to meet his basic needs.	☐	☐
3. Van Gogh was at times optimistic about eventually seeing the conditions of his life improve.	☐	☐
4. Maintaining his mental health was a constant challenge for Van Gogh.	☐	☐
5. One reason for Van Gogh's sadness may have been his lack of faith in the value of art.	☐	☐

B Close Reading

Read the quotes from the reading. Circle the statement that best explains each quote. Share your answers with a partner.

1. "I find something touching and almost sad in these workers, who are generally represented as a class of criminals and thieves by a very false and unjust public opinion." (*letter 1*)

   a. Van Gogh is sad because the workers are criminals and thieves.

   b. Van Gogh feels the workers are unfairly portrayed.

   c. Van Gogh wants public opinion to be represented.

2. "Through me, you [Theo] have a role in the actual production of paintings, which will retain their calm even in the catastrophe." (*letter 7*)

   a. You are my partner in the creation of art.

   b. You are my protection against disaster.

   c. You will remain calm even in my troubles.

3. "For my work, I have risked my life and my reason." (*letter 7*)

   a. I have become irrational.

   b. I have given up on thinking.

   c. I have sacrificed everything.

VOCABULARY

A Guessing from Context

Work with a partner. Look at the list of words from the reading. Locate each word in the reading and try to guess its meaning from other words in the context. Write your guess and then the dictionary meaning. Was your guess correct?

1. **poverty**
   (*letter 1*)

   Guess: _being poor_

   Dictionary: _having little or no money, goods, or means of support_

2. **excluded**
   (*letter 1*)

   Guess: _____

   Dictionary: _____

3. **sympathy**
   (*letter 1*)

   Guess: _____

   Dictionary: _____

4. **conception**
   (*letter 2*)

   Guess: _____

   Dictionary: _____

5. **eccentric**
   (*letter 2*)

   Guess: _____

   Dictionary: _____

6. **enchanted**
   (*letter 3*)

   Guess: _____

   Dictionary: _____

7. **refuge**
   (*letter 4*)

   Guess: _____

   Dictionary: _____

8. **recover**
   (*letter 5*)

   Guess: _____

   Dictionary: _____

9. **unbearable**
   (*letter 5*)

   Guess: _____

   Dictionary: _____

10. **catastrophe**
    (*letter 7*)

    Guess: _____

    Dictionary: _____

B Synonyms

Complete the essay with the words from the box. Use the synonym in parentheses to help you select the correct word. Compare answers with a partner.

catastrophe	eccentric	excluded	recover	sympathy
conception	enchanted	poverty	refuge	unbearable

Seeing beauty in this life and creating art were Vincent Van Gogh's only aims

in life. His strange behavior _____excluded_____ him from acceptance
1. (barred)

by the rest of society. Despite his rich inner life, Van Gogh lived a life of such

_____ that he often tried to pay people with his paintings
2. (impoverishment)

rather than with money. As a stranger with _____ behavior,
3. (odd)

he found few friends.

Van Gogh was _____ with the natural world. In
4. (delighted)

such works as *The Starry Night*, with its broad brushstrokes and passionate

lines and colors, he found _____ from ordinary life.
5. (shelter)

Van Gogh's _____ was that art is a way into the heart,
6. (idea)

a deep emotional experience rather than just a simple amusement. However,

his extreme isolation and constant work led to a mental breakdown and he

was never able to _____ his strength and hope. He
7. (regain)

experienced an _____ sadness. His early death was a
8. (extremely painful)

_____: think what else he could have accomplished if he had
9. (disaster)

lived. We feel great _____ for Van Gogh; when he died, his
10. (compassion)

mother threw away many of Vincent's paintings as worthless.

*Wheatfield
with Crows*

NOTE-TAKING: Identifying Supporting Details

Go back to the reading and read it again. Notice the four major topics in Van Gogh's letters: (1) an artist's life; (2) social injustice; (3) love; and (4) depression. Then fill in the chart. Next to each topic, list details that reflect the artist's life and concerns.

Topic	Supporting Details
1. An artist's life	• Wants his art to touch people • Wants his art to express his feelings • •
2. Social injustice	• •
3. Love	• •
4. Depression	• •

CRITICAL THINKING

Several weeks after Vincent Van Gogh died, his brother went to their friend Emile Bernard to arrange a private showing of hundreds of Vincent's paintings in Theo's Paris apartment.

Work with a partner. Complete the discussion between Theo Van Gogh and Emile Bernard. Then role play the discussion.

EMILE: I am so sorry for your loss. I know you and Vincent were very close. Why do you think he wrote that he had risked his life and his reason for his work? What did he mean?

THEO: _____

EMILE: He often spoke of you as a partner in his work.

THEO: _____

EMILE: How should we explain Vincent's work to the public? What was he trying to accomplish?

THEO: _____

EMILE: Vincent was very concerned about social issues, wasn't he?

(continued on next page)

THEO: _____

EMILE: _____

THEO: _____

EMILE: _____

THEO: _____

LINKING READINGS ONE AND TWO

Fill in the chart with the missing information.

TOPIC	READING ONE (BIOGRAPHY)	READING TWO (LETTERS)
Relationship with Theo	Paragraphs 1, 4, and 5	Letters 4 and 7
Criticism of society		
Painting		
Sadness		

Now answer the questions with a partner.

1. How do the letters add to our understanding of Van Gogh's life? What do they tell us that the biography doesn't?

2. What does the biography give the reader that the letters do not provide?

READING THREE: *Portrait of Dr. Gachet*—A Timeline

 Warm-Up

Discuss the questions with a partner.

Van Gogh sold only one painting in his lifetime — to a woman artist. He exchanged most of his paintings for art supplies or gave them away to his brother and to people who showed him kindness.

1. How much do you think a painting by Vincent Van Gogh would be worth today?

2. Should great art be private property, or should it be available for everyone to see?

Scanning for Dates to Understand Sequence

Some texts are organized by dates, years, or time periods, and the events associated with them. Scanning a text for dates allows you to understand the **sequence (order) of events** it describes.

Scan the reading for dates. After each date circle the keywords that will help you remember the events that took place at that time. Then answer the question.

How many years are covered in this story? _____

Now read the text to learn more about the life of a famous Van Gogh painting.

Portrait of Dr. Gachet: A Timeline

1890 Vincent Van Gogh paints a portrait of his doctor. When Van Gogh dies, his brother Theo inherits the painting.

1897 After Theo's death, Theo's widow, Johanna, sells it for 300 francs ($58) to an art collector in Copenhagen.

1910 The portrait is sold to Galerie Druet in Paris.

1912 The Stadel, a famous museum in Frankfurt, obtains the painting from a rich private **donor**.

1933 The Stadel's director hides the painting inside the museum because he is afraid that the Nazi **regime**, known for hating modern art, will destroy it.

1937 Hermann Göring, an important Nazi military leader, **confiscates** the painting as "degenerate"[1] art. He keeps it in his private collection for a while and then sells it to Franz Koenigs, a German, for $53,000. Koenigs immediately resells it to Siegfried Kramarsky, who lives in a safer place in the Netherlands.

1941 Kramarsky **flees** the Nazi invasion of the Netherlands and goes to New York City, taking the picture with him. For almost 50 years, the family allows the Metropolitan Museum of Art in New York to exhibit the painting **on loan**.

1990 After the death of their parents, the Kramarsky children sell the painting for the **sensational** price of $82 million to Ryoei Saito, the head of a Japanese paper company. He keeps it in a warehouse until his death, when the painting disappears. The art world still hopes the painting will **resurface** once again.

---

[1] *degenerate:* having very low standards, being immoral. The Nazi government hated all modern art and called it "degenerate" because it was not nationalistic or racially pure and because modern artists (Picasso, Chagall, Van Gogh) often criticized society.

Art History: *The Life and Letters of Vincent V*

COMPREHENSION

A Main Ideas

Complete the sentences with information from the reading.

1. Although Theo's wife sold the painting for $58 in 1897, _____

_____ .

2. A Nazi leader took the painting away because he said it was "degenerate" art, but

_____ .

3. The painting was taken to New York City because _____

_____ .

4. The painting was sold in 1990 and _____

_____ .

B Close Reading

Read the quotes from the reading. Circle the statement that best explains each quote. Share your answers with a partner.

1. "The Stadel, a famous museum in Frankfurt, obtains the painting from a rich private donor." (*1912*)

   a. The museum bought the painting.

   b. Museum funds were not used.

2. "Hermann Göring, an important Nazi military leader, confiscates the painting as 'degenerate' art." (*1937*)

   a. The Nazi government condemned Van Gogh's art.

   b. The Nazi government bought Van Gogh's art.

3. "For almost 50 years, the family allows the Metropolitan Museum of Art in New York to exhibit the painting on loan." (*1941*)

   a. The museum bought the painting.

   b. The museum showed the painting.

4. "The art world still hopes the painting will resurface once again." (*1990*)

   a. No one knows where the painting is.

   b. No one can buy the painting any more.

VOCABULARY

Ⓐ Synonyms

Read each sentence. Match the word or phrase in bold with the correct synonym from the box below. There is one extra synonym. Compare answers with a partner.

__g__ 1. The Nazis **confiscated** modern art everywhere they went: in all the museums in Germany and in the countries they occupied.

_____ 2. Some of the art the Nazis took never **resurfaced** again because it was burned; the rest they sold for foreign currency.

_____ 3. In Göring's case, the money he received for the sale of the *Portrait of Dr. Gachet* was never officially reported to the **regime**.

_____ 4. Europeans **fleeing** from German invasion took their paintings to safer countries, and much of the artwork ended up in the United States.

_____ 5. In 1986, the Reagan tax codes took away tax benefits for rich **donors** who would agree to contribute their art collections to the nation's museums so everyone could see them.

_____ 6. Although the *Portrait of Dr. Gachet* was **on loan** from the Kramarskys for many years, the Metropolitan Museum could not afford to pay $82 million in a public sale.

_____ 7. The **sensational** amount of money paid by a Japanese buyer was a sign of the economic strength of his country.

a. appeared	**c.** escaping	**e.** government	**g.** seized
b. borrowed	**d.** gift givers	**f.** known	**h.** shocking

Ⓑ Word Root: *sen-*

> The **root** of a word is the **basic part** of a word that shows its **main meaning**.
>
> **EXAMPLE:**
> sensational contains the root *sen-*, from a Latin word meaning "sense" or "feel"

Read each sentence. Write a definition for the word in bold. Compare definitions with a partner. Then check your definitions in a dictionary.

1. The painting was sold for the **sensational** price of $82 million.

   giving a shocking or exciting feeling _____

(continued on next page)

2. Van Gogh was a very **sensitive** child.

_____

3. If anyone comes too close to the painting, an alarm goes off because the painting is protected by a motion **sensor**.

_____

4. Van Gogh's life should not be **sentimentalized** into the myth of the madman painter; he was a well-educated and careful artist.

_____

CRITICAL THINKING

> **Irony** describes a situation that is **unusual or absurd** because it is the **opposite** of what is expected.

There are many ironies in the story of Van Gogh, some of them tragic. State the ironies in your own words and then discuss them with a partner.

1. A lack of money never prevented Van Gogh from creating art, _____

   _but too much money made his art disappear_____.

2. He never sold a painting _____

   _____.

3. His own mother _____

   _____.

4. Van Gogh wanted his paintings to hang in the homes of the poor _____

   _____.

5. He wanted artists to be protected from the money makers _____

   _____.

6. The Nazis said his art was "degenerate" _____

   _____.

BRINGING IT ALL TOGETHER

Work in groups of four. Debate the topic. Two students will defend the statement (pro) given for the topic, and two will oppose the statement (con). Each team will write a list of points to support its side. The debate begins with a short presentation from each side. Then everyone gets a turn to speak. Use some of the vocabulary you studied in the chapter (for a complete list, go to page 138).

TOPIC: Art should be censored by the government.

PRO	CON
- *Some art is immoral, and people need to be protected from it.*	- *Adults should decide for themselves what they see; they aren't children.*
-	-
-	-

When you are finished, discuss which team presented the better arguments.

WRITING ACTIVITY

Write two paragraphs about one of the paintings shown in the chapter or another painting by Vincent Van Gogh.

- **First paragraph:** Write a description of the painting.
- **Second paragraph:** Write about your response to it. Using what you know about Van Gogh, what do you think the artist was trying to communicate?

Use at least five of the words you studied in the chapter.

DISCUSSION AND WRITING TOPICS

Discuss these topics in a small group. Choose one of them and write a paragraph or two about it. Use the vocabulary from the chapter.

1. Imagine that you could go back in time and speak to Vincent Van Gogh. What would you tell him about how we feel about him and his work today? What do you think his reaction would be?

2. Many people think that paintings are international. Do you agree or disagree? Explain your views.

3. Did Van Gogh have a successful life?

VOCABULARY

Nouns	Verbs	Adjectives	Phrase
catastrophe	confiscate	eccentric	on loan
commitment *	dismiss	enchanted	
conception *	flee	excluded *	
donor	found *	impoverished	
poverty	inspire	introverted	
refuge	quarrel	sensational	
regime *	recover *	unbearable	
rejection *	resurface	vibrant	
self-confidence			
sympathy			

* = AWL (Academic Word List) item

SELF-ASSESSMENT

In this chapter you learned to:

○ Preview a text using visuals

○ Skim letters for a quick overview:
   names, places, dates

○ Scan a text for dates to understand the
   sequence of events

○ Guess the meaning of words from the
   context or from their Latin roots

○ Understand and use synonyms and
   connotations

○ Use dictionary entries to learn the
   meanings of words

○ Take notes to identify supporting details

What can you do well? ✓

What do you need to practice more? ✓

CHAPTER 7

FORENSICS:
Science and Fiction

FORENSICS: the study of the scientific methods for finding out about a crime

OBJECTIVES

To read academic texts, you need to master certain skills.

In this chapter, you will:

- Skim a text by reading the topic sentences

- Predict the content of a text from the title and subheadings

- Read the last paragraph first to understand the point of a text

- Understand and use synonyms, idioms, and collocations

- Recognize the different forms and meanings of a word

- Use underlining and margin notes to identify who said what

- Organize study notes chronologically to clarify the sequence of events

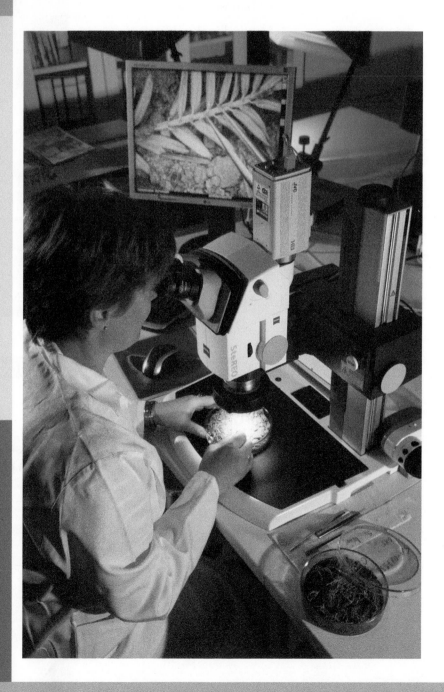

Consider These Questions

1 Look at the crime scene picture. What aspects of this scene would be examined by a forensic scientist? Check (✓) the appropriate boxes. Discuss your answers with a partner.

☐ **a.** outline of body on floor

☐ **b.** footprints on floor

☐ **c.** fingerprints on jewelry box

☐ **d.** bedroom door

☐ **e.** hair on dresser

☐ **f.** window by dresser

2 What other things do you think forensic scientists investigate at crime scenes? Check (✓) the appropriate boxes. Share your answers with a partner.

☐ **a.** fibers

☐ **b.** blood

☐ **c.** bullets

☐ **d.** credit records

☐ **e.** tire tracks

☐ **f.** visas

READING ONE: Basic Principles of Forensics

A Warm-Up

What kind of person would be a good forensic scientist? List the traits you think he or she should have. Share your answers with a partner.

_____

_____

_____

_____

B Reading Strategy

Skimming by Reading Topic Sentences

In academic writing, the **topic sentence** (the first sentence of a paragraph) often gives the **main idea** of the paragraph. Reading the topic sentence of a paragraph and especially the **keyword** in it will help you **get the gist** of each paragraph in a text.

Look at the four topic sentences in the reading and circle the keywords that preview the main ideas. Then write these keywords here.

PARAGRAPH 1: _trace_

PARAGRAPH 2: _____

PARAGRAPH 3: _____

PARAGRAPH 4: _____

Now read the text to find out more about the basic principles of forensics.

BASIC PRINCIPLES OF FORENSICS

By Dr. Zakaria Erzinçlioglu, from *An Illustrated Guide to Forensics*

1   More than 80 years ago, Dr. Edmond Locard of Paris expressed the basic principle of forensic science: "Every contact leaves behind a trace." The burglar who touches a window with his bare hands leaves fingerprints behind; the criminal who steps on the flower-bed leaves his tracks and carries away some soil on his boots. The robber who smashes a window carries tiny fragments of glass on his clothes. The murderer may be **contaminated** with his victim's blood; the victim may retain some fibers from the murderer's clothes. "Leaving a trace" is the idea that all forensic science is based on.

2   Locard's Principle may be clear—the trace will be there—but our ability to *find* the trace will be limited by our talents, our knowledge, and the techniques and machines **at our disposal**. Chemical analysis of the soil may **reveal** decomposition products from a body. The change in the microscopic plant and animal life in the soil may provide a clue to the person who **committed** the crime. So may today's DNA evidence. The trick lies in finding and analyzing the trace.

3   Forensic science is concerned with finding out what happened in the past—specifically discovering the truth about past events that are of interest to the law. But the practice of forensic science is not simply a set of laboratory techniques. It is the habit of starting with a doubt, of being **eager** and willing to question the evidence. The practice of forensic science needs people who can develop a "suspicious mind."

4   Suspicion, of course, is of little use by itself; suspicion not supported by facts is useless. Suspicion based only on emotional reactions is worse than useless and can cause great **harm**. For suspicion to be **productive**, it must be based on, and **followed up** by, **sound** reasoning. This mixture of suspicion and reason is essential for the forensic scientist.

COMPREHENSION

A Main Ideas

Work with a partner. Match the keywords from the topic sentences of the reading with their meanings in the reading.

_C_ 1. trace   a. previous events that relate to a crime

_d_ 2. find   b. belief in someone's guilt or in how something
                         is connected to a crime
_a_ 3. past
                      c. small mark or sign that can explain what
_b_ 4. suspicion   happened

                      d. discover

B Close Reading

Read the quotes from the reading. Circle the statement that best explains each quote. Share your answers with a partner.

1. "The trace will be there — but our ability to find the trace will be limited by our talents, our knowledge, and the techniques and machines at our disposal." (*paragraph 2*)

   a. Machines show the limits of our abilities and talents.

   b. We may not always be able to find the traces.

2. "The trick lies in finding and analyzing the trace." (*paragraph 2*)

   a. The difficulty is finding out where the trace comes from.

   b. Finding the trace involves all kinds of tricky techniques.

3. "It is the habit of starting with a doubt, of being eager and willing to question the evidence." (*paragraph 3*)

   a. Questioning people is part of doing the job.

   b. Going beyond appearances is important.

4. "Suspicion based only on emotional reactions is worse than useless and can cause great harm." (*paragraph 4*)

   a. Suspicion should never involve emotions.

   b. Suspicion without facts is dangerous.

SCANNING...

VOCABULARY

A Synonyms

Complete each sentence with a word or phrase from the box. Use the synonym in parentheses to help you select the correct word or phrase. Compare answers with a partner.

at our disposal	contaminate	follow up	productive	sound
committed	eager	harm	reveal	

1. We need to have forensic evidence because eyewitnesses and even victims can be wrong about who _____committed_____ a crime.
   (carried out)

2. People involved in a crime are often too hurt and disoriented to make a _____sound_____ decision about the identity of the criminal.
   (reliable)

3. Sometimes eyewitnesses can do more _____harm_____ than good;
   (damage)
   in 75% of the cases in which DNA evidence has proved that the wrong man went to prison, it was mistaken eyewitness testimony that sent him there.

4. Eyewitnesses are certainly _____eager_____ to do their duty, but
   (more than willing)
   research studies have shown, for example, that it is especially difficult to identify the faces of people of another race in conditions of great stress.

5. Another problem with eyewitnesses is that some police procedures may _____contaminate_____ the accuracy of the identification process.
   (spoil)

6. In addition, witnesses looking at police photos may sometimes see information or notes that _____reveal_____ what the police think of a certain suspect.
   (disclose)

7. In the police lineup, witnesses have to _____follow up_____ their
   (continue)
   identification by picking out a suspect, but sometimes they just pick out the person whose photo they already saw at the police station.

8. We must do everything _____at our disposal_____ to reform the laws.
   (available)

9. If we do not make changes in witness identification, our criminal investigations will not be very _____productive_____.
   (effective)

B Word Usage: *sound*

1 Noun, Verb, or Adjective

Sound can be a noun (*n.*), a verb (*v.*), or an adjective (*adj.*). Each word form has a different meaning:

sound *n.*   something you hear
- There were strange **sounds** coming from the crime scene. (*count noun*)
- The TV is broken: the picture is on, but the **sound** is off. (*noncount noun*)

sound *v.*   how something seems
- The job of crime scene investigator **sounds** exciting.

sound *adj.* sensible, correct, and likely to produce the right result
- We're looking for someone who can make **sound** decisions.

Which form of the word *sound* appears in the reading? Write it on the line.

_____

2 Idioms with *sound*

Sound often appears in idioms such as:

a sound mind in a sound body   to have a healthy mind, you need a healthy body

Match the idioms using *sound* with their meanings.

__d__ **1.** The psychologist told us that the criminal is **of sound mind**.

_____ **2.** He was **sound asleep**.

__c__ **3.** The nuclear reactor is not **structurally sound**.

__b__ **4.** We need to **sound out** the boss to see if he is going to hire another investigator.

__e__ **5.** I do **not like the sound of** that machine; it may be broken.

_____ **6.** That idea **sounds good,** but we have to check the facts.

a. can't be easily awakened

b. see what someone thinks

c. be worried by

d. not mentally ill

e. in good condition

f. appears to be fine

C Collocations

Remember that **collocations** are "word partners." They are words that are used together frequently.

EXAMPLE:
The adjective **sound** is often paired with certain nouns, like **reasoning**.
- For suspicion to be productive, it must be based on **sound reasoning**.

1 With *sound*

Check (✓) the words that are often paired together. Discuss your answers with a partner.

☐ 1. sound judgment   ☐ 4. sound happiness

☐ 2. sound plan   ☐ 5. sound advice

☐ 3. sound decision

2 With *harm*, *damage*, and *crime*

Check (✓) the words that are often paired together. Discuss your answers with a partner.

☑ 1. do harm to   ☑ 5. commit a crime

☐ 2. make harm   ☑ 6. do a crime

☑ 3. do damage to   ☐ 7. make a crime

☐ 4. make damage

CRITICAL THINKING

Discuss the questions in a small group. Be prepared to share your answers with the class.

1. In what ways do all our contacts with other people "leave traces"? Give some examples. What has left a trace in your life? What trace would you like to leave in other people's lives?

2. The author of this textbook says forensic scientists must "doubt the evidence" and rely only on "sound reasoning." What do you think he means?

3. Both Socrates, a Greek philosopher, and the Buddha, a religious leader, believed that we should doubt everything — question everything. How can that idea be applied to life?

Ⓐ Warm-Up

Discuss the questions with a partner.

1. Do you like watching the *CSI* series on TV or other shows like *Bones* with forensics investigators and scientists? Why or why not?

2. Do you think that television and movies give the public a good idea of what a real crime scene investigator does? Why or why not?

Ⓑ Reading Strategy

Predicting Content from Title and Subheadings

Predicting or getting some idea of the content of a text before you start reading it will help you to improve your reading speed and comprehension. The **title and subheadings** of a text can help you **predict or guess its content**.

1 Complete the statement. Circle the appropriate completion.

A "mixed blessing" is _____.

a. a good thing

b. a good thing with some difficulties

c. a bad thing

2 Answer the question. Write the answer on the lines. Share your answer with a partner.

Look at the title and the subheadings in the reading. What do you expect to learn in this reading?

_____

_____

_____

_____

Now read the text to find out if your guess was correct.

The "*CSI* Effect" Is a Mixed Blessing for Real Crime Labs

Stefan Lovgren, *National Geographic News*

1 Because of the popularity of television programs that feature forensic scientists, universities have seen a dramatic increase in applications to their forensic science programs. Lawyers and police are facing greater pressure from the public and juries to present **sophisticated** forensic evidence in court. "It's **a double-edged sword**," said Captain Chris Beattie, a bald man with glasses who has been head of the Los Angeles County Crime Lab for 32 years. "We have a larger **pool** of qualified people to do the job. But it's also created unreasonable expectations that we can **solve** every crime the way they do on television."

CSI on TV

2 The public has been fascinated with crime on television for a long time. But TV shows now focus attention on the use of science in solving crimes. On CBS's *CSI: Crime Scene* **Investigation** — and its spin-off series *CSI: Miami* and *CSI: NY* — **sharp-minded** investigators, armed with **high-powered** forensic **equipment**, descend on crime scenes to study the evidence. Much of the action takes place in a laboratory. "In the old shows, no one could figure out how to make the science interesting," said Elizabeth Devine, a supervising **producer** on *CSI: Miami*, who worked for 15 years as a forensic scientist at the L.A. sheriff's office. "What we did was slow things down. We wanted to show people that this is cool stuff," she said. "We wanted people to look through the microscope and see what forensic scientists are looking at. This is **the heart and soul of** a lot of investigations."

3 Jay Siegel used to run the Michigan State program and now heads a new undergraduate forensic science program at Indiana-Purdue University in Indianapolis. He says the field is so **competitive** that it attracts the very brightest students, though many come with unreasonable expectations. "A lot of them have watched *CSI* and say, 'That's what I want to do, go to crime scenes and collect evidence, analyze it, and confront [the criminals] and **testify** in court,'" Siegel said. "But no one person does all of those things in real life, so people have to let go of these expectations."

4 Forensic pathologists are not police detectives. They don't investigate and solve crimes. On *CSI* the characters do it all. They collect the evidence (what a real "CSI" would do). They analyze the evidence (actually, the job of a criminalist). They interrogate witnesses (the job of a detective). They get shot at. But in real life, CSIs rarely get shot at. They contribute to solving a case, but it's someone else, usually the police detective, who actually puts it all together and solves the case.

(continued on next page)

Gadgets

5 While the cool technology in the *CSI* crime lab may seem to have come from a *Star Trek* movie, real-world experts say the equipment used on the shows is firmly based on reality. "The gadgetry that you see on TV is very close to what we have in real life," said Dean Gialamas, the director of the forensics laboratory at the Orange County Sheriff-Coroner Department in Santa Ana, California. "The major difference is the way the technology is used."

6 For example, on *CSI*, a computer automatically matches fingerprints to those in its database. But in real life, scientists themselves must perform such detailed work. And while DNA testing on the show is instant, in real life it takes at least a week. In real life, suspect matches don't just miraculously happen. Hours, days, and weeks of work can go into matching a bullet to a gun or DNA to a suspect.

7 Real-life investigations, of course, take a lot longer than they do on television. "We don't show any of the large amount of paperwork that has to be done in the field," said Devine, the *CSI* producer. "Nobody wants to see someone sitting at a desk taking notes and writing reports." Real-life forensic scientists are also often too busy to focus on a single case.

The Big Picture

8 So what makes a great forensic scientist? "Strong technical ability, first of all," said Harley Sagara, an assistant director at the L.A. County crime lab. "But [he or she] should also be open-minded and have the ability to analyze the big picture and test a hypothesis." Forensic scientists have to enjoy and do well in math and science. They must also be able to explain their science in the courtroom. Sagara, who has more than 30 years of field experience, says he has given 300 to 400 court testimonies.

9 The field is still dominated by men, who run 75 percent of U.S. crime labs. But that may be changing. The vast majority of students applying to university forensic science programs are now women.

COMPREHENSION

A Main Ideas

Complete this summary of the main ideas of the reading with the appropriate information from the box below. Write the letter of the words that best complete the sentence on the line.

CSI programs on television are very popular. This is good because more students

__b__. However, there are some problems because most of the students _____.
1.   2.
For example, real CSIs are not police detectives; their job is _____. Although lab
3.
equipment on TV is very similar, _____. Real investigations take longer and involve
4.
_____. To be a good CSI, you need good technical skills, but you also need _____.
5.   6.

> a. much more paperwork
> b. are taking university forensic science courses these days
> c. to go to the crime scene, collect evidence, and analyze it
> d. it is not used in the same way in real life
> e. to be able to explain your work in the courtroom
> f. don't realize that in real life some things are different from TV

B Close Reading

Read the quotes from the reading. Circle the statement that best explains each quote. Share your answers with a partner.

1. "Lawyers and police are facing greater pressure from the public and juries to present sophisticated forensic evidence in court." (*paragraph 1*)

   a. People expect DNA evidence to be used a lot in court.

   b. People distrust DNA evidence used in court.

   c. Lawyers and police don't approve of DNA evidence.

2. "Nobody [watching TV] wants to see someone sitting at a desk taking notes and writing reports." (*paragraph 7*)

   a. Taking notes and writing reports are not important.

   b. Taking notes and writing reports are not realistic.

   c. Taking notes and writing reports are not interesting for viewers.

3. "They must also be able to explain their science in the courtroom." (*paragraph 8*)

   a. They have to be able to speak English well enough for everyone to understand.

   b. They have to know how to explain science to people who do not have scientific training.

   c. They have to be good in college courses such as science and math.

VOCABULARY

A Word Forms

1 Fill in the chart with the correct word forms. Some categories can have more than one form. Use a dictionary if necessary. An **X** indicates there is no form in that category.

	NOUN	VERB	ADJECTIVE	ADVERB
1.	competition / *competitor*		competitive	
2.	equipment			X
3.	hypothesis			
4.	investigation /			X
5.	producer /	produce		
6.		solve	X	X
7.		X	sophisticated	X
8.		testify	X	X

2 Complete the sentences with the correct form of a word from the chart. One word is used twice, but in a different form.

1. One of the _____*producers*_____ on the *CSI* TV program actually worked in the field of forensic science for many years.

2. The television programs *CSI*, *Bones*, and *NCIS* all use forensic science to investigate and _____ crimes.

3. The crimes on TV are not real; they are just _____ situations that entertain viewers.

4. These programs have fully _____ "crime labs" that show the public how the machines work.

5. The TV programs may differ in their focus, but they are all committed to making scientific _____ an important component of their success.

6. Forensic science is a very _____ field, and students have to have good technical skills in order to get a job.

7. Scientists start with a possible theory (otherwise called a working _____) based on logic, and then they test it against the evidence until they find out whether the theory is true or false.

8. _____ machinery allows scientists to work more

productively and get more done in a day.

9. Forensic scientists or their supervisors may be called into court to

_____ at a trial.

B Idioms

Match the idioms in bold with the underlined phrases in the sentences that explain their meaning.

_____ 1. be high-powered   _____ 4. be sharp-minded

_____ 2. be a double-edged sword   _____ 5. be the heart and soul of

_____ 3. be open-minded

> a. Having students see so much about forensic science on TV can have both positive and negative consequences.
> b. A forensic scientist should look at evidence in a flexible, unprejudiced, and understanding way.
> c. Forensic science procedures are the essence of the *CSI* TV shows.
> d. Being a scientist is a very important job with good financial rewards.
> e. A forensic scientist must have excellent analytical skills.

C Word Usage: *pool*

Read the sentences. Each one uses the word *pool*, but with a different meaning. Match the word as used in the sentence with one of the meanings from the box below.

_____ 1. We have a large **pool** of qualified people to do the job.

_____ 2. At a crime scene, each **pool** of blood is subject to investigation.

_____ 3. Scientists cooperate internationally; they **pool** their resources to solve medical and other scientific problems.

_____ 4. Betting on games of chance, such as **pool**, is against the law in some parts of the United States.

_____ 5. On a hot day, people cool off in the **pool**.

> a. a hole filled with water that people can swim in
> b. a recreational activity in which you use a stick to knock numbered balls into holes in a table
> c. a small area of liquid or light on a surface
> d. a group of people or things available to do an activity when needed
> e. to combine your money, ideas, skills, etc. with other people so that you can all use them

NOTE-TAKING: Identifying Who Said What

1   Go back to the reading. Underline the names and titles of the people interviewed. Write notes in the margin to remember the main points of their statements.

EXAMPLE:

Because of the popularity of television programs that feature forensic scientists, universities have seen a dramatic increase in applications to their forensic science programs. Lawyers and police are facing greater pressure from the public and juries to present sophisticated forensic evidence in court. "It's a double-edged sword," said Captain Chris Beattie, a bald man with glasses who has been head of the Los Angeles County Crime Lab for 32 years. "We have a larger pool of qualified people to do the job. But it's also created unreasonable expectations that we can solve every crime the way they do on television."

BEATTIE: TV attracts better students, but unrealistic ideas.

2   Use your notes to match the people with what they contributed to the reading.

_____ 1. Beattie, head of L.A. County Crime Lab

_____ 2. Devine, producer, *CSI*, formerly worked at L.A. County Crime Lab

_____ 3. Siegel, head of under-graduate forensics program at Indiana-Purdue U.

_____ 4. Gialamas, director, forensics lab, Orange County, CA

_____ 5. Sagara, asst. director, L.A. County Crime Lab

a. TV shows use real technology in unrealistic ways.

b. Forensic scientists have to specialize in the lab; they don't do all the jobs.

c. *CSI* TV shows give an exciting but inaccurate view of forensic science.

d. Forensic scientists must have good presentation skills in order to explain evidence in court during trials.

e. In real life, the job includes a lot more paperwork than we ever see on TV.

CRITICAL THINKING

Discuss the questions in a small group. Be prepared to share your answers with the class.

1. Popular TV programs usually aim to appeal to viewers so that they will become a loyal audience from week to week. Given this basic motivation, should TV executives be criticized for misrepresenting the true nature of the forensic science profession on screen? Why or why not?

2. Unlike characters on television programs, real-life people have to specialize when they go into forensics. Not everyone does everything: blood work, fingerprints, ballistics, interviews, and so on. Why do you think this is necessary?

3. Why do you think men dominated this field at the beginning? Is it important to see role models of women scientists on TV? Explain your answer.

LINKING READINGS ONE AND TWO

Fill in the chart with the missing information.

	READING ONE	READING TWO
Characteristics of a forensic scientist	• *a suspicious mind* •	• • • •
College courses needed	• • •	• • •

You and a partner want to apply for forensic science courses. Discuss whether or not you have the right qualifications and type of mind for this kind of work. Share your conclusions with the class.

A Warm-Up

Discuss the questions with a partner.

1. If someone is unjustly found guilty of a crime and put into prison, how can he or she convince people of the truth?

2. Is it ever too late to uncover the truth?

B Reading Strategy

Reading Last Paragraph First

When you read the last paragraph of a text first, you see **how the text concludes** (ends). Knowing the author's **conclusion**, you can then read the events or arguments that led up to it. This can give you a **better understanding** of the text.

Read the last paragraph of the reading. Then answer the questions on the lines.

1. When was Anderson pardoned? _____

2. Why was he pardoned? _____

Now read the text to find out what events led to Anderson's pardon.

The Forensic Use of DNA

By James Watson with Andrew Berry

James Watson and Francis Crick discovered the double-helix structure of DNA in 1953. Crick described their discovery as finding "the secret of life."

1   The forensic use of DNA was first discovered in 1984 by a British geneticist named Alec Jeffreys, who was doing research at Leicester University. According to Jeffreys, DNA technology had the power to identify an individual with what he called a "DNA fingerprint."

2   In 1998, Marvin Lamont Anderson had been in a Virginia prison for fifteen years. He had been **convicted** of a brutal assault in 1983. The victim identified him from a photograph and she picked him out in a police line-up.[1] However, a closer look

[1] *line-up:* a row of people looked at by a witness to a crime to try to identify the criminal

Chromosome with DNA double helix

at the case for **the prosecution** might have revealed some problems. Anderson didn't have a very effective **defense** lawyer. His **attorney** didn't point out that when the victim was shown photographs, Anderson's was the only one in color. Of all the men whose pictures she was shown, he alone was placed in the line-up. The police knew that another man, John Otis Lincoln, had stolen the bicycle used in the crime just 30 minutes before the crime was committed. But Anderson's attorney did not even call Lincoln to testify in court.

3   Five years after Anderson's **trial**, John Lincoln **confessed** to the crime, but the trial **judge** called him a liar and refused to act. Anderson meanwhile continued to protest his innocence. He asked the authorities to do a DNA analysis on the physical **evidence** from the crime scene. He was told that all the evidence had been destroyed after the trial. That was normal procedure at that time. It was then that Anderson contacted the lawyers of the Innocence Project, a group that had gained national attention using DNA analysis to find evidence of guilt or innocence in criminal cases.

4   In the end, Anderson was saved because of the sloppiness of the police technician who had performed the first analysis on the crime scene material in 1982. The technician hadn't returned the samples for destruction, and so they still existed when Anderson asked for a reexamination. The Director of the Virginia Department of Criminal Justice, however, refused the request. He argued that it might establish an "unwelcome **precedent**." But under a new law, the Innocence Project attorneys won a court order calling for the tests to be performed, and in December 2001, the results proved that Anderson could not have committed the crime. The DNA "fingerprint" matched John Otis Lincoln's. Anderson was **pardoned** and freed by Governor Mark Warner of Virginia in 2002.

COMPREHENSION

A Main Ideas

Read each statement. Decide if it is *True* or *False*. Check (✓) the appropriate box. If it is false, change it to make it true. Discuss your answers with a partner.

	TRUE	FALSE
1. Without DNA evidence, Anderson would never have been freed.	☐	☐
2. Anderson was accused of a nonviolent crime.	☐	☐
3. The police, lawyers, and judges were careful not to commit an injustice.	☐	☐
4. As a result of this case, new laws were passed.	☐	☐
5. The Innocence Project tried to help but couldn't.	☐	☐

Close Reading

Read the quotes from the reading. Circle the statement that best explains each quote. Share your answers with a partner.

1. "However, a closer look at the case for the prosecution might have revealed some problems." (*paragraph 2*)

   a. A closer look would have saved Anderson.

   b. A closer look could have saved Anderson.

2. "In the end, Anderson was saved because of the sloppiness of the police technician who had performed the first analysis on the crime scene material in 1982." (*paragraph 4*)

   a. If it hadn't been for the sloppiness of the police technician, Anderson's case would have been hopeless.

   b. Because the technician was sloppy, Anderson went to prison.

3. "He [the Director of the Virginia Department of Criminal Justice] argued that it might establish an 'unwelcome precedent.'" (*paragraph 4*)

   a. The authorities didn't want to waste time and money on prisoners.

   b. The authorities didn't believe in DNA evidence.

VOCABULARY

Definitions

These words are often used in the **courtroom** or in **legal** situations. Match the words with their meanings.

__j__	1. the judge	**a.** to act as a witness in court
_____	2. the jury	**b.** to admit that you committed a crime
_____	3. the defense	**c.** found guilty of a crime
_____	4. the prosecution	**d.** the lawyers who try to prove someone is guilty of a crime
_____	5. attorney	
_____	6. confess	**e.** a court decision that will influence future cases
_____	7. convicted	**f.** the lawyers who try to prove someone is not guilty of a crime
_____	8. pardoned	
_____	9. precedent	**g.** the people who decide guilt or innocence
_____	10. trial	**h.** a legal process to find out whether or not someone committed a crime
_____	11. testify	**i.** forgiven for a crime and freed from punishment
_____	12. evidence	**j.** the official in control of a court who decides how criminals should be punished
		k. information and objects presented in court
		l. a lawyer

NOTE-TAKING: Organizing Material Chronologically

1 Go back to the reading. Read it again to understand what happened to Marvin Anderson. Then read it a third time and take notes. Organize the events of the story in chronological order, to make the sequence of events easier to understand.

1. _CSIs take crime scene material from a violent assault on a woman_

2. _____

3. _____

4. _____

5. _____

6. _____

7. _____

8. _____

2 Using your notes, give the details supporting the main ideas of the reading. Do not copy from the text. Use your own words. Write the paragraph number next to the information you give.

1. Anderson was convicted of a brutal crime.

   The victim identified his photograph. (paragraph 2)

   The victim picked him out in a line-up. (paragraph 2)

2. His attorney did not do a good job of defending him.

   _____

   _____

3. The authorities refused to listen to him.

   _____

   _____

4. Only DNA evidence freed him.

   _____

   _____

   _____

   _____

CRITICAL THINKING

Discuss the questions in a small group. Be prepared to share your answers with the class.

1. What makes DNA evidence so important? Why can it save people when nothing else will?

2. Why do you think the police and court authorities refused to help Anderson? What was their attitude toward him?

3. In your opinion, what motivates the lawyers in the Innocence Project? Why do they bother helping convicts for free?

AFTER YOU READ

BRINGING IT ALL TOGETHER

Work with a partner. Choose one of the interviews and role-play the interview. Use some of the vocabulary you studied in the chapter (for a complete list, go to page 160).

INTERVIEW ONE

A professor in the forensic science department of a university is interviewing a student who is applying to the forensic science program. These points should be discussed in the interview:

- the principles of forensic science
- character traits needed to be successful in the field
- what classes to take in the program
- a comparison with what we see on TV
- the use of DNA evidence
- the student's reasons for choosing forensic science

INTERVIEW TWO

A student reporter for a college newspaper is interviewing a lawyer from the Innocence Project. Discuss these subjects in the interview and add others of your own:

- the goal of the Innocence Project
- whether or not it is important to give help to prisoners
- how DNA can help forensic science
- the case of Marvin Anderson

WRITING ACTIVITY

Write a letter to apply for a job as a crime scene investigator. Base your letter on the information in the readings and use your imagination. Write about the following topics.

- your motivation to do this kind of work
- your studies
- personal characteristics you would bring to this kind of job

Be convincing! Use at least five of the words and idioms you studied in the chapter.

DISCUSSION AND WRITING TOPICS

Discuss these topics in a small group. Choose one of them and write a paragraph or two about it. Use the vocabulary from the chapter.

1. What do you think about the work of the Innocence Project? Would you want to work with such an organization? Why or why not?

2. Can you think of other uses of DNA? For identity? For medicine?

3. How can we improve the accuracy of eyewitness testimony? How can we avoid mistakes?

4. Many people get their ideas for a career when they are young. They may be inspired by literature, comic books, movies, or TV. For example, some scientists say they got their inspiration from science fiction books or movies: Apollo 15 astronauts named a place on the moon "Dandelion Crater" after *Dandelion Wine*, a novel by the science fiction writer Ray Bradbury. What are the advantages and disadvantages of deciding on a career this way?

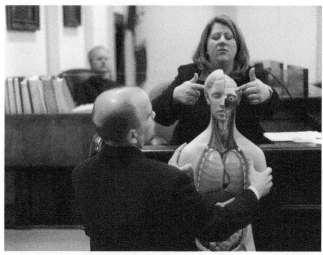

Forensic scientist giving testimony in court

VOCABULARY

Nouns	Verbs	Adjectives	Phrases and Idioms
attorney	commit *	competitive	at one's disposal
defense	confess	eager	be a double-
equipment *	contaminate	productive	edged sword
evidence	convict	sophisticated	be the heart and
harm	pardon	sound	soul of
hypothesis *	reveal *		be high-powered
investigation	solve		be open-minded
judge	testify		be sharp-minded
jury			
pool	**Phrasal Verb**		
precedent *	follow up		
producer			
prosecution			
trial			

* = AWL (Academic Word List) item

SELF-ASSESSMENT

In this chapter you learned to:

○ Skim a text by reading the topic sentences

○ Predict the content of a text from the title and subheadings

○ Read the last paragraph first to understand the point of a text

○ Understand and use synonyms, idioms, and collocations

○ Recognize the different forms and meanings of a word

○ Use underlining and margin notes to identify who said what

○ Organize study notes chronologically to clarify the sequence of events

What can you do well? ✓

What do you need to practice more? ✓

CHAPTER 8

PREHISTORY: From Wolf to Dog

PREHISTORY: the scientific study of history before the time of written records, including the study of archaeology, anthropology, paleontology, genetics, and other fields

OBJECTIVES

To read academic texts, you need to master certain skills.

In this chapter, you will:

- Preview a text using visuals
- Predict the type of text from the title
- Use paraphrasing to identify the main ideas
- Guess the meaning of words from the context or from their Greek and Latin roots
- Understand and use synonyms, homonyms, and suffixes
- Recognize idioms, phrasal verbs, and compound words
- Use note-taking to review and remember details, and to prepare for a test

Consider These Facts

There were no dogs on earth 20,000 years ago, only wolves. Somewhere and sometime after this point, a new animal evolved from the wolf — the dog. In a sense, dogs are domesticated wolves. Were the wolves tamed by humans, or did some wolves tame themselves to survive better?

Look at the timeline showing two eras of the past: the **Paleolithic** and the **Neolithic**. Read some of the characteristics of each era.

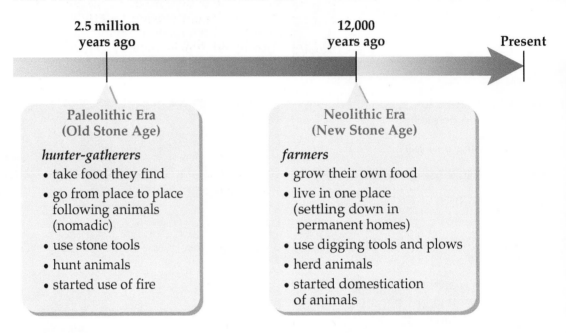

2.5 million
years ago

12,000
years ago

Present

**Paleolithic Era
(Old Stone Age)**

hunter-gatherers
- take food they find
- go from place to place following animals (nomadic)
- use stone tools
- hunt animals
- started use of fire

**Neolithic Era
(New Stone Age)**

farmers
- grow their own food
- live in one place (settling down in permanent homes)
- use digging tools and plows
- herd animals
- started domestication of animals

Now read each statement. Decide if the activity mentioned was more common in the **Paleolithic** or the **Neolithic** era. Check (✓) the appropriate box. Discuss your answers with a partner.

	PALEOLITHIC	NEOLITHIC
1. Humans hunted for food and primarily ate meat.	☐	☐
2. Humans began to eat wheat and other grains.	☐	☐
3. Humans lived in permanent settlements.	☐	☐
4. Humans began to cook their food.	☐	☐

A Warm-Up

Discuss the questions with a partner.

1. Thousands of years ago, human beings dreamed about animals as protectors and allies, even as the ancestors of their clans. Why do you think animals had this important place in the human imagination? Do you know any myths about wolves?

2. Do you think there is a special bond between dogs and man? Can you describe it? Why do we say that dogs are "man's best friend"?

3. Do you have a pet? Would you like to have a pet? What pets, if any, are popular with people you know?

B Reading Strategy

Previewing Using Visuals

Looking at the pictures (drawings or photographs) that illustrate a text first, before you read the text, can help you **predict what the text is about**.

1 Look at the pictures of a wolf and a dog that illustrate the reading. List the ways that dogs differ from wolves. Share your answers with a partner.

WOLVES	DOGS
1. _Wolves have a long, narrow "nose."_	_Dogs have a shorter, wider "nose."_
2. _____	_____
3. _____	_____
4. _____	_____
5. _____	_____

2 Look again at the pictures in the reading. What do you think you will learn from this reading? Discuss your answer with a partner. Write it on the line.

_____

Now read the text to find out if the pictures that illustrate it give you a good idea of its contents.

More Than Man's Best Friend

By Jarrett A. Lobell and Eric A. Powell, *Archaeology*

1   Today there are **some** 77 million dogs in the United States alone. But 20,000 years ago, it's possible there wasn't a single animal on the planet that looked like today's *canis lupus familiaris*. All scientists today accept the fact that dogs descend from the gray wolf, *canis lupus*. But biologists and archaeologists still debate when, where, and how gray wolves first evolved into dogs. Were the dogs first **domesticated** in China, the Middle East, or possibly Africa? The answers are important since dogs were the first animals to be **tamed** by man. They probably played an important role in what is called the "Neolithic Revolution," the time when human beings began to settle down in permanent homes and grow their own food instead of wandering around from place to place as they did in the Paleolithic **era**.

A wolf

A dog

2   What is it that tells us this animal is a "dog" and that one is a "wolf"? Modern wolves and dogs can be easily identified by their appearance. The most important difference is in the snout or nose area. In almost all dogs, the snout is shorter and wider than wolf snouts. Another **crucial** difference is the animal's manner and attitude toward humans. Dogs are genetically **predisposed to** want human attention and approval and to accept human leadership. Wolves are not.

3   Because early dogs looked more like wolves than dogs do today, it can be difficult to **distinguish** between wolf and dog skeletons from the far past. But recently, a team led by paleontologist Mietje Germonpré of the Royal Belgian Institute of Natural Sciences reported a **stunning** new finding in the February 2009 issue of *Journal of Archaeological Science*. Her team found a nearly complete fossil dog skull dating back 31,700 years ago. The skull, found in the Goyet Cave in Belgium, could represent the change from wolf to dog. However, there is a large **gap** in <u>time</u> between the age of the Goyet Cave "dog" and the next oldest dog-like skeletons from western Russia dating from 14,000 years ago. Was the appearance of the Goyet skull just an isolated event? What happened in between? We don't know.

4   Another way to **estimate** when and where domestic dogs originated is to study the genetic differences between dogs and wolves from different locations. In 2009, Peter Savolainen of the Royal Institute of Technology in Sweden published a genetic analysis of DNA indicating that dogs were first

domesticated 16,300 years ago south of the Yangtze River in China. This was about the same time and place as the beginning of rice agriculture.

5   In 2010, another team led by biologist Robert Wayne of the University of California, Los Angeles, came to a different conclusion. Using a larger sample of dog and wolf DNA, their genetic analysis showed that DNA from dogs overlaps most closely with that of Middle Eastern wolves, not those in China. "We know that dogs from the Middle East were closely associated with humans because they were found in ancient human burial sites," Wayne said. "In one case, a puppy is curled up in the arms of a buried human." Wayne and his colleagues suggested that dogs were first domesticated somewhere in the Middle East and then mated with other gray wolves across the globe.

6   University of Victoria (Canada) archaeozoologist[1] Susan Crockford, who did not take part in either study, suspects that searching for a single moment when dogs were domesticated is not useful. The process probably happened more than once. "We have evidence that there was a separate origin of North American dogs, different from the Middle Eastern origin," says Crockford. This supports the idea of at least two "birthplaces." "I think we need to think about dogs becoming dogs at different times in different places," states Dr. Crockford.

---

[1] archaeozoologist: someone who analyzes animal bones at archaeological sites

COMPREHENSION

A Main Ideas

Read each statement. Decide if it is *True* or *False* according to the reading. Check (✓) the appropriate box. If it is false, change it to make it true. Discuss your answers with a partner.

	TRUE	FALSE
1. Scientists' investigation of physical and genetic differences is central to the research about the domestication of dogs.	☐	☐
2. It is easy for scientists to distinguish between dog and wolf skeletons from thousands of years ago.	☐	☐
3. It is safe to say that dogs became dogs at least 31,700 years ago.	☐	☐
4. The natural evolution of a species depends on the success of scientists' intervention.	☐	☐
5. Wolf DNA does not help biologists in their dog and wolf research.	☐	☐
6. Where, when, and how gray wolves evolved into dogs is still open to interpretation.	☐	☐

B Close Reading

Read the quotes from the reading. Circle the statement that best explains each quote. Share your answers with a partner.

1. "Dogs are genetically predisposed to want human attention and approval and to accept human leadership. Wolves are not." (*paragraph 2*)

   a. Wolves want human leadership.

   b. Dogs are born with a desire for human contact.

   c. Dogs can get human approval when they show leadership.

2. "In one case, a puppy is curled up in the arms of a buried human." (*paragraph 5*)

   a. This shows that human beings and dogs had a close intimate relationship.

   b. This shows that humans were buried with their families.

   c. This shows that dogs have always aimed to please their masters.

3. "This supports the idea of at least two 'birthplaces.'" (*paragraph 6*)

   a. This proves that different breeds of dogs were born in different places.

   b. This attests to the fact that it would be easier to agree on one moment in time when dogs were domesticated.

   c. This confirms the idea that there may be two or more origins for the domestication of dogs.

VOCABULARY

A Guessing from Context

Read the essay and guess the meanings of the words in bold from the context. Write these meanings above the words.

The Domestication of Dogs: Making Dogs into Friendly Helpers

We do not know exactly when human beings first walked on the earth. Biologists and archaeologists believe we have to go back __some__ six million years. They
_{1.}
__estimate__ the number of years based on the fossils and stone tools that have been
_{2.}
found at certain archaeological __sites__.
_{3.}

The information that different scientists have gathered about when the

__domestication__ of dogs took place is also not exact. Nevertheless, despite the
_{4.}
__gaps__ that exist between one finding and another, all the information we have is
_{5.}
__crucial__ to our understanding of the evolution of both human beings and animals.
_{6.}

It is generally agreed that dogs were first __tamed__ by man in the Neolithic __era__,
7.   8.

when human beings started to abandon the nomadic life and settle in one place. The

fact that dogs evolved from wolves is commonly accepted. However, since wolves

still exist, it is important to understand that only those wolves __predisposed to__
9.

enter into relationships with humans eventually became the dogs that we have today.

As research shows, when and where this transformation occurred is not clear

because it is difficult to __distinguish__ between early dogs and wolves in the fossils
10.

record. Their physical difference was not as obvious in prehistoric times as it is now.

Without __stunning__ proof to the contrary, it seems reasonable to accept the idea that
11.

dogs may have emerged in many different places on earth.

Now match the words with their meanings.

_c_	1. some	a. trained a wild animal to obey
___	2. estimate	b. very important
___	3. sites	c. approximately
___	4. domestication	d. recognize a difference
___	5. gaps	e. period in history
___	6. crucial	f. guess
___	7. tamed	g. very impressive
___	8. era	h. locations
___	9. predisposed to	i. differences, disparities
___	10. distinguish	j. the act of making a wild animal live with humans as a pet or worker
___	11. stunning	k. tending to behave in a particular way

B Greek and Latin Names and Roots

The **gray wolf** is the *canis lupus* (*canis* = dog; *lupus* = wolf), the wolf that was most inclined to evolve into the *canis lupus familiaris* (*familiaris* = belonging to a family or household), or "domesticated dog." The Latin names make the close relationship between wolves and dogs immediately clear.

Scientists **classify plants and animals** and many other things by using **Greek and Latin names and roots**. This tradition goes back to the Middle Ages when early scientists used Greek and Latin to communicate with each other.

LATIN	ENGLISH
bi(s)	two
canis	dog
domesticus	relating to the home
erectus	erect, upright
familiaris	belonging to a family or household
gen-	create, produce, give birth to
habilis	handy, able
homo	man
lupus	wolf
*ped-**	foot
pedalis	a foot in length
sapiens	wise, able to reason

*The Greek root *ped-* means "child" and is part of words like **pediatrician** (a doctor for children).

1 Work with a partner. Look at the timeline showing the stages of human development. Guess what characteristics these human beings had. Use the "Latin and English" chart for help.

homo habilis (2.5–1.8 million years ago)	*homo erectus* (0–0.5 million years ago)	*homo sapiens* (150,000 years ago–present)

1. *homo habilis:* _____

2. *homo erectus:* _____

3. *homo sapiens:* _____

2 Guess the meanings of these English words with Latin roots. Use the "Latin and English" chart for help.

1. ability: _____

2. generate: _____

3. bicycle: _____

4. pedestrian: _____

5. familiarity: _____

3 Read the definitions of words using Greek and Latin roots.

ACADEMIC FIELDS OF STUDY
- **anthropology:** the study of primitive human social organization
- **archaeology:** the study of long-gone civilizations by examining what remains of their buildings, graves, tools, etc.
- **archaeozoology:** the study of animal remains from archaeological sites
- **biology:** the scientific study of living things
- **genetics:** the study of human reproduction
- **paleontology:** the study of prehistoric times by examining fossils (ancient animals and plants that have been preserved in rock)

HISTORICAL PERIODS
- The **Neolithic:** the more recent period of the Stone Age
- The **Paleolithic:** the earlier period of the Stone Age

Now match the roots with their meanings.

__g__ 1. anthrop-   a. the study of

____ 2. archaeo-   b. old

____ 3. bio-   c. new

____ 4. lith-   d. one who studies

____ 5. neo-   e. life

____ 6. paleo-   f. source, beginning

____ 7. -logist   g. human

____ 8. -logy   h. produce, give birth to

____ 9. gen-   i. stone

NOTE-TAKING: Reviewing Details to Help You Remember

Go back to the reading and read it again. Circle each expert's name and field of study. Underline his or her findings so far. Then fill in this organizer.

	NAME	FIELD	FINDINGS
1.	Mietje Germonpré	Paleontology	Found dog skull in Goyet Cave in Belgium, indicating domesticated dogs dated back 31,700 years in Belgium
2.			
3.			
4.			

CRITICAL THINKING

Discuss the questions in a small group. Be prepared to share your ideas with the class.

1. Why do you think dogs were so much help in the Neolithic Revolution?

2. In this reading, experts disagree about the facts of the past. Does this mean that students can't learn anything? What can you learn when experts disagree? In what ways might disagreements among experts lead to more insights about things than agreements would?

3. When can being able to say "We don't know" or "I don't know" be a sign of strength rather than one of weakness?

A Warm-Up

Discuss the questions with a partner.

Wolves lift up their heads to howl. Dogs bark.

1. What are other differences in the way wolves and dogs behave?

2. Are there any similarities in their behavior?

B Reading Strategy

Paraphrasing to Identify Main Ideas

A **paraphrase** is a statement that expresses something someone has said or written in a shorter, clearer way.

When a text is difficult, stopping to think after each paragraph may be useful on the first or second reading. It may also be useful to write a **one-sentence paraphrase** for **each paragraph**. The paraphrase will help you **identify the main ideas.**

EXAMPLE PARAGRAPH:

Paleolithic humans, as cave paintings show, were brilliant students of animal behavior. The first human hunters probably observed the wolves' cooperative strategies for hunting. Wolves are watchful, too. Rather than compete with these new hungry hunters, wolves may have chosen to give them their trust and work with them. They would join these humans in their chase, combining their better sense of smell and speed with the deadly aim of human weapons. They may have hoped that these two-leggers would prove trustworthy and share with them.

EXAMPLE PARAPHRASE:

Early humans and wolves may have joined together to hunt more efficiently and began to trust each other.

As you read the text, write a one-sentence paraphrase in the margin next to each paragraph.

Domesticating Wolves

By Meg Daley Olmert, from *Made for Each Other*

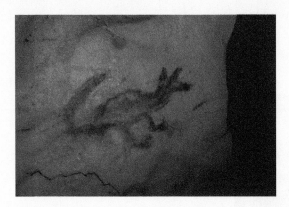

1   Paleolithic humans, as cave paintings show, were brilliant students of animal behavior. The first human hunters probably observed the wolves' cooperative strategies for hunting. Wolves are watchful, too. Rather than compete with these new hungry hunters, wolves may have chosen to give them their trust and work with them. They would join these humans in their chase, combining their better sense of smell and speed with the deadly aim of human weapons. They may have hoped that these two-leggers would prove trustworthy and share with them.

2   Humans didn't just hunt like wolves; they lived like them as well. Humans lived in "packs" or groups and cooperatively cared for their young. Besides being socially compatible, these two-legged carnivores[1] cooked their kill, offering a smell that some wolves probably couldn't resist. Those wolves that dared to come near discovered that these cooking animals threw away some of the best parts. (Early human hunters seem to have been more interested in bone marrow[2] than meat). Scavenging the garbage from early human camps may be what lured wolves into cave dwellings as long as 400,000 years ago. That's when wolf bones started appearing in the caves humans lived in.

3   If some wolves entered human dens voluntarily, they must have been the boldest, most genetically predisposed to be adventurous. It would have been the least nervous wolf, or the hungriest, who made the most successful cave raids. If their presence kept more dangerous animals away, humans may have repaid this service by throwing these adventurous animals a bone. Soon the animals would decide to stay. Eating leftovers doesn't make a wolf into a dog, but it's a start. A bone or two would have sent a powerful trust symbol to the wolf. What we do know is that perhaps as early as 40,000 years ago, something environmental, social, or both started some Eurasian wolves on their genetic journey toward dogdom.

4   The gentlest wolves followed us into our new homes.[3] The final transformation wouldn't have taken long once we began to selectively mate our favorite — most cooperative — wolves and help raise their young. . . . Sometime between 40,000 and 15,000 years ago, genetic tuning knobs started turning and wolves became affectionate to people and youthful in their personality and bodies. They came to lick the hand that fed them.[4] They also kept their best wolf manners, offering their services to their new human family.

---

[1] *carnivores:* meat-eaters (humans are omnivores and will eat everything; most animals are either herbivores like cows and eat only plants, or carnivores like wolves and eat meat)

[2] *bone marrow:* the soft tissue inside bones

[3] Human societies eventually moved away from caves.

[4] *lick the hand that fed them:* The expression is "Don't bite the hand that feeds you," which means "Don't be ungrateful." Daley Olmert is making a play on words meaning "love the hand that feeds you."

5   As the most socially desirable wolves moved deeper and deeper into human society, they brought with them the wolf culture of respect and loyalty. Wolves need each other to survive. Belonging to a family is more important than their rank in the family. That wolf logic explains their devotion and submission to the humans they came to see as their parents, their betters. The primitive humans would no doubt have noticed that their pet wolves treated them with the deference shown a pack leader. . . . It's fascinating to imagine our early ancestors' amazement and thrill at being able to interact in friendly ways with wild animals. These cave dwellers found themselves in a completely new social arrangement with animals that brought a host of pleasing emotions. Wolves would teach us a new idea called "tame," and it would change the world.

COMPREHENSION

A Main Ideas

Put these paraphrases into logical order (from *1* to *5*) according to the paragraphs in the reading.

_____ a. Through natural selective mating of the tamest wolves, genetic changes began to happen, causing differences in behavior and personality in the wolves closest to humans.

_____ b. Early humans and wolves may have joined together to hunt more efficiently and began to trust each other.

_____ c. The bravest wolves protected and cooperated with humans in return for food.

_____ d. Domesticated wolves obeyed humans, becoming very valuable in human civilization.

_____ e. Domesticated wolves formed a family with humans, showing deference and submission, opening the way to the further taming of animals.

B Close Reading

Read the quotes from the reading. Circle the statement that best explains each quote. Share your answers with a partner.

1. "[The wolves] would join these humans in their chase, combining their better sense of smell and speed with the deadly aim of human weapons." (*paragraph 1*)

   a. Wolves did the killing, and humans organized the chase.

   b. Wolves led the chase, and humans did the killing.

2. "Scavenging the garbage from early human camps may be what lured wolves into cave dwellings as long as 400,000 years ago." (*paragraph 2*)

   a. Wolves may have come to humans for food.

   b. Wolves may have been used as human food.

(continued on next page)

3. "What we do know is that perhaps as early as 40,000 years ago, something environmental, social, or both started some Eurasian wolves on their genetic journey toward dogdom." (*paragraph 3*)

   a. We don't know exactly when dogs first appeared.

   b. We know exactly when dogs first appeared.

4. "The final transformation wouldn't have taken long once we began to selectively mate our favorite — most cooperative — wolves and help raise their young." (*paragraph 4*)

   a. With each generation wolves became more dangerous.

   b. Cooperative wolves got tamer in each generation.

5. "Genetic tuning knobs started turning and wolves became affectionate to people and youthful in their personality and bodies." (*paragraph 4*)

   a. The change from wolf to dog made the animal more loving and playful, with a different body size and shape.

   b. Humans became more affectionate to wolves and started tuning their genes.

6. "Wolves need each other to survive. Belonging to a family is more important than their rank in the family." (*paragraph 5*)

   a. For a wolf, self is more important than the group.

   b. For a wolf, the group is more important than self.

VOCABULARY

Ⓐ Guessing from Context

Look at the list of words from the reading. Locate each word in the reading and try to guess its meaning from the context clues. Write down the clues, your guess, and then the dictionary meaning. Was your guess correct?

1. **cooperative**
   (*paragraph 1*)

   Clues: *rather than compete / work with / join / share*

   Guess: *working together*

   Dictionary: *willing to cooperate (work together)*

2. **scavenge**
   (*paragraph 2*)

   Clues: _____

   Guess: _____

   Dictionary: _____

3. **lure**
   (*paragraph 2*)

   Clues: _____

   Guess: _____

   Dictionary: _____

4. dwelling
(paragraph 2)

Clues: _____

Guess: _____

Dictionary: _____

5. rank
(paragraph 5)

Clues: _____

Guess: _____

Dictionary: _____

6. devotion
(paragraph 5)

Clues: _____

Guess: _____

Dictionary: _____

7. deference
(paragraph 5)

Clues: _____

Guess: _____

Dictionary: _____

8. thrill
(paragraph 5)

Clues: _____

Guess: _____

Dictionary: _____

B Synonyms

Complete each sentence with a word or phrase from the box. Use the synonym in parentheses to help you select the correct word or phrase. Compare answers with a partner.

a host of	devotion	rank	trust
deference	lured	thrilled	

1. Even though Daley Olmert has no official _____ rank _____ in a
   (position)
   university, she has been able to join university research groups because of her

   respected work.

2. According to her work, there is a physical basis for the _____
   (love)
   we feel for our dogs and cats. Oxytocin, the same hormone that prepares humans

   to bond to each other, is also at work in the relationship between today's animal

   lovers and their pets.

(continued on next page)

3. Oxytocin produces _____ positive physical and
   (many)

   psychological changes: it calms stress hormones and makes you feel warmth and

   attachment.

4. Wolves may have been _____ to us by food, but they have
   (attracted)

   become "man's best friend" in the process.

5. According to Daley Olmert, dogs show us _____ because
   (submissive behavior)

   domesticated animals see us as one of them.

6. And humans were surely _____ to be able to get closer to
   (very pleased)

   nature by gaining the friendship of helpful animals.

7. The bond of _____ created between wolf and man and
   (confidence)

   then dog and man was the beginning of a worldwide process of the domestication

   of animals — an essential step in civilization.

C **Suffix: -worthy**

> **Worthy** is an adjective that means "deserving." It can be added as a **suffix** to
> certain nouns, creating an adjective: **noun** + worthy = **adjective**.
>
> **EXAMPLE:** *trust* + *-worthy* = trustworthy
> - When you deserve trust, you are **trustworthy**.
> - A **trustworthy** person would not betray a friend.

Make words to describe these qualities.

1. When you deserve praise, you are _____.

2. When something deserves to be in the news, it is a _____ item.

3. When something deserves to be noted (remembered), it is _____.

4. Unacceptable behavior for which someone is to blame is _____
   behavior.

5. A ship that is well built for the sea is _____.

D Homonyms: *site* / *sight* / *cite*

> **Homonyms** are words that **sound alike** but have different spellings and different meanings. For instance, site, sight, and cite all sound alike [**saIt**] but are used differently:
>
> site *n.*   a place; a location
>
> sight *n.*   the ability to see; the act of seeing; the thing you see
>
> cite *v.*   to mention something as an example that supports, proves, or explains a particular idea; to give someone's exact words

Complete the paragraph with *site*, *sight*, or *cite* in the appropriate places. Compare answers with a partner.

More than one archaeological _____*site*_____ has dug up wolf
            1.

bones in caves. However, it is difficult to _____ accurate data
                                            2.

about how the close relationship between humans and wolves evolved. It is believed

that in the Stone Age, both humans and wolves caught _____
                                                        3.

of one another hunting for food. A kind of companionship developed when the

bravest wolves approached the _____ of human dwellings.
                                4.

Within their _____ were the leftovers from the humans'
              5.

meals. Humans may have rewarded the wolves for their protection with a bone; soon

wolves and humans working together may have

become a familiar _____.
                    6.

To _____ the words of Meg
    7.

Daley Olmert, author of *Made for Each Other: The*

Biology of the Human-Animal Bond, "Eating leftovers

doesn't make a wolf into a dog, but it's a start."

NOTE-TAKING: Preparing for a Test

Go back to the reading and read it again. Read over your paraphrases. Then make up questions a teacher might ask on an exam. Make one question for each paragraph and then answer it for practice. Remember to answer in your own words.

1. Q: _Why would wolves and humans find an advantage in working together?_

   A: _Wolves were faster and had a better sense of smell; humans could use their_ _efficient tools for the kill. Together they could have more to eat._

2. Q: _What attracted wolves to humans?_

   A: _____

   _____

3. Q: _____

   A: _____

   _____

4. Q: _____

   A: _____

   _____

5. Q: _____

   A: _____

   _____

CRITICAL THINKING

Fact or Opinion?

Recognizing the difference between a **fact** and an **opinion** is an important reading skill.

EXAMPLES:
- The humans cooked their kill.
  *This is a **fact** because there is physical evidence of fire and bones of animals cooked for food.*

- The wolves would join the humans in their chase.
  *The author is expressing a professional **opinion**, based on logical reasoning. There is no physical evidence for this statement.*

Read each statement from the reading. Decide if it expresses a *Fact* or an *Opinion*. Check (✓) the appropriate box. Discuss your answers with a partner.

	FACT	OPINION
1. "Scavenging . . . may be what lured wolves into cave dwellings as long as 400,000 years ago."	☐	☑
2. "That's when wolf bones started appearing in the caves humans lived in."	☐	☐
3. "If some wolves entered human dens voluntarily, they must have been the boldest, most genetically predisposed to be adventurous."	☐	☐
4. "It would have been the least nervous wolf, or the hungriest, who made the most successful cave raids."	☐	☐
5. "Paleolithic humans, as cave paintings show, were brilliant students of animal behavior."	☐	☐
6. "[The wolves] may have hoped that these two-leggers would prove trustworthy and share with them."	☐	☐

LINKING READINGS ONE AND TWO

Discuss the questions in a small group. Be prepared to share your answers with the class.

1. Anthropologists and archaeologists often have to piece together the story of the past like a puzzle. They have to draw logical conclusions from very limited remaining evidence. How is this "guessing" different from our guesses as nonexperts? Do you think this kind of speculation (guessing) and opinion has a place in prehistory books? Why or why not?

2. During class, professors often ask students if they have any questions about the readings. What questions would you ask about Readings One and Two?

3. In Reading One, there were contradictions because the experts don't agree. In Reading Two there is another kind of contradiction. First, the author claims that only the bravest wolves would have dared to approach humans. Then the author says the most socially desirable wolves were gentle. Has she made a mistake? What might be her answer to such a question?

4. Genetic changes happen by chance as gene cells reproduce. If the changes improve the animal's adaptation to the environment, the animal will have a better chance of survival. Those genes will be passed to future generations. In this way, over thousands and thousands of years genetic changes created dogs from their wolf ancestors. What traits [characteristics of personality] did these changes give dogs that helped them survive with humans better than wolves could?

5. At the beginning of this chapter you were asked this question: "Were the wolves tamed by humans, or did some wolves tame themselves to survive better?" After reading the information in Readings One and Two, how would you answer the question?

A Warm-Up

Discuss the questions with a partner.

1. How do you think dogs helped humans in the Neolithic period?

2. How do dogs help us today?

3. Is this help the same as in the past?

B Reading Strategy

Predicting Type of Text from Title

The title of a reading reflects what **type of text** you are going to read. If, like the title of Reading Three, it includes a name like "Frisky," you can guess that this text is going to be an anecdote.

An **anecdote** is a personal **story that illustrates a larger point**. An anecdote is often told in informal speech.

What else can you predict from the title of the reading? Answer the questions on the lines. Discuss your answers with a partner.

1. When someone is "frisky," it means they are playful and full of energy. Can you guess who Frisky is?

_____

2. If you were in a hurricane or a natural disaster, what would you do about your animals?

_____

3. Do you think this is going to be a happy story or a sad one? (Look at the word "rescue.")

_____

Now read the text to find out if your guesses were correct.

Frisky to the Rescue in Hurricane Katrina
By Jennifer Wulff, *People Magazine*

1   His neighbors tried to get him to leave, but **lifelong** Biloxi, Mississippi resident George Mitchell, a widower, insisted on **riding out the storm**. Yes, that terrible storm Katrina. "I said, 'Nope, Hurricane Camille[1] was **as bad as it gets**,' says Mitchell, 'and I survived it.'" He turned 80 the day Katrina[2] hit. Stubbornly, he took his schnauzer-poodle mix Frisky (who was a senior citizen himself for a dog at age 18) to an empty neighbor's home and waited. Soon Mitchell was chest-deep in water. He put Frisky on an inflatable mattress and **hung on** to keep himself afloat. "It was like being in a washing machine," says the retired Navy man turned real estate agent.

2   After treading water[3] for hours, he began to fade. "I was ready to let go," says Mitchell, who was **on the verge of passing out**. Not if Frisky had anything to do with it. The dog, which Mitchell found on his porch in 1987 as a **stray** puppy, went to the corner of the mattress and began **frantically** licking his master's face. "He would not stop licking until I **snapped out of it**," says Mitchell. Realizing his best friend's own life would be in danger if he died, Mitchell fought to stay alive. Finally, at daybreak, the water began to **recede**, and Mitchell could once again stand.

3   He spent the next 12 days at a nearby hospital being treated for dehydration[4] and cuts. Frisky was right by his side. "He slept on me the whole time," says Mitchell, who now lives in a Biloxi retirement community[5] with his pup. "He's **quite a boy**. I wouldn't give him up for a million dollars."

---

[1] *Hurricane Camille* was a category 5 hurricane that hit the Gulf states in 1969, killing more than 200 people and causing more than $8 billion of damage.

[2] *Hurricane Katrina,* one of the worst hurricane disasters in U.S. history, hit the Gulf states in 2005, killing 1,800 people and causing $81 billion dollars of damage due to flooding. The river levees (walls) broke, and water flooded 80% of New Orleans and many cities along the Mississippi River.

[3] *tread water:* to stay floating upright in deep water by moving your legs as if you were riding a bicycle

[4] *dehydration:* If you don't drink enough water, you will suffer from dehydration.

[5] *retirement community:* a place where senior citizens choose to live together

COMPREHENSION

Ⓐ Main Ideas

Complete the sentences with information from the reading. Use your own words. Compare answers with a partner.

1. George Mitchell didn't want to leave Biloxi because _____

_____.

2. He stayed at a neighbor's house, and when he was chest-deep in water, _____

_____.

3. He was too tired to hold on, but Frisky _____

_____.

4. Today Mitchell _____.

Ⓑ Close Reading

Read the quotes from the reading. Circle the statement that best explains each quote. Share your answers with a partner.

1. "'I said, 'Nope, Hurricane Camille was as bad as it gets,' says Mitchell, 'and I survived it.'" (*paragraph 1*)

   a. I need to evacuate.

   b. I don't need to evacuate.

2. "Stubbornly, he took his schnauzer-poodle mix Frisky (who was a senior citizen himself for a dog at age 18) to an empty neighbor's home and waited." (*paragraph 1*)

   a. Advanced age was common to dog and owner.

   b. The dog was old but not his owner.

3. "It was like being in a washing machine." (*paragraph 1*)

   a. The water was agitated.

   b. The water was deep.

4. "He began to fade. . . . Not if Frisky had anything to do with it." (*paragraph 2*)

   a. Frisky couldn't do anything to fade.

   b. Frisky wouldn't let Mitchell die.

5. "Realizing his best friend's own life would be in danger if he died, Mitchell fought to stay alive." (*paragraph 2*)

   a. Mitchell fought to live in order to save his dog.

   b. His dog fought his owner to survive in the storm.

VOCABULARY

A Words and Idioms

Work with a partner. Match the words and idioms with their meanings. If you need help, look back at the reading to find them in context.

_i_	1. ride out the storm	**a.**	lost or without a home
___	2. as bad as it gets	**b.**	start paying attention
___	3. on the verge of	**c.**	just about to happen
___	4. frantically	**d.**	a great dog
___	5. pass out	**e.**	go back or down from a certain level
___	6. hang on	**f.**	hold on tightly
___	7. stray	**g.**	lose consciousness, faint
___	8. snap out of it	**h.**	the worst
___	9. recede	**i.**	wait for something to get better
___	10. quite a boy	**j.**	with great agitation and worry

B Phrasal Verbs with *pass* and *hang*

Read these sentences with phrasal verbs with *pass* and *hang*.

1. Many people **passed away** during Hurricane Katrina but could not be buried immediately.

2. Mitchell tried not to **pass out** and fall into the water.

3. In the storm, people lost precious things they wanted to **pass down** to their children and grandchildren.

4. Frisky never **passed up** an opportunity to lick or encourage his master.

5. Frisky encouraged his master to **hang on** and not let go.

6. Now Mitchell and his dog **hang out** together at the retirement home.

Now match the phrasal verbs with their meanings.

_f_	1. pass away	**a.**	faint
___	2. pass out	**b.**	lose a chance
___	3. pass down	**c.**	give to the next generation
___	4. pass up	**d.**	spend a lot of time
___	5. hang on	**e.**	keep going
___	6. hang out	**f.**	die

C Compound Words with *-long*

> **Compound words** ending in *-long* usually relate to a **time period**.
>
> **EXAMPLES:**
> - He was a **lifelong** resident of Biloxi. = He resided in Biloxi **all his life**.
> - It was a **weeklong** vacation. = She was away on vacation **for a week**.

Rewrite each description, using a compound word with *–long*.

1. A job that lasted a year = _____

2. A class that lasted a month = _____

3. A conversation that lasted an hour = _____

4. A meeting that lasted the whole day = _____

CRITICAL THINKING

Discuss the questions in a small group. Be prepared to share your answers with the class.

1. This heartwarming story is an anecdote: a personal story to illustrate a point. What is the point Mitchell is trying to make? Why did the journalist think it was important to put this story in a magazine?

2. How does this story illustrate the traits dogs got from wolves? How does it show the bond between man and dog and also between dog and man? Why did Mitchell hang on so long in the storm?

3. Do you agree with Mitchell's decision to try to ride out the storm? What would have happened to him without his dog? Explain.

4. Do you think dogs can be heroes? In what sense?

AFTER YOU READ

BRINGING IT ALL TOGETHER

Organize a panel discussion about the evolution of dogs from wolves. Follow these instructions:

- One student is the panel organizer who explains that this is a special panel allowing students to learn more about how dogs evolved from wolves.
- Some of the students play the roles of the people mentioned in the chapter (see page 185). Each person explains what he or she knows about the process of evolution from wolf to dog.
- The remaining students ask questions of the experts and offer their own contributions about dogs after the presentation.

TOPIC: The evolution of dogs from wolves

ROLES:

- Panel organizer
- Mietje Germonpré, Belgium
- Peter Savolainen, Sweden
- Robert Wayne, US
- Susan Crockford, Canada
- Meg Daley Olmert, US
- George Mitchell, US

Before starting the panel discussion, each student should look at the chapter vocabulary (for a complete list, go to page 186) and pick the words and idioms he or she will need for the discussion.

WRITING ACTIVITY

Write a two-paragraph anecdote about a family pet.

- **First paragraph:** Tell the story.
- **Second paragraph:** Explain the aspects of the animal-human bond demonstrated in the story.

Use at least five of the words and idioms you studied in the chapter.

DISCUSSION AND WRITING TOPICS

Discuss these topics in a small group. Choose one of them and write a paragraph or two about it. Use the vocabulary from the chapter.

1. Summarize orally or in writing the evolution of wolf to dog based on the scientific findings mentioned in the readings. Is this type of research important or not? What do we learn from this kind of research?

2. In the early 19th century, there were thousands of wolves in the western United States, but the government offered money to people who would kill wolves. As a result, their numbers were reduced to hundreds, and they became an endangered species. Why do some cultures hate and fear wolves? Can you think of stories from different cultures where wolves were the enemy?

3. Jack London wrote a very famous novel in which wolf howls were described as "the call of the wild." What did he think wolves symbolized? Would this be a positive or negative symbol for you?

4. Some dogs are bred and trained to be cruel fighters. Do these characteristics come from wolves? Do you think it is a good thing to train dogs to be vicious?

5. Give other examples of the bond between animals and humans.

VOCABULARY

Nouns	Verbs	Adjectives	Adverbs
deference	distinguish	cooperative *	frantically
devotion *	domesticate *	crucial *	some
dwelling	estimate *	lifelong	
era	lure	stray	**Phrases and Idioms**
gap	recede	stunning	a host of
rank	scavenge	trustworthy	as bad as it gets
site *	tame		be on the verge of
thrill			(doing something)
trust	**Phrasal Verbs**		be predisposed to
	hang on		be quite a boy
	pass out		ride out the storm
			snap out of it

* = AWL (Academic Word List) item

SELF-ASSESSMENT

In this chapter you learned to:

○ Preview a text using visuals

○ Predict the type of text from the title

○ Use paraphrasing to identify the main ideas

○ Guess the meaning of words from the context or from their Greek and Latin roots

○ Understand and use synonyms, homonyms, and suffixes

○ Recognize idioms, phrasal verbs, and compound words

○ Use note-taking to review and remember details, and to prepare for a test

What can you do well? ✓

What do you need to practice more? ✓

CHAPTER 9

EDUCATION STUDIES:
Overcoming Inequalities

EDUCATION STUDIES: the theory and practice of teaching and the principles of school administration

OBJECTIVES

To read academic texts, you need to master certain skills.

In this chapter, you will:

- Identify the issues from the first paragraph of an essay

- Understand the most important idea by reading the last paragraph first

- Skim a text by reading the topic sentences

- Understand and use synonyms, antonyms, and different word forms

- Guess the meaning of words from the context and use them in a new context

- Use dictionary entries to learn the meanings of words

- Use note-taking to summarize an argument and identify important details

A Consider These Questions

Discuss the questions in a small group.

1. Many people talk about getting "a good education." How would you describe a good education? What kinds of things does it include?

2. Who is responsible for providing us with an education? The government? Parents? Ourselves?

B Your Personal Experiences

Discuss the questions with a partner.

1. Is education important to you? What benefits do you hope to enjoy from your education?

2. How would you evaluate the education you have received so far?

READING ONE: Savage Inequalities: Children in America's Schools

A Warm-Up

Discuss the questions with a partner.

In 2008–2009, New York City spent $17,696 on the education of each child, while Great Neck and Manhasset, neighboring wealthy suburban communities, spent $26,316 and $25,360, respectively, on each child. There are comparable differences in other metropolitan areas. Do you think this is fair? Why or why not?

B Reading Strategy

Identifying Issues from First Paragraph of an Essay

The **first paragraph** (*introduction*) of an **essay** presents the issues that the author is going to discuss in the body of the essay. Reading the first paragraph of an essay will allow you to spot the **keywords** and identify the **issues**. This in turn will help you follow the ideas in the rest of the essay.

Read the first paragraph of the reading. Circle the keywords that tell the reader what the author is going to discuss in this essay. Write them on the lines.

_____   _____

_____   _____

Now read the rest of the essay to find out how the author develops the issues mentioned in the introduction.

Savage Inequalities: Children in America's Schools

By Jonathan Kozol

1   The differences in spending between very wealthy suburbs and poor cities are not always extreme. However, when relative student needs have been taken into consideration, the **disparities** in funding are enormous. **Equality**, after all, does not mean simply equal funding. Equal funding for unequal needs is not equality. Lack of money is not the only problem, but the **gulf** in funding we have seen is so remarkable and seems so **unfair** that it strikes many thoughtful citizens at first as unbelievable. How can it be that **inequalities** as great as these exist in neighboring school districts?

2   The answer is found, at least in part, in the way we finance public education. Most public schools in the United States depend on a local property tax. The property tax depends, of course, on the value of homes and local industries. A **typical** wealthy suburb in which homes are often worth more than $800,000 enjoys a larger tax base in proportion to its student population than a city occupied by thousands of poor people. Typically, in the United States, very poor communities place a high priority on education, and they often tax themselves at higher rates than the very **affluent** communities. But even if they tax themselves at a much higher rate than an extremely wealthy district, they still end up with much less money for each child in their schools.

3   All of these disparities are also **heightened**, in the case of larger cities, by the number of entirely tax-free institutions — colleges and hospitals and art museums, for instance — that are sited in such cities. Police expenses are higher in crime-ridden cities than in most suburban towns. Fire department costs are also higher where old and run-down housing is a problem. Public health costs are also higher where poor people cannot pay for private hospitals. All of these costs plus the expenses for public schools create a great **challenge** for poor neighborhoods.

4   Many people tend to grow angry if invited to look closely at these inequalities. "Life isn't **fair**," one parent in Winnetka[1] answered flatly when I raised the issue. "Wealthy children also go to summer camp. All summer. Poor kids maybe not at all. Or maybe, if they're lucky, for two weeks. Wealthy children have the chance to go to Europe and they have **access** to good libraries, encyclopedias, computers, better doctors, nicer homes. Some of

---

[1] **Winnetka:** a well-to-do Chicago suburb

(continued on next page)

my neighbors send their kids to schools like Exeter and Groton.[2] Is government supposed to equalize these things as well?"

5　But government, of course, does not assign us to our homes, our summer camps, our doctors — or to Exeter. It does assign us to our public schools. Indeed, it forces us to go to them. Unless we have the wealth to pay for private education, we are **compelled** by law to go to public school — and to the public school in our district. Thus the state, by requiring attendance but refusing to require equality, effectively requires inequality.

6　The point is often made that, even with a genuine equality of schooling for poor children, other forces still would work against their school performance. Teen-age pregnancy, drug use, and other problems still would make many families in these neighborhoods all but **dysfunctional**. Nothing I have said should leave the **misimpression** that I do not think these factors are enormously important. Also some people place the emphasis on schools and others emphasize family and neighborhood; the truth is that both are essential in a child's life.

7　The family, however, differs from the school in the significant respect that government is not responsible, or at least not directly, for the inequalities of family background. It *is* responsible for inequalities in public education. Schools could make dramatic changes almost overnight if financial equality were a reality.

---

[2] *Exeter and Groton:* private boarding schools for the wealthy

COMPREHENSION

Ⓐ Main Ideas

Read each statement. Decide if it is *True* or *False* according to the reading. Check (✓) the appropriate box. If it is false, change it to make it true. Discuss your answers with a partner.

	TRUE	FALSE
1. People in very poor neighborhoods do not care about education as much as people in very rich neighborhoods.	☐	☐
2. Urban areas in general have greater expenses than suburban areas.	☐	☐
3 Rich people in the suburbs work hard and are willing to share with poor people.	☐	☐
4. To ensure equality in education, the government should favor poor children over rich children in regard to funding.	☐	☐
5. The government is responsible for the welfare of its schoolchildren.	☐	☐

Close Reading

Read the quotes from the reading. Circle the statement that best explains each quote. Share your answers with a partner.

1. "Equal funding for unequal needs is not equality." (*paragraph 1*)

   a. Equality means treating all people the same.

   b. Equality means taking into account unequal needs.

2. "Lack of money is not the only problem, but the gulf in funding we have seen is so remarkable and seems so unfair that it strikes many thoughtful citizens at first as unbelievable." (*paragraph 1*)

   a. Thoughtful citizens can't understand the basis of educational funding.

   b. Thoughtful citizens can't understand why educational funding is so unfair.

3. "But even if they [people in a poor district] tax themselves at a much higher rate than an extremely wealthy district, they still end up with much less money for each child in their schools." (*paragraph 2*)

   a. Poor people may pay a higher percentage in taxes and yet end up with less at their disposal.

   b. Rich people may pay a higher percentage in taxes and yet end up with less at their disposal.

4. "Thus the state, by requiring attendance but refusing to require equality, effectively requires inequality." (*paragraph 5*)

   a. Government education policy makes inequality inevitable.

   b. Government education policy refuses to accept inequality.

5. "Teen-age pregnancy, drug use and other problems still would make many families in these neighborhoods all but dysfunctional. Nothing I have said should leave the misimpression that I do not think these factors are enormously important." (*paragraph 6*)

   a. The author thinks families wouldn't be so dysfunctional if schooling were better.

   b. The author doesn't want readers to think he sees school money as the only problem in poor areas.

6. "The family, however, differs from the school in the significant respect that government is not responsible, or at least not directly, for the inequalities of family background." (*paragraph 7*)

   a. The government is not required by law to equalize family backgrounds, so it shouldn't bother trying to equalize schools.

   b. The government is not required by law to equalize family backgrounds, but it is required to operate a school system.

VOCABULARY

Ⓐ Prefixes of *Not*-Words or Antonyms

Different **prefixes** tell us the **opposite** — the **antonym** — of a word:

typical *(adj.)*	**atypical** = not typical
parity *(n.)*	**disparity** = lack of parity
functional *(adj.)*	**dysfunctional** = not functional
equality *(n.)*	**inequality** = lack of equality
impression *(n.)*	**misimpression** = wrong impression
fair *(adj.)*	**unfair** = not fair

Fill in the chart with the *antonym* of each word (using prefixes) and the meaning of the antonym. Compare answers with a partner.

	ANTONYM	MEANING OF THE ANTONYM
1. political *(adj.)*	apolitical	not having any interest in politics
2. fairness *(n.)*		
3. equal *(adj.)*		
4. experience *(n.)*		
5. ability *(n.)*		
6. communication *(n.)*		
7. utopia *(n.)*		

Ⓑ Synonyms

Complete the text with the words from the box. Use the synonym in parentheses to help you select the correct word. Discuss your answers with a partner.

access	challenge	disparities	gulf	misimpression	unfair
affluent	compelled	dysfunctional	heightened	typically	

It is not too difficult to imagine that a poorly educated America will run the

risk of becoming a _____dysfunctional_____ society in the future. If equal
                    1. (broken)

_____ to the opportunities of a quality education is not
      2. (admittance)

given to all Americans, the _____ that Kozol describes
                      3. (differences)

between the _____ and the poor in America will no longer
     4. (wealthy)

be the primary issue. America, _____ regarded as one of
5. (normally)
the world's strongest economies, will suffer an economic decline because of the

_____ between its many "uneducated" citizens and better-
6. (great gap)
educated citizens in other countries. In fact, the crisis that Kozol writes about will

be _____ considerably when the countries that now invest
7. (intensified)
more than America does in their people's education start to enjoy the benefits of

their investment.

All Americans, no matter what their socioeconomic background, should be

_____ to go beyond the "class wars" and correct their
8. (forced)
_____ of the needs of our country. Questions about what
9. (false idea)
is fair or _____ for individuals will certainly lose their
10. (not fair)
significance if we cannot assure a prosperous future for our children. Education is

essential to our society's future. Our _____ is to improve the
11. (test)
educational system in our country.

NOTE-TAKING: Summarizing the Argument

Go back to the reading. Read each paragraph again, following Kozol's argument
(the reasons for his point of view) closely. Then write a one-sentence summary.
Use your own words; do not copy the text.

PARAGRAPH	SUMMARY OF ARGUMENT
1	**Inequalities:** *Schools in poor neighborhoods get less money than schools in rich areas even though they need it more.*
2	**Why? Tax system . . .**
3	**Why? City expenses . . .**
4	**What rich people say:**
5	**Kozol's answer:**
6	**Other factors:**
7	**But government . . .**

CRITICAL THINKING

(A) Analyzing the Argument

Discuss the questions in a small group.

1. In your opinion, is Kozol's argument effective?
2. What are the strong points of his argument? The weak points?
3. How does he show what his opponents would say?
4. How does he answer them?
5. What do you think Kozol sees in the future if his advice is not followed?
6. Can you think of anything that could strengthen his argument?

(B) Brainstorming a Letter

Imagine you are a parent and want to write a letter to Kozol, either to object to his argument or to support it. Brainstorm at least three reasons in defense of your point of view with a partner.

1. Letter from a parent living in an affluent suburb (objecting to Kozol's argument)

   a. _Why should we be compelled to care about social inequalities?_

   It's not our problem.

   b. _____

   _____

   c. _____

   _____

2. Letter from a parent living in a poor city neighborhood (supporting Kozol's argument)

   a. _People from the affluent suburbs have access to the theaters and cultural_

   institutions in the cities.

   b. _____

   _____

   c. _____

   _____

Now write your letter.

A Warm-Up

Discuss the questions with a partner.

1. How did you learn to read as a child?

2. Did you face any challenges when you learned to read?

B Reading Strategy

Skimming by Reading Topic Sentences

In academic writing, the **topic sentence** (the first sentence of a paragraph) often gives the **main idea** of the paragraph. Reading the topic sentence of a paragraph and especially the **keyword** in it will help you get the gist of each paragraph in a text.

Look at the seven topic sentences in the reading and circle the keywords that preview the main ideas. Then write these keywords here.

PARAGRAPH 1: _envy / knowledge_

PARAGRAPH 2: _____

PARAGRAPH 3: _____

PARAGRAPH 4: _____

PARAGRAPH 5: _____

PARAGRAPH 6: _____

PARAGRAPH 7: _____

Now read the text to find out more about how Malcolm X taught himself to read.

The Autobiography of Malcolm X

Malcolm X was one of the leaders of the African-American community in the 1960s.

1   It had really begun back in the Charlestown Prison, when Bimbi first made me **envy** his great knowledge. Bimbi had always **taken charge of** any conversation he was in, and I had tried to copy him. But every book I **picked up** had very few sentences which didn't contain words that might as well have been in Chinese. When I just **skipped** those words, of course, I really ended up with little idea of what the book said. So I had come to the Norfolk Prison Colony still **going through** only book-reading **motions**. Pretty soon, I would have quit even these motions, unless I had received the **motivation** I did.

2   I saw that the best thing I could do was **get hold of** a dictionary — to study, to learn some words. I spent two days just turning the pages of the dictionary. I'd never realized so many words existed! I didn't know *which* words I needed to learn. Finally, just to start some kind of action, I began copying.

3   In my slow and terrible handwriting, I copied into my notebook everything printed on that page, **down to** the punctuation marks.

4   I believe it took me a day. Then, aloud, I read back, to myself, everything I'd written in the notebook. Over and over, aloud, to myself, I read my own handwriting.

5   I woke up the next morning, thinking about those words — very proud to realize that not only had I written so much at one time, but I'd written words that I never knew were in the world. Moreover, with a little effort, I also could remember what many of these words meant. I reviewed the words whose meanings I didn't remember.

6   I was so **fascinated** that I went on — I copied the dictionary's next page. And the same experience came when I studied that. With every succeeding page, I also learned of people and places and events from history. Actually, the dictionary is like a small encyclopedia. Finally the dictionary's A section had filled a whole notebook — and I went on into the Bs. Between what I wrote in my notebook, and writing letters, during the rest of my time in prison I would guess I wrote a million words.

7   I suppose it was **inevitable** that as I learned more and more words, I could for the first time pick up a book and read and now begin to understand what the book was saying. Anyone who has read a great deal can imagine the new world that opened. Let me tell you something: from then until I left prison, in every free moment I had, if I was not reading in the library, I was reading on my bed. There was nothing you could have done to take me away from my books. Between my correspondence, my visitors, and my reading of books, months passed without my even thinking about being imprisoned. In fact, up to then, I never had been so truly free in my life.

COMPREHENSION

A Main Ideas

Work with a partner. Complete the sentences that reflect the steps Malcolm X went through in teaching himself to read.

1. When Malcolm X went to jail, he _____

  _____ .

2. The first thing he did was _____

  _____ .

3. In his own handwriting, he _____ .

4. Then, after a night's sleep, he would _____

  _____ .

5. He learned not only words but _____ .

6. Reading became _____ .

B Close Reading

Read the quotes from the reading. Circle the statement that best explains each quote. Share your answers with a partner.

1. "So I had come to the Norfolk Prison Colony still going through only book-reading motions." (*paragraph 1*)

   a. Malcolm had limited reading skills.

   b. He could read the words and understood what he was reading.

2. "In my slow and terrible handwriting, I copied into my notebook everything printed on that page, down to the punctuation marks." (*paragraph 3*)

   a. He copied everything but the punctuation marks into his notebook.

   b. He also copied the punctuation marks into his notebook.

3. "With every succeeding page, I also learned of people and places and events from history. Actually, the dictionary is like a small encyclopedia." (*paragraph 6*)

   a. By reading the dictionary, he learned a lot more than just words.

   b. Reading the dictionary helped him read the encyclopedia.

4. "There was nothing you could have done to take me away from my books. Between my correspondence, my visitors, and my reading of books, months passed without my even thinking about being imprisoned. In fact, up to then, I never had been so truly free in my life." (*paragraph 7*)

   a. According to the author, reading is part of the pathway to freedom.

   b. According to the author, freedom is having time to read.

VOCABULARY

A Guessing from Context

Go back to the reading and reread the sentences in which these words and idioms appear. Be sure that you understand what they mean according to the context. Then match them with their meanings.

_f_ 1. envy

_____ 2. take charge of

_____ 3. skip (something)

_____ 4. go through the motions

_____ 5. motivation

_____ 6. get hold of

_____ 7. down to

_____ 8. fascinated

_____ 9. inevitable

a. ignore

b. inspiration

c. impossible to avoid

d. passionately interested

e. do something mechanically

f. be jealous of

g. find

h. take control of

i. including

B Synonyms

Complete the story with the words and idioms from the box. Use the synonym or paraphrase in parentheses to help you select the correct word or idiom. Compare answers with a partner.

down to	fascinated	inevitable	skipping
envy	gone through the motions	motivation	take charge of

People who have learned to _____*take charge of*_____ their lives reveal the
1. (take control of)

very best of the human spirit. Before he was "rescued" by the Metropolitan Regional

Career and Technical Center — otherwise known as the "Met" — tenth grader Cesar

had only _____ of going to school. Between hanging out
2. (attended school in a mechanical way)

on street corners with fellow gang members, getting into trouble with the police,

and visiting his father and brother in jail, he never did his homework and had very

limited reading and writing skills as a result. Dropping out of school was surely

going to be the _____ consequence of this lifestyle.
3. (impossible to avoid)

However, at the Met, Cesar found the _____ to turn
4. (inspiration)

his life around and become an exceptional student. The Met was a unique public

high school in Providence, Rhode Island, where students received a lot of personal attention while designing their own programs according to their interests and needs. Cesar's teachers taught him to become _____ with the

5. (passionately interested)

learning experience by giving him interesting books to read. Eventually, Cesar's old habit of _____ the words that he didn't know disappeared

6. (not reading)

as he started to read every word on the page _____ the last

7. (including)

footnote. This was especially true when he picked up *The Autobiography of Malcolm X*. Malcolm X became Cesar's role model. With the Met's help and the inspiration of Malcolm X finding freedom through education, Cesar was able to find himself as a person and chart his destiny. This former gang member, whose childhood friends would most likely _____ his good fortune, became a poet and

8. (be jealous of)

went to a small private college on a full scholarship.

C Using the Dictionary

Read the dictionary entry for the phrasal verb *pick up*. The dictionary entry gives some of the verb's many meanings. Then read each sentence. Decide which meaning is being used. Write the number of the appropriate meaning.

---

pick up *phr. v.*

1 LIFT UP   to take something (from a table or a shelf)

2 GET BETTER   to improve (one's business or social life)

3 LEARN   to learn something without much effort or without being taught in a class

4 START AGAIN   to begin something (a conversation, a meeting, a life) again, starting from the point where it stopped earlier

5 POLICE   to find someone and take him/her to the police station for questioning

---

__2__   **a.** After Cesar learned the benefits of pursuing an education, his life **picked up** in every possible way.

_____   **b.** As his reading skills improved, he could easily understand most of the books he **picked up**.

_____   **c.** This dramatic change in his life gave him confidence in himself and made him realize that he could readily **pick up** whatever new ideas were presented to him.

_____   **d.** His friends, however, continued to engage in criminal activities and were constantly **picked up** by the police.

_____   **e.** After being released from prison, many of his friends just **picked up** where they had left off and continued their old life of crime.

CRITICAL THINKING

Discuss the questions in a small group. Be prepared to share your answers with the class.

1. In the brief preface to his book, Malcolm X wrote: "Many who today hear me somewhere in person, or on television, or those who read something I've said, will think I went to school far beyond the eighth grade. This impression is due entirely to my prison studies."

   Malcolm X invented his "prison studies" program completely on his own. Do you think government and state agencies should implement a similar educational program in all prisons? Why or why not? What do you think Malcolm X would say?

2. Simple copying is not a method encouraged by today's teachers because it is a very slow process and does not develop creativity. Without memorization, it won't work at all. Why did Malcolm X choose this method? How did he make it work for him? Would it work for you? Since you are making an effort to improve your reading comprehension skills, you probably have some ideas about the best way to achieve this goal. What are your methods?

3. Malcolm X writes that he was "very proud to realize that not only had [he] written so much at one time, but [he'd] written words that [he] never knew were in the world" (*paragraph 5*).

   Besides improving one's vocabulary and, consequently, one's ability to read different types of books, what can be the impact of learning words that one never knew existed before? How can such "discoveries" open up "new world[s]" (*paragraph 7*)?

4. Despite the fact that he was in prison, Malcolm X said that when he learned how to read, he "never had been so truly free in [his] life" (*paragraph 7*). What did he mean? What makes a person feel free? How can someone be in prison and feel free? Does reading make you feel free? Why or why not?

The 42nd Street Library in New York

LINKING READINGS ONE AND TWO

Work in groups of four. Role-play an interview with Jonathan Kozol and Malcolm X about educational issues. Two journalists ask the questions suggested below.

Fill in the chart to prepare for the role-play. The group should add one or two "journalist's questions" and answer all questions based on information in Readings One and Two .

	JOURNALIST'S QUESTION	JONATHAN KOZOL'S ANSWER	MALCOLM X'S ANSWER
1.	Do you believe that education leads to freedom?	"Yes I do. Education provides our young people with opportunities for better jobs and more freedom of choice in life."	"Yes I do. When I taught myself to read in prison, I never felt freer in my life. Reading gave me intellectual and spiritual freedom even though I was in prison."
2.	Do you believe that children who don't go to good schools might end up in prison?		
3.	If the schools aren't good, should people teach themselves?		
4.			
5.			

Now role-play the interview.

A Warm-Up

Work with a partner. Match the words with their meanings.

_____ 1. shiftless   a. sad

_____ 2. egotistical   b. very strong

_____ 3. dejected   c. mysterious, difficult to explain

_____ 4. intense   d. lazy

_____ 5. enigmatic   e. self-centered

B Reading Strategy

Understanding Most Important Idea from Last Paragraph

Reading the **last paragraph (*conclusion*) first** is sometimes a very effective way of seeing where the author is going with his or her story or argument. It can be very helpful in **understanding the most important idea** of a text.

First, read the last paragraph of the reading. Then read the beginning of the text and think about the author's idea in telling you about this part of his life. Write this idea on the line.

_____

Now read the whole text from beginning to end to find out if you got this idea right.

Where I Learned to Read

By Salvatore Scibona

1   I did my best to flunk out of high school. I failed English literature, American literature, Spanish, pre-calculus, chemistry, physics. Once, I burned my report card in the sink of the KFC where I worked. The television stayed on day and night, singing like a Siren[1] in the crowded house. "Come sit by me and die a little," it said.

2   Sometimes, to break my addiction to the tube, I used to read or, anyway, swing my eyes over the pages of library books. As long as nobody had assigned the book, I could **stick with it**. I didn't know what I was reading. I didn't really know *how* to read. Reading messed with my brain in an **unaccountable** way. It made me happy, or something.

---

[1] *Siren:* In Greek mythology, Sirens were bird-women whose enchanting voices lured sailors to their deaths.

3   Early senior year, a girl in homeroom passed me a brochure that a college had sent her. The college's **curriculum** was an **outrage**. No electives. Not a single book in the **seminar** list by a living author. However, no tests. No grades, unless you asked to see them. No textbooks — I was confused. In place of an astronomy manual, you would read Copernicus.[2] No books about Aristotle,[3] just Aristotle. Like, you would read *book*-books. The Great Books, so called, though I had never heard of most of them. I loved this whole beautiful idea. I would scrap everything (or so I usefully believed) and go to that place [St. John's College] and ask them to let me in.

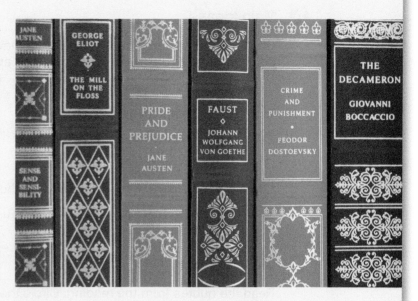

4   Loans. Grants[4] from the college and the government. Jobs from asbestos remover[5] to library clerk. I carried bricks and mortar to rooftops during the summers, but if I hadn't made time to read the night before, my legs wore out by noon. Even my body needed to read.

---

[2] *Copernicus:* Polish astronomer (1473–1543); first to demonstrate that Earth and other planets rotate around the Sun

[3] *Aristotle:* Greek philosopher (384–322 B.C.), student of Plato; one of the founders of Western philosophy

[4] *grant:* an amount of money given to someone by an organization for a particular purpose; does not have to be paid back

[5] *asbestos remover:* Asbestos was used as building insulation against fire; it was found to cause cancer and had to be removed.

5   On weekends, I hung out with my friends. The surprise, the wild luck: I had friends. One sat in my room with a beer and Hegel's *The Phenomenology of Spirit*,[6] reading out a sentence at a time and stopping to ask, "All right, what did that mean?" The **gravity** of the whole thing would have been laughable if it hadn't been so much fun, and if it hadn't been such a gift to find my tribe.

6   In retrospect, I was a sad little boy and a standard-issue, **shiftless**, **egotistical**, **dejected** teen-ager. Everything was going to hell, and then these strangers let me come to their school and showed me how to read. **All things considered**, every year since has been a more intense and **enigmatic** joy.

---

[6] *Hegel:* German philosopher (1770–1831); revolutionized European philosophy

COMPREHENSION

A **Main Ideas**

Check (✓) the statements that express a main idea the author wishes to communicate in the reading. Discuss your answers with a partner.

☐ **1.** Every student deserves a chance.

☐ **2.** Reading can change a life.

☐ **3.** High school is a terrible place.

☐ **4.** There are many types of pleasure.

☐ **5.** Students learn to read better when they are motivated.

☐ **6.** An educational institution can be unusual and still successful.

B **Close Reading**

Read the quotes from the reading. Circle the statement that best explains each quote. Share your answers with a partner.

1. "The television stayed on day and night, singing like a Siren in the crowded house. 'Come sit by me and die a little,' it said." (*paragraph 1*)

   a. According to the author, television made him feel better.

   b. According to the author, television is a dead end.

2. "As long as nobody had assigned the book, I could stick with it. I didn't know what I was reading." (*paragraph 2*)

   a. Scibona would only try to read books he had chosen for himself.

   b. Scibona gave himself the chance to read the assigned books.

3. "Reading messed with my brain in an unaccountable way. It made me happy, or something." (*paragraph 2*)

   a. Reading confused the author for some unknown reason.

   b. Reading brought him pleasure for some unknown reason.

4. "Like, you would read *book*-books. The Great Books, so called, though I had never heard of most of them. I loved this whole beautiful idea." (*paragraph 3*)

   a. Scibona hungered for some knowledge he couldn't explain.

   b. Scibona wanted to go to college so he could get a job.

5. "I carried bricks and mortar to rooftops during the summers, but if I hadn't made time to read the night before, my legs wore out by noon. Even my body needed to read." (*paragraph 4*)

   a. Reading was necessary for his summer job.

   b. Reading became essential for his existence.

VOCABULARY

 Synonyms

Complete the summary of Salvatore Scibona's college experience with the words and idioms from the box. Use the synonym or paraphrase in parentheses to help you select the correct word or idiom. Compare answers with a partner.

all things considered	egotistical	seminar	unaccountable
curriculum	enigmatic	shiftless	
dejected	gravity	stick with it	

Salvatore Scibona was very impressed with the _____*curriculum*_____
                        1. (program of courses)

at St. John's College. This unconventional college with its emphasis on Great

Books and primary sources, along with its policy of no electives, no tests, and no

grades, was indeed a total shock to his ideas of a proper education, but in a good

way. He did not know why the description of this school inspired him, but for

some _____ reason, he decided not to let the opportunity
      2. (difficult to explain)

go to waste, and he applied. Despite the fact that his high school record reflected

the unsatisfactory work of a _____, irresponsible,
                      3. (lazy)

_____, and _____ teenager, the
    4. (self-centered)   **5. (sad)**

Admissions Office decided to take a chance on him, and he was accepted.

Right from the start, Scibona understood the intense focus on the

reading experience that characterized studies at St. John's. He knew that

he would be held responsible for all the readings assigned, but he was

determined to _____ and not give up. Students
          6. (keep trying)

read great works of philosophy and literature from the Western tradition.

As an active participant in the learning process at the college, he came to

appreciate the _____ of the ideas he was asked to
         7. (seriousness)

discuss at each _____ he attended. After the
    8. (class meeting for small groups of students)

_____ qualities of each difficult text were questioned,
    9. (mysterious)

analyzed, and finally understood, he realized the joy that an education can bring.

_____, going to St. John's was the best experience of his life.
  10. (Taking everything into account)

B Word Forms

1 Fill in the chart with the correct word forms. Use a dictionary if necessary. An **X** indicates there is no form in that category.

	Noun	Adjective
1.	curriculum	curricular
2.		dejected
3.		egotistical
4.		enigmatic
5.	gravity	
6.	outrage	
7.	seminar	X
8.	X	unaccountable

2 Complete the sentences with the correct form of the words. Choose from the two forms (noun, adjective) in parentheses.

1. Finding a way to reduce inequalities in education is a great _____enigma_____.
   (enigma / enigmatic)

2. The consequences of educational problems could be very _____
   (gravity / grave)

   for the United States in the global market.

3. Our youth might end up in a _____ state without any
   (dejection / dejected)

   prospects for the future.

4. In such an _____ situation, more and more social
   (outrage / outrageous)

   problems would develop.

5. That's why a revision of the public school _____ is
   (curriculum / curricular)

   urgently needed.

NOTE-TAKING: Identifying Important Details

Go back to the conclusion of the reading. The sentences in that last paragraph review the author's journey from *high school* to *college* to his *post-college* years. Use these sentences as a frame for note-taking as you reread the text. First circle the important details. Then write appropriate explanatory notes here, in the respective sections.

High School	"I was a sad little boy and a standard-issue, shiftless, egotistical, dejected teen-ager. Everything was going to hell." *Failed major courses . . .*
College	"Then these strangers let me come to their school and showed me how to read."
Post-College	"All things considered, every year since has been a more intense and enigmatic joy."

Now discuss these questions with a partner.

1. Do you have the same amount of notes for each section? Which section leaves a lot of room for your imagination? Why?

2. Is every part of the reading now clear to you? If not, what aspects of the reading do you still not understand? Write down questions that you would like to discuss with a partner.

Discuss the questions in a small group. Be prepared to share your answers with the class.

1. Why does Scibona fear the TV? Why did he leave it on all the time as a young man?

2. Below are some examples of "Great Books." Match them with their subject matter. Some books will fit into more than one category. See answers below.

__d__ **1.** Plato: *Dialogues*		**a.** literature
_____ **2.** Shakespeare: *Romeo and Juliet*		**b.** science
_____ **3.** Machiavelli: *The Prince*		**c.** politics
_____ **4.** Galileo: *The Starry Messenger*		**d.** philosophy
_____ **5.** Jane Austen: *Pride and Prejudice*		
_____ **6.** Hegel: *Phenomenology of Spirit*		
_____ **7.** Dickens: *A Tale of Two Cities*		
_____ **8.** Darwin: *On the Origin of the Species*		
_____ **9.** John Stuart Mill: *On Liberty*		
_____ **10.** Freud: *The Interpretation of Dreams*		
_____ **11.** Tolstoy: *War and Peace*		

Why did Scibona feel so excited about reading some of these books? Would you want to read any of them? Would you enjoy taking a course in which you sat around and discussed ideas from these books in a small group? Would this be a good education in your opinion?

3. Reading consists of sweeping your eyes across a page and understanding the symbols in your brain. Why is it so pleasurable for some? Why do you think every year is now a "more intense and enigmatic joy" for Scibona? What might reading bring you?

4. What kind of "tribe" did Scibona find in college? Why was this so important to him?

ANSWERS:
1. d **2.** a **3.** c, d **4.** b **5.** a **6.** d **7.** a **8.** b **9.** c, d **10.** b **11.** a

BRINGING IT ALL TOGETHER

Work in groups of three or four. Discuss each quotation to explain what it means. Th
decide how Kozol, Malcolm X, and Scibona would respond to it. Be prepared to shar
your point(s) of view with the class. Use some of the vocabulary from the chapter (for
complete list, go to page 210).

1. "It is not the biggest, the brightest or the best that will survive, but those who
   adapt the quickest."

   — *Charles Darwin, English naturalist, 1809–1882*

2. "A mind is not a vessel to be filled but a fire to be ignited."

   — *Plutarch, Greek historian and biographer, 46–120* A.D.

3. "It was in making education not only common to all, but in some sense
   compulsory on all, that the destiny of . . . America . . . was practically settled."

   — *James Russell Lowell, American poet and diplomat, 1819–1891*

4. "It is only the ignorant who despise education."

   — *Publilius Syrus, Latin writer, 1st century* B.C.

5. "The direction in which education starts a man will determine his future life."

   — *Plato, Greek philosopher, 429–347* B.C.

WRITING ACTIVITY

Write a report about a book you read or were forced to read. Answer these questions:
- Did you like the book or not?
- What did reading the book bring to you?
- Did you experience Scibona's "intense and enigmatic joy"? Why or why not?

Use at least five of the words and idioms you studied in the chapter.

DISCUSSION AND WRITING TOPICS

Discuss these topics in a small group. Choose one of them and write a paragraph or
two about it. Use the vocabulary from the chapter.

1. How could more funding make schools better? Give some concrete examples.
   Use your experience as a guide.

2. If Malcolm X was able to teach himself to read, why do we need schools to
   educate people? Is there a danger in having a society of only self-taught people?

3. Why is it important for a free society to have good public schools?

4. Would you recommend that future teachers be asked to read Kozol, Malcolm X,
   and Scibona? What could they learn from these writers about their job
   as teachers?

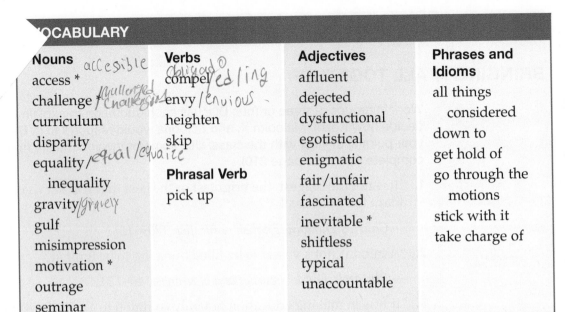

VOCABULARY

Nouns	Verbs	Adjectives	Phrases and Idioms
access * *accesible*	compel *compelled/ing* *obliged*	affluent	all things considered
challenge * *challenged/challenging*	envy / *envious*	dejected	down to
curriculum	heighten	dysfunctional	get hold of
disparity	skip	egotistical	go through the motions
equality / *equal/equalize*		enigmatic	stick with it
inequality	**Phrasal Verb**	fair / unfair	take charge of
gravity / *gravely*	pick up	fascinated	
gulf		inevitable *	
misimpression		shiftless	
motivation *		typical	
outrage		unaccountable	
seminar			

. * = AWL (Academic Word List) item

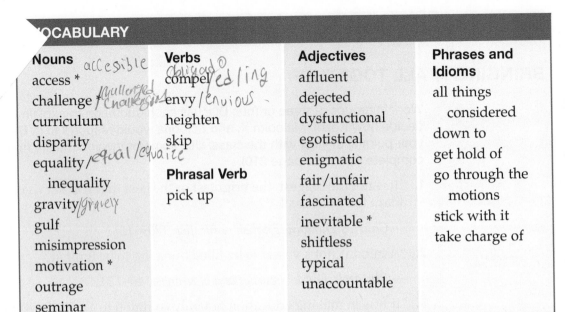

(handwritten margin notes: -ly, -sure, -ed, -ing, -ence, -ness)

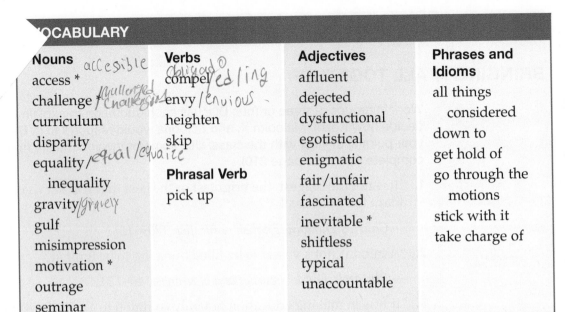

SELF-ASSESSMENT

In this chapter you learned to:

○ Identify the issues from the first paragraph of an essay

○ Understand the most important idea by reading the last paragraph first

○ Skim a text by reading the topic sentences

○ Understand and use synonyms, antonyms, and different word forms

○ Guess the meaning of words from the context and use them in a new context

○ Use dictionary entries to learn the meanings of words

○ Use note-taking to summarize an argument and identify important details

What can you do well? ☑

What do you need to practice more? ☑

SOCIOLOGY:
Crime and Punishment

SOCIOLOGY: the scientific study of societies and the behavior of people in groups

OBJECTIVES

To read academic texts, you need to master certain skills.

In this chapter, you will:

- Predict the content of a text from the first sentence or title and subheadings

- Deal with difficult scientific names

- Guess the meaning of words from the context

- Understand and use synonyms, suffixes, "scientific" verbs, different word forms, and words of different intensity

- Use dictionary entries to learn the meanings of words

- Take notes using a map outline to remember details

- Write a summary to understand main ideas and remember details

A Consider These Questions

Discuss the questions with a partner.

1. Have you ever been the victim of a crime?

2. Are there ways to avoid becoming a victim of crime?

3. Most people in society are not criminals. Criminals deviate (or differ) from normal behavior. Why do you think some people fall into criminal behavior?

4. How does society punish deviant behavior such as criminality? Are all offenders treated equally, or do some escape harsh punishment? How?

A burglar

B Crime Words

Read the definitions of the words in bold.

- **burglary:** the crime of entering a building to steal things
- **correctional institution:** a prison or place where people are sent as punishment for crimes (also a "penal institution" from "penalty" or punishment)
- **counterfeiting:** copying something (money, handbags, etc.) exactly in order to deceive people
- **homicide:** the crime of murder
- **incarceration:** the state of being kept in prison
- **inmate:** someone who is kept in a prison or a mental hospital
- **offender:** someone who is guilty of a crime
- **recidivism:** a tendency to go back to criminal activity even after spending time in prison
- **rehabilitation:** a program that restores a person to a useful or healthy life

Now match the words with their meanings.

_i_	1. burglar	a.	a lawbreaker
___	2. correctional institution	b.	fake
___	3. counterfeit	c.	put in prison
___	4. homicide	d.	reform or cure someone
___	5. incarcerate	e.	a repeat offender
___	6. inmate	f.	a prisoner
___	7. offender	g.	killing someone
___	8. recidivist	h.	a jail
___	9. rehabilitate	i.	someone who robs houses

READING ONE: The Global Context

Ⓐ Warm-Up

Discuss the questions in a small group. Share your answers with the class.

1. Which countries do you think would rank in the top ten in terms of high crime rates?

2. Would the United States be in the top ten with the highest crime rates?

3. Are some countries safer than others? Can you think of why?

Ⓑ Reading Strategy

Predicting Content from First Sentence

The **first sentence** usually tells us the **topic** of the text. You can predict the content of a text by reading its first sentence.

The reading is a passage from a sociology textbook. Underline its first sentence and write it on the line.

_____

Discuss the questions with a partner.

1. Why would a sociology textbook want to discuss crime in a global context?

2. What do you think the reading is about?

Now read the text to find out if your prediction was correct.

THE GLOBAL CONTEXT

By Linda A. Mooney, David Knox, Caroline Schacht, from *Understanding Social Problems*

1 Several facts about crime are true all over the world. First, crime is **ubiquitous** — there is no country where crime does not exist. Second, most countries have the same components in their criminal justice systems: police, courts, and prisons. Third, adult males make up the largest category of crime suspects worldwide; and fourth, in all countries, stealing is the most common crime committed, whereas violent crime is a relatively rare event.

2 Even so, **dramatic** differences do exist in international crime rates. First, the United States does not have the highest crime rate in the world. The United States ranks 12th among 165 nations, with Sweden, Denmark, Australia, and Great Britain in rank order each having a higher crime rate than the United States.

3 In the category of violent crime, the United States is once again not in the top ten. Several **developing countries** (Namibia and Swaziland) as well as **developed countries** (Australia and Sweden) have higher crime rates than the United States. Property crimes show a similar pattern. The United States ranks 13th in property crimes (car theft, burglary, and larceny[1]) with Sweden, Denmark, Australia, and Great Britain topping the list.

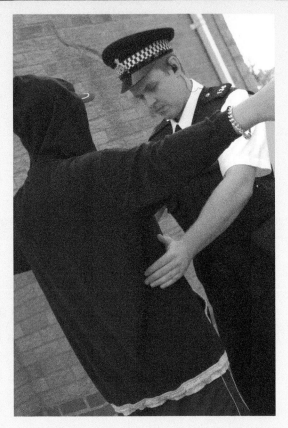

4 Violent crime and property crimes represent just two types of crimes that take place worldwide. Although we are concerned about these types of crimes and the possibility of victimization, Interpol[2] has identified six global priority areas:
1. fighting drugs and criminal organizations (e.g. drug trafficking)
2. going after financial and high-tech crimes (e.g. counterfeiting, business and financial fraud, and cybercrime)
3. finding fugitives[3]
4. **countering** terrorism
5. stopping the trafficking of human beings
6. fighting corruption (e.g. enforcing the rule of law)

5 Each of these priority areas contains a relatively new category of crimes — **transnational** crime. As defined by the U.S. Department of Justice, "transnational crime" is "organized criminal activity across one or more national borders." Human trafficking for sexual exploitation, forced labor, and child soldiers are other examples of transnational crimes.

---

[1] *larceny:* the crime of stealing

[2] *Interpol:* an international police organization that helps national police forces catch criminals

[3] *fugitive:* someone who is trying to avoid being caught, especially by the police

COMPREHENSION

A Main Ideas

Read each statement. Decide if it is *True* or *False* according to the reading. Check (✓) the appropriate box. If it is false, change it to make it true. Discuss your answers with a partner.

	TRUE	FALSE
1. According to the data in this reading, the United States has a higher general crime rate than Sweden, Denmark, Australia, and Great Britain.	☐	☐
2. According to the same sources, the United States has a higher violent crime rate than Sweden and Australia.	☐	☐
3. Women in every country are less likely to commit crimes than men.	☐	☐
4. In recent years, violent crime has been the priority for Interpol.	☐	☐
5. Transnational crime is a new category of crime that has been given priority status.	☐	☐

B Close Reading

Read the quotes from the reading. Circle the statement that best explains each quote. Share your answers with a partner.

1. "Dramatic differences do exist in international crime rates." (*paragraph 2*)

   a. Crime is different all over the world.

   b. Crime rates are different all over the world.

2. "The United States ranks 12th among 165 nations, with Sweden, Denmark, Australia, and Great Britain in rank order each having a higher crime rate than the United States." (*paragraph 2*)

   a. Great Britain has more crime than the United States.

   b. Denmark has less crime than Great Britain.

3. "Violent crime and property crimes represent just two types of crimes that take place worldwide. Although we are concerned about these types of crimes and the possibility of victimization, Interpol has identified six global priority areas." (*paragraph 4*)

   a. Both property crime and violent crime get the most attention from Interpol.

   b. Neither property crime nor violent crime gets the most attention from Interpol.

VOCABULARY

A Guessing from Context

One way to guess the meaning of an unknown word in a reading is to look for a **definition** within the reading. Another way is to look for **examples** that would give you an idea of what the word means.

- There has been a **dramatic** decrease in crime rates in New York City in the past ten years. This remarkable decline is considered to be partly the result of new policing techniques in the city. The New York City Police Department has been praised for its success in lowering the crime rate in the nation's largest city. In 2001, there were 649 murders in the city compared with 329 murders in 2010; this represents a 50 percent drop in a ten-year period.

LOOK FOR A DEFINITION:
The "**dramatic**" decrease is "remarkable." It is a positive decrease (a "success"), one for which the Police Department "has been praised."

LOOK FOR EXAMPLES:
With the statistics given — of a 50 percent drop in the murder rate in ten years — it is clear that the word "**dramatic**" refers to something that is very impressive.

Guess the meaning of each word or phrase by going back to the reading and finding a *definition* or an *example* for it. Check (✓) the appropriate box. Then write the definition or example(s) on the first line and your guess on the second line. Compare answers with a partner.

	DEFINITION	**EXAMPLE**
1. **ubiquitous** (*paragraph 1*)	☐	☐

D/E: _____

Guess: _____

| 2. **developing countries** (*paragraph 3*) | ☐ | ☐ |

D/E: _____

Guess: _____

| 3. **developed countries** (*paragraph 3*) | ☐ | ☐ |

D/E: _____

Guess: _____

| 4. **transnational** (*paragraph 5*) | ☐ | ☐ |

D/E: _____

Guess: _____

B Using the Dictionary

Read the dictionary entries for the word *counter*.

> **counter** *v.* **1** to react to a statement, criticism, argument, action etc. by saying or doing something that will prove the statement is not true or that will have an opposite effect **2** to do something to reduce the bad effects of something or to defend yourself against them
>
> **counter** *adv.* against [something]
>
> **counter** *n.* **1** a flat surface in a kitchen or store where you work or prepare food **2** a flat narrow surface where you are served or where you pay in a bank or store **3** a piece of electrical equipment that counts something
>
> **counter** *prefix* **1** the opposite of something **2** given as a reaction to something **3** matching something

Now read each sentence. Decide which word form is being used and what its specific meaning is. Write the name of the word form and the number of the appropriate definition.

_____prefix (2)_____ **a.** The **counter**terrorism task force is organizing defense for the region.

_____ **b.** To **counter** the tendency to recidivism, prisons have set up new programs to help inmates.

_____ **c.** The lawyer **countered** the accusation against his client by calling a witness who said his client was at home at the time of the crime.

_____ **d.** Some bank robbers go right up to the bank **counter** to threaten the employee and demand money.

_____ **e.** It runs **counter** to American law to allow child labor.

_____ **f.** The inspector told us that the $50 bills were all **counter**feit.[1]

C Gradations of Intensity

How intense is the growth? Give a number to each one, with *1* being least intense and *5* being most intense. Discuss with a partner. Some disagreement is possible.

__1__ **slight** growth

_____ **explosive** growth

_____ **significant** growth

_____ **considerable** growth

_____ **dramatic** growth

---

[1] *counterfeit:* from the French words "contre" and "faire," meaning "made in opposition to the real thing"

CRITICAL THINKING

Discuss the questions in a small group. Be prepared to share your answers with the class.

1. The authors repeatedly state that the United States is NOT in the top 10 crime-ridden countries. What did the authors expect readers to think? Why do Americans often think they live in the most crime-ridden country in the world?

2. What are some factors that could explain why males commit more crimes than females all over the world?

3. Why is Interpol more concerned about terrorism and trafficking than ordinary violent crimes or property crimes?

READING TWO: Sociological Theories of Crime

Ⓐ Warm-Up

Why do some people commit crimes? Read the different explanations.

There are *psychological* explanations that focus on the individual personalities of offenders, unhealthy relationships, and mental illness. There are also *biological* studies that focus on the role of stress hormones, nervous system problems, and genetic predispositions. *Sociological* theories of crime, on the other hand, focus on social problems and environmental factors leading to criminal behavior.

Which of these types of explanations do you agree with? Discuss with a partner. Circle your answer(s).

a. psychological

b. biological

c. sociological

Ⓑ Reading Strategy

Dealing with Difficult Scientific Names

Don't worry about the complicated names that some scientists use. As you read a scientific text like this one, just think of the **perspectives** as "A" and "B" and "C," for example, and think of the **theories** as "1," "2," "3," and so on. Later, after you have finished reading and have gotten a general idea of the text, you can think about the names, look up the definitions of some of the terms, and take notes with the correct names.

Look at the reading. Write *A, B, C* next to each perspective, and write *1, 2, 3* above each theory. Share your answers with a partner.

Now read the text to find out more about each perspective and each theory.

SOCIOLOGICAL THEORIES OF CRIME

By Linda A. Mooney, David Knox, Caroline Schacht, from *Understanding Social Problems*

Structural-Functionalist Perspective

1   According to Emile Durkheim,[1] and other **structural functionalists**, crime serves a function in society. One of the functions of crime is that it unites the rest of society against the criminal. The criminal violates the rules of behavior that the rest of the society respects. When people come together to express their anger about the crime, they develop tighter **bonds** of **solidarity** and unity.

2   Crime can also lead to social change. For example, a crime may lead to improvements in laws and public services. It may make the police more **responsive** to citizens, and create partnerships with business to improve conditions and to make reforms.

3   Two of the major theories of crime that have come from structural functionalism are "strain theory" and "control theory." **Strain theory** was developed by Robert Merton. It uses Durkheim's concept of *anomie:* the absence of **norms** to guide people's behavior. Merton argued that when the structure of society doesn't permit people to reach their goals (such as obtaining enough money to live on), the strain (or tension) that results may lead to crime. Society encourages everyone to want the same things (a job, money) but doesn't provide opportunities for everyone.

4   Strain theory explains criminal behavior as a result of blocked opportunities. However, if blocked opportunities are responsible for crime, why don't more people become

Emile Durkheim

criminals? **Control theory** may answer that question. Hirschi (1969) suggests that strong **social bonds** prevent people from violating social norms or rules. A crucial aspect of these social ties is attachment to other people. Ford (2005), using data from the National Youth Survey, concludes that a strong family bond lowers the **likelihood** of substance abuse (drugs and alcohol) and criminal behavior among young people. Bell (2009) reports that weaker attachment to parents is associated with a greater likelihood of gang membership for both males and females.

(continued on next page)

---

[1] *Emile Durkheim:* a French university professor (1858–1917) who helped to establish the principles of sociology

Conflict Perspective

5   **Conflict theories** of crime suggest that deviance[2] is inevitable whenever two groups have different degrees of power in society. The more inequality there is in a society, the greater the crime rate in that society. Social inequality leads individuals to commit crimes such as larceny and burglary as a means of economic survival. Other individuals, who are angry and frustrated by their low position in society, express their rage and frustration through crimes such as drug use, violence, and **homicide**. Rather than viewing law as something that protects all members of society, conflict theorists focus on how laws are created by those in power to protect themselves and their interests.

Symbolic Interactionist Perspective

6   Two important theories of crime come from the symbolic interactionist perspective. The first, **labeling theory**, focuses on what happens when someone is **labeled** a criminal.

---

[2] **deviance:** behavior that is different from what is considered normal or acceptable

Being officially described as a deviant or criminal often leads a person to further criminal behavior because he or she may be **denied** opportunities for engaging in positive behavior. The labeled person may be expelled from school or be unable to get work. In addition, he or she may **internalize** the judgment: being a criminal becomes the major definition of his or her personality.

7   In **differential association theory**, Edwin Sutherland proposed that through interaction with others, individuals learn the values and attitudes associated with crime as well as the techniques and motivations for criminal behavior. Individuals who are more exposed to the idea that laws exist to be broken ("crime pays") rather than the idea that laws should be obeyed ("do the crime, you'll do the time") are more likely to engage in criminal activity. Thus, children who see their parents benefit from crime or who live in high crime neighborhoods where success is associated with illegal behavior are more likely to engage in criminal behavior.

COMPREHENSION

Ⓐ Main Ideas

Complete the sentences according to your understanding of the reading.

1. According to Durkheim, crime has two functions in society: _____

   _____

2. *Anomie* is a feeling of being lost because _____

   _____

3. According to Merton's "strain theory," _____

   _____

4. Not everyone facing blocked opportunities falls into crime; control theory

explains that _____.

5. Conflict theory says that crime is _____

_____.

6. Labeling a person a criminal after a misdeed will _____

_____.

7. A person is more likely to engage in criminal activities when he or she _____

_____.

B Close Reading

Read the quotes from the reading. Circle the statement that best explains each quote. Share your answers with a partner.

1. "The criminal violates the rules of behavior that the rest of society respects. When people come together to express their anger about the crime, they develop tighter bonds of solidarity and unity." (*paragraph 1*)

   One could generalize from this statement that . . .

   a. collective anger can be a unifying force in society.

   b. criminal behavior tears society apart because it victimizes people.

   c. criminals commit antisocial acts that put society in danger.

2. "[Strain theory] uses Durkheim's concept of *anomie:* the absence of norms to guide people's behavior." (*paragraph 3*)

   One might infer from what is said here that . . .

   a. people do not have to be taught to distinguish right from wrong.

   b. when society's values break down, people feel unstable.

   c. a free society can be dangerous.

3. "Conflict theories of crime suggest that deviance is inevitable whenever two groups have different degrees of power in society. The more inequality there is in a society, the greater the crime rate in that society." (*paragraph 5*)

   Based on this statement alone, we might be comfortable saying that conflict theorists . . .

   a. blame the poor for the crimes they commit.

   b. believe that capitalism's free-market economy can cure all social problems.

   c. believe that capitalism's injustices create criminals.

(continued on next page)

4. "Through interaction with others, individuals learn the values and attitudes associated with crime as well as the techniques and motivations for criminal behavior." (*paragraph 7*)

This statement about the differential association theory shows that the symbolic interactionist perspective . . .

   a. places an emphasis on the positive and negative effects of our relationships with others.

   b. explains criminal behavior as a separate force that has nothing to do with our interpersonal relations.

   c. sees the source of criminal behavior in human differences.

VOCABULARY

Ⓐ Guessing from Context

Look at the list of words or phrases from the reading. Locate each word or phrase in the reading and try to guess its meaning from the context clues. Write down the clues, your guess, and then the dictionary meaning. Was your guess correct?

1. **solidarity**
   (*paragraph 1*)

   Clues: *come together / develop tighter bonds / unity*

   Guess: *a feeling of loyalty, sympathy, and community*

   Dictionary: *loyalty and general agreement between all the people in a group*

2. **norms**
   (*paragraph 3*)

   Clues: _____

   Guess: _____

   Dictionary: _____

3. **social bonds**
   (*paragraph 4*)

   Clues: _____

   Guess: _____

   Dictionary: _____

4. **labeled**
   (*paragraph 6*)

   Clues: _____

   Guess: _____

   Dictionary: _____

5. **internalize**
   (*paragraph 6*)

   Clues: _____

   Guess: _____

   Dictionary: _____

B Synonyms

Complete the essay with the words from the box. Use the synonym in parentheses to help you select the correct word. Compare answers with a partner.

bonds	internalized	likelihood	solidarity
denied	label (v.)	responsive	

The Social Cost of White Collar Crime

The sociologist Edwin Sutherland was the first to _____ label _____

1. (call)

a crime a "white collar crime." In a speech given to the American Sociological Society

in 1939, he referred to white collar criminals as "respectable people" who violate

our laws by manipulating stocks on Wall Street, giving bribes for business, creating

pollution, and so on. Today other crimes such as computer and corporate crimes

have joined the category. Since in all _____ the person who

2. (probability)

commits a white collar crime will hold a powerful position in society, we may have

to change our ideas about which criminals do the most damage in society.

According to the Federal Bureau of Investigation, it is estimated that white collar

crime costs the United States more than $300 billion annually. However, it is crucial

to understand that the social costs of white collar crime are not only monetary but

psychological and moral as well. For many different reasons, the justice system is not

as _____ to the harm done by white collar crimes as it is to

3. (ready to react)

the harm done by street crimes: White collar offenders almost never go to jail, even

though the average dollar loss of their crimes is much greater than the losses from

street crime. Poor people are _____ the same opportunity to

4. (refused)

get a good lawyer as rich people. As a result, the idea that people with power can

get away with the crimes they commit has become _____

5. (part of the thinking)

by most people in society. In addition, we have created a society lacking in

_____ between people from different social classes because

6. (loyalty)

the justice system has permitted a certain kind of financial lawlessness to exist

without punishment. This has loosened social _____ .

7. (ties)

C Suffix: -cide/-icide/-ocide

> The suffix *-cide/-icide/-ocide* means "killing."
>
> **EXAMPLE:**
> homicide = murder (the killing of a human being—*homo* in Latin)

Write the meanings of these kinds of crimes. Use the meanings of the Latin roots (in parentheses) for help.

1. fratricide _____ (*frater* = brother)

2. genocide _____ (*genus* = people)

3. matricide _____ (*mater* = mother)

4. patricide _____ (*pater* = father)

5. suicide _____ (*sui* = self)

D Verbs for Presenting Theories, Giving Reasons, and Explaining

1 When social scientists (sociologists, psychologists) present theories, they may argue that / suggest that / propose that their theories are valid.

Find three sentences in the reading using *argued that / suggests that / proposed that*. Write them on the lines.

a. _____

_____

b. _____

c. _____

_____

2 When social scientists (sociologists, psychologists) do an experiment, they may report / show / demonstrate their findings or conclude from the data. *

Find sentences with two of these verbs in the reading. Write them on the lines.

a. _____

_____

b. _____

_____

---

*In the social sciences, the word *prove* is rarely used. We can "prove" that water boils, and a lawyer can "prove" that his client was not at the scene of the crime. But we cannot "prove" that one theory of crime is absolutely correct. That is why there are many different "perspectives" on crime in the reading.

NOTE-TAKING: Making a Map Outline

Go back to the reading and read it again. Use this map outline as you read to take notes. Write the name of the sociologist who represents each theory (if a name has been given) and what each theory proposes. Share your answers with a partner. This note-taking technique is a good way to study for an exam.

A. STRUCTURAL-FUNCTIONALIST PERSPECTIVE

Sociologist: _Durkheim_

Functions of crime: (1) _unites the rest of society_ ; (2) _leads to social change_

Strain Theory

Sociologist: _____

Cause of crime: _____

_____

Control Theory

Sociologist: _____

Cause of crime: _____

_____

B. CONFLICT PERSPECTIVE

Conflict Theories

Sociologist: _____

Cause of crime: _____

_____

C. SYMBOLIC INTERACTIONIST PERSPECTIVE

Labeling Theory

Sociologist: _____

Cause of crime: _____

_____

Differential Association Theory

Sociologist: _____

Cause of crime: _____

_____

CRITICAL THINKING

Read each situation, and discuss in a small group which perspective or theory the information supports. Be prepared to share your ideas with the class.

1. After the economic crash in 2008, the unemployment rate was 37% for people in their twenties. This has stopped many young people from finding jobs and starting careers. Some may become desperate.

2. A Hollywood actor or actress will serve a few weeks or months at most for committing the same drug crime that may cost a poor person many years in prison.

3. The public has been informed about domestic violence against women and child abuse. Laws have been passed to protect women and children.

4. A young person caught using drugs can either be encouraged to change or be led to adopt the persona of a "druggie" depending on how he or she is treated.

5. Getting into the wrong crowd and having friends who are always bragging about illegal activities can lead a person into criminal behavior more easily.

6. Despite the challenges of extreme poverty, there are many poor children who have loving and caring parents and attentive teachers. These children have very good prospects for the future.

LINKING READINGS ONE AND TWO

Work in a group of four to complete the chart on page 227 in the context of this scenario.

> **SCENARIO**
> You have been appointed to an international commission that has been formed to fight some transnational crimes that have become international law enforcement agencies' top priority (Reading One). The commission seeks the advice of expert sociologists in this initiative.

For each transnational crime, write the proposal a given theorist might make to eliminate the specific crime from the world stage. Review the explanations for the theories in Reading Two as you consider your replies.

	CRIME	EXPERT	EXPERT'S PROPOSAL TO ELIMINATE TRANSNATIONAL CRIMES
1.	Drug trafficking	Control theorist	The way to eliminate drug trafficking is to eliminate the market. We have to reverse the trend of dysfunctional families and start rebuilding family ties. If we succeed, family bonds will be strengthened, and substance abuse will no longer be as much of a temptation.
2.	Financial fraud	Differential association theorist	
3.	Fugitives fleeing justice	Conflict theorist	
4.	Trafficking of women and children	Structural functionalist	
5.	Corruption	Strain theorist	

Ⓐ Warm-Up

Discuss the question with a partner.

There are several reasons we send criminals to prison: (1) to protect society; (2) to punish them for deviant behavior; and (3) to rehabilitate them so they will change their lives. Which reason do you think is the most important?

Ⓑ Reading Strategy

Predicting Content from Title and Subheadings

Predicting or getting some idea of the content of a text before you start reading will help you improve your reading speed and comprehension. The **title and subheadings** of a text can help you **predict or guess its content**.

Look at the title of the reading and then at the subheadings that follow. What do you think will be the main point of each paragraph? Write your predictions on the lines. Share your answers with a partner.

PARAGRAPH 1: _Prisoners can take part in programs that will help them change their lives._

PARAGRAPH 2: _____

PARAGRAPH 3: _____

PARAGRAPH 4: _____

PARAGRAPH 5: _____

PARAGRAPH 6: _____

Now read the text to find out if your predictions were correct.

PRISON PROGRAMS THAT WORK

By Linda A. Mooney, David Knox, Caroline Schacht, from *Understanding Social Problems*

1   An estimated 1.7 million people are behind bars in the United States, adding to the **skyrocketing** cost of corrections. Each of the following correctional practices has been evaluated and found to be associated with positive changes in the inmates who participate. The programs reduce recidivism rates, **enhance** self-esteem, lower aggression, and increase the possibility of employment after prison. These programs are not only cost-effective, they are humane.

Puppies Behind Bars (PBB)

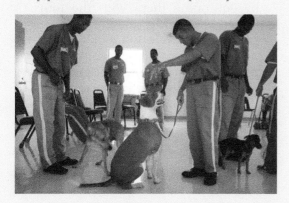

2   Puppies Behind Bars was discussed on the Oprah Winfrey television show. It works like this. For 16 months puppies live in a prison cell with an inmate-trainer who teaches them basic obedience skills. At the end of that time, the dogs are **evaluated** to see if they can become service dogs for the disabled or bomb squad dogs for homeland security. If approved, the dogs go to schools where they are trained. In 2006, PBB also began a program called Dog Tags. The PBB service dogs are donated to injured soldiers coming home from Iraq and Afghanistan (PBB 2009).[1]

---

[1] There are **scholarly references** in this reading because prison programs must be evaluated carefully by social scientists and government officials.

Prison University Project

3   Thousands of inmates across the country participate in programs for college study. San Quentin's Prison University Project in California is just such a program. Taught by college professors, graduate students and other **volunteers**, this program offers 12 courses per semester leading to a two-year associate of arts degree. The goal is to prepare students to lead thoughtful and productive lives inside and outside prison, and to provide them with the skills needed to obtain employment and economic **stability**.

Habitat for Humanity Prison Partnership

4   Since the first Partnership started in Texas in 1999, prisons throughout the United States have become partners with Habitat for Humanity to build homes for **needy** and low-income families. Although some inmates work within the prison walls, low-risk prisoners work side by side with other Habitat for Humanity volunteers at the construction site. The Partnership allows prisoners to develop confidence, provides them with marketable skills, and makes them feel proud of their accomplishments. "The prisoners who participate with Habitat for Humanity will gain a **renewed** belief

(continued on next page)

in themselves," said Millard Fuller, founder and president of Habitat for Humanity International. "Habitat for Humanity is building more than houses. We are building lives."

Nebraska's Prison Nursery Program

5   Between 1977 and 2007, the number of women in prison in the United States increased by 832 percent (WPA 2009). With about 4 percent of female inmates pregnant when they enter prison, there has been a growing trend to provide prison nursery programs. Nebraska's Prison Nursery Program provides inmates with prenatal care[2] education, parenting skills, information on child development, "hands-on training" for new and expectant mothers, and community resources available when they are released. An **assessment** of the program, 10 years after it was in operation, showed lower misconduct rates and lower recidivism rates when compared to inmates who were forced to give up their infants when entering prison (Carlson 2009).

Prison Entrepreneurship Program

6   When Catherine Rohr, a Wall Street investor, visited a Texas prison, she had a brainstorm: criminals and people in business are a lot alike. They both assess risk, live by their instincts, share profits, network,[3] and compete with one another. It was then that she founded the Prison Entrepreneurship Program (PEP). Today, corporate leaders and faculty volunteers teach business skills to PEP participants — former drug dealers, gang leaders, and others — by equipping them with the tools of success. Over 90 percent of the 440 graduates have found jobs within four weeks of being released from prison, 57 have started their own businesses, and recidivism rates are as low as 5 percent (PEP 2009; Beiser 2009).

---

[2] *prenatal care:* care for mothers and babies before the babies are born

[3] *network (v):* to meet other people who do the same type of work in order to share information, help each other, and so on.

COMPREHENSION

 Main Ideas

Working with a partner, check (✓) the statements that best express the main ideas in the reading.

☐ **1.** Convincing prison inmates that they have something to offer society is a crucial step toward an effective rehabilitation process.

☐ **2.** Prison programs that are responsive to the emotional, physical, educational, and moral needs of inmates should be more common than they are now.

☐ **3.** Inmates and people in business have similar strengths.

☐ **4.** Making prison inmates responsible for helping other beings while they are in prison provides them with the skills needed to do well in society when they leave prison.

☐ **5.** The costs of special programs designed to bring out the humanity in prisoners are too high for implementation throughout the nation.

☐ **6.** Nothing special should be done for prison inmates who are serving life terms.

B Close Reading

Read the quotes from the reading. Circle the statement that best explains each quote. Share your answers with a partner.

1. "An estimated 1.7 million people are behind bars in the United States, adding to the skyrocketing cost of corrections." (*paragraph 1*)

   a. Prison costs are too high.

   b. More people should be in prison.

   c. The high prison expenses reflect the high crime rate in the United States.

2. "'The prisoners who participate with Habitat for Humanity will gain a renewed belief in themselves,' said Millard Fuller, founder and president of Habitat for Humanity International. 'Habitat for Humanity is building more than houses. We are building lives.'" (*paragraph 4*)

   a. The people who get the houses are the ones who benefit most.

   b. The people who build the houses are the ones who benefit most.

   c. Both the builders and the people who receive the homes benefit.

3. "Catherine Rohr, a Wall Street investor . . . had a brainstorm: criminals and people in business are a lot alike. They both assess risk, live by their instincts, share profits, network, and compete with one another." (*paragraph 6*)

   a. Wall Street investors have a lot to learn from prisoners.

   b. Successful businessmen have a criminal side to them.

   c. Lawful business and unlawful business may require some of the same skills.

VOCABULARY

A Word Forms

1 Fill in the chart with the correct word forms. Use a dictionary if necessary. An **X** indicates there is no form in that category.

	NOUN	VERB	ADJECTIVE	ADVERB
1.	assessment	assess		X
2.		enhance		X
3.		evaluate		X
4.			needy	X
5.			renewed	X
6.	X	skyrocket		X
7.	stability			X
8.	volunteer			X

2 Complete the sentences with the correct form of the words. Choose from the two forms in parentheses. Compare answers with a partner.

1. Society is not always fully equipped to cure all social ills. In order to reduce the recidivism rate, there is a _____need_____ for more effective
   (need / needy)
   rehabilitation programs.

2. For instance, former convicts who have not had job training in prison cannot find jobs and end up taking part in illegal activities because their lives are not economically _____.
   (stability / stable)

3. As federal, state, and local government expenses continue to _____, it becomes more and more necessary to find
   (skyrocket / skyrocketing)
   alternative prison programs that will ensure inmates' rehabilitation.

4. Alternative prison programs that value the human being in the inmate have been known to generate a _____ of self-worth in
   (renewal / renewed)
   prisoners' minds.

5. Former convicts with _____ self-esteem usually have
   (enhancement / enhanced)
   a better chance of becoming productive members of society than those who maintain a negative view of themselves.

6. Through cooperative projects involving inmates and civilians, it has become clear that work that is done _____ is often as valuable for the
   (voluntary / voluntarily)
   people who give as it is for those who receive.

7. Elected officials cannot make reasonable decisions about the funding of certain activities unless they receive an accurate _____ of the
   (assess / assessment)
   effectiveness of related social programs.

8. Experts must _____ all kinds of social programs before
   (evaluate / evaluation)
   they make recommendations about how taxpayers' money should be spent.

B Synonyms

Complete the essay with the words from the box. Use the synonym in parentheses to help you select the correct word. There is one extra word. Compare answers with a partner.

assess	enhance	volunteer	renew	skyrocketed	stability

Serial Killers in the Media

The interest in serial killers has _____ in the United

1. (increased greatly)

States in the past 30 years. There has been an explosive growth in media stories

about serial murder. If any film genre could help restore a degree of economic

_____ to the country during these difficult times, it is

2. (steadiness)

Hollywood's violent films.

Why are normal people so attracted to the portrayal of behavior that is so far

from the norm? Why, for instance, have such films as *The Silence of the Lambs* been

so popular? It is difficult to _____ why people are attracted

3. (evaluate)

to stories about individuals who have committed a series of murders over a period

of time. Perhaps serial killers' evil deeds leave us thrilled and horrified at the same

time. Serial killers may be the new symbol for the inexplicable and unstoppable

nature of evil. In truth, however, most of the evil in our world is the result of

economic greed and political indifference. The question is not how to protect

ourselves from a few sick monsters but how to _____ life for

4. (improve)

all our citizens and _____ the bonds of social solidarity.

5. (re-establish)

NOTE-TAKING: Writing a Summary for Studying

> **Writing a summary** of textbook material in your own words will help you understand the main idea of the text and the connections between the different details. It can also help you remember details for an exam.
> - The first sentence of the summary gives the overall main idea.
> - The concluding sentence (last sentence) restates the overall main idea.

1. Go back to the reading. List details about how each of these programs works. Does the program appeal to the emotions or the intellect? What does it do for inmates?

PROGRAM	HOW PROGRAM WORKS
Puppies Behind Bars	• It gives inmates the opportunity to take care of and love a young and innocent animal. • It appeals to the emotions. • It gives inmates a sense of responsibility.
Prison University	• • •
Habitat Partnership	• • •
Prison Nursery	• • •
Prison Entrepreneurship	• • •

2 Complete the one-paragraph summary of the reading. The summary can then be used as study material. You can use the words in the box to introduce the individual programs.

First. . . .   Second. . . . .   Another . . .   Next . . .   Finally . . .

SUMMARY

Society has an interest in rehabilitating inmates. Starting programs that encourage them to change will make it easier for them to rejoin society. The first program suggested is Puppies Behind Bars. It appeals to the emotions by giving inmates the opportunity to take care of and love a young and innocent animal. The second program is

CRITICAL THINKING

Discuss the questions in a small group. Be prepared to share your answers with the class.

1. What social values do all the programs described in the reading appeal to? Would any of them be particularly suitable for your community? Why or why not?

2. Should we be educating people in prison for free when our other citizens can't get a free education? Why or why not?

3. Should women be given special consideration in prison? Why or why not?

BRINGING IT ALL TOGETHER

1   Match the theory with the people it describes as likely to commit crimes.

_____ 1. strain theory

_____ 2. control theory

_____ 3. conflict theory

_____ 4. labeling theory

a. people who feel powerless in society

b. people who have been called criminals and have internalized it

c. people who lack the skills or the opportunity to reach a goal

d. people who lack social bonds; don't feel connected; lack family ties

2   Match the program with the groups of people it is most likely to help.

_b, d_ 1. **Puppies Behind Bars**

_____ 2. **Prison University Project**

_____ 3. **Habitat for Humanity Partnership**

_____ 4. **Prison Nursery Program**

_____ 5. **Prison Entrepreneurship Program**

a. people who feel powerless in society

b. people who have been called criminals and have internalized it

c. people who lack the skills or the opportunity to reach a goal

d. people who lack social bonds; don't feel connected; lack family ties

3   Work in a small group. Discuss rehabilitation programs and how they can be linked to crime theories. Use some of the vocabulary you studied in the chapter (for a complete list, go to page 238). Follow these instructions:

- Form groups of five students. Each student will defend one of the five programs in the reading (one student per program). When the presentations are over, the group will decide on the two best programs based on the presentations.
- As you present the programs, show the ways in which they respond to the different theories of crime and how they give inmates what they have been deprived of in society.

EXAMPLE:

Puppies Behind Bars works well for people described by the labeling theory. They have internalized the idea that they are criminals and think that they are worthless people. They can't seem to get rid of that identity.

Puppies Behind Bars also works well for people described by the control theory. They lack social bonds and family ties and don't feel connected to the emotions of sharing and nurturing.

Puppies Behind Bars works well for these two types of people because it offers them the possibility of building self-esteem through a positive relationship with a loving animal.

WRITING ACTIVITY

Write a short essay in response to this question: "How can a society reduce crime?" Each section of the essay should answer a question:

- **Introduction:** Why do crimes happen? Choose certain crimes as examples.
- **Body:** How can we improve society and have fewer of these types of crimes?
- **Conclusion:** What can prisons do to help people rediscover their humanity?

Use at least five of the words and idioms you studied in the chapter.

DISCUSSION AND WRITING TOPICS

Discuss these topics in a small group. Choose one of them and write a paragraph or two about it. Use the vocabulary from the chapter.

1. When Malcolm X, the African-American leader, was in prison, he used the time to improve his reading skills. His love of reading became so strong that in spite of his imprisonment, he believed that he had never been as "free" before in his life.

   Do you support rehabilitation programs similar to the one Malcolm X devised for himself? Why or why not? Do you believe one can find "freedom" when one is physically prevented from moving around? Why or why not? In what way would you define this kind of "freedom"?

2. In Reading Two, one basis for Merton's strain theory is explained this way: "Society encourages everyone to want the same things (a job, money) but doesn't provide opportunities for everyone" (*paragraph 3*).

   Is it up to society to "provide opportunities for everyone," or is it up to the individual to "provide opportunities" for himself or herself?

3. Which theory explained in Reading Two do you agree with most? Why?

4. Which rehabilitation program described in Reading Three do you think is the best one? Why? Are there others that you would recommend? If so, which ones?

VOCABULARY

Nouns	Verbs	Adjectives	Phrases and Idioms
assessment *	counter	dramatic *	correctional institution
bond *	deny *	needy	developed countries
burglary	enhance *	renewed	developing countries
counterfeiting	evaluate *	responsive	social bonds
homicide	internalize *	transnational	
incarceration	label *	ubiquitous	
inmate	skyrocket		
likelihood			
norm *			
offender			
recidivism			
rehabilitation			
solidarity			
stability *			
volunteer *			

* = AWL (Academic Word List) item

SELF-ASSESSMENT

In this chapter you learned to:

○ Predict the content of a text from the first sentence or title and subheadings

○ Deal with difficult scientific names

○ Guess the meaning of words from the context

○ Understand and use synonyms, suffixes, "scientific" verbs, different word forms, and words of different intensity

○ Use dictionary entries to learn the meanings of words

○ Take notes using a map outline to remember details

○ Write a summary to understand main ideas and remember details

What can you do well? ✔

What do you need to practice more? ✔

VOCABULARY INDEX

The number following each entry is the page where the word, phrase, or idiom first appears. Words followed by an asterisk (*) are on the Academic Word List (AWL). The AWL is a list of the highest-frequency words found in academic texts.

CREDITS

TEXT CREDITS

PHOTO CREDITS

ILLUSTRATION CREDITS